Jewish–Christian Difference and Modern Jewish Identity

Jewish–Christian Difference and Modern Jewish Identity

Seven Twentieth-Century Converts

Shalom Goldman

LEXINGTON BOOKS
Lanham • Boulder • New York • London

Published by Lexington Books
An imprint of The Rowman & Littlefield Publishing Group, Inc.
4501 Forbes Boulevard, Suite 200, Lanham, Maryland 20706
www.rowman.com

Unit A, Whitacre Mews, 26-34 Stannary Street, London SE11 4AB

British Library Cataloguing in Publication Information Available

Library of Congress Cataloging-in-Publication Data

Goldman, Shalom, author.
Jewish-Christian difference and modern Jewish identity : seven twentieth-century converts / Shalom Goldman.
pages cm.
Includes bibliographical references and index.
ISBN 978-0-7391-9608-3 (cloth : alk. paper) -- ISBN 978-0-7391-9609-0 (electronic)
1. Jews--Identity. 2. Jewish converts--Biography. 3. Judaism--Relations--Christianity. 4. Christianity and other religions--Judaism. I. Title.
DS143.G6137 2015
261.2'6--dc23
                            2015010969
ISBN 978-0-7391-9610-6 (pbk: alk paper)

∞ ™ The paper used in this publication meets the minimum requirements of American National Standard for Information Sciences Permanence of Paper for Printed Library Materials, ANSI/NISO Z39.48-1992.

Printed in the United States of America

In memory of Jacob Goldman and Rhoda Miller

Contents

Acknowledgements

This book benefited greatly from careful readings by colleagues, friends and students.
Among them are:
Yaakov Ariel , Shlomit Finkelstein, Rabbi Daniel Greyber, Susannah Heschel , Hannah Jacobs, Ruby Lal, Brian Mahan, Joel Marcus, Gyan Pandey, and Alan Tansman.

To my brothers Ari and Dov and to my son Daniel, elef todot.

For editorial and technical assistance, kudos are due to Nick Fabian, who has sharpened the prose of my last three books.

To the librarians of Duke University Libraries, and especially to Rachel Ariel, Jewish Studies librarian, many thanks.

And to my partner Laurie Patton, who saw the shape of this book before I did, todah mikerev halev.

Prologue: Demons' Wager

This book is an exploration of the shifting contours of Jewish identity in the twentieth century, the century of the Holocaust and the establishment of Israel. In that century, definitions of Jewishness, elusive and mutable, have been the subject of intense debate and controversy. At a fundamental level, the questions "Who is a Jew?" and "How does one become a Jew?" lead us to examine the relationships between ethnicity, religion, and nationalism in the post-war world. Thus this book focuses on what novelist Joseph Kanon has dubbed "the pivot of the century—the aftermath of World War II, which is still the central event of our time."[1]

Two twenty-first-century international news stories highlight the unresolved and shifting nature of Jewish identity and demonstrate the complexity of the continuing debates surrounding this issue. In November 2009, Britain's Supreme Court ruled that the Jews' Free School of London could not apply Orthodox Jewish standards in formulating its admissions policies. The rabbis who run the school had denied admission to a twelve-year-old boy because his mother's conversion to Judaism had been supervised by a rabbi from a liberal denomination. As Orthodox Jews, the rabbis of the Jews' Free School followed a strict definition of Jewish identity, which only acknowledged conversions directed by Orthodox rabbis. They did not recognize the mother's conversion; therefore, the boy was not Jewish and thus denied admission. The British court, however, found that the school's admissions policy, rather than relying on a religious standard, was in fact a "test of ethnicity which contravenes the Race Relations Act." As a result of the case, the court forced the relaxation of the school's admissions standards in favor of the liberal denominations, but the issue was far from settled. In fact, some Orthodox Jews spoke of an irreparable break with their liberal co-religionists.[2]

The second story focuses on the daughter and son of Theodore Herzl, the founder of political Zionism. Herzl died in 1904 and was buried in Vienna. In his will, he requested that "when the Jewish state was founded" (such was his certainty) he and his children be reburied in Jerusalem. In 1949 Herzl was exhumed and reburied in a Jerusalem cemetery on a mountain renamed in his honor. But the Israeli Rabbinate opposed the reburial of his daughter Pauline, who had been a morphine addict and died of an apparent overdose in 1930, and his son Hans, who had converted to Catholicism and later committed suicide upon learning of his sister's death. According to Jewish law the actions of the Herzl children rendered them unfit for burial in a Jewish cemetery. After reconsidering the case at the beginning of the twenty-first century, the Chief Rabbinate declared that Hans Herzl's actions, as well as Pauline's actions, were the result of mental illness and that they could be buried in a Jewish cemetery. In 2006 both Pauline and Hans Herzl's bodies were exhumed in France and at last reburied near their father's grave in Jerusalem. Israeli nationalist considerations had thus trumped religious sensibilities.

As these stories suggest, conversion to, or apostasy from, the Jewish religion provides a unique lens through which to approach the complicated question of Jewish identity. How one *becomes* a Jew through conversion reveals much about the "meaning" of Jewish identity. Similarly, apostasy, the attempt to *leave* the Jewish people and join another faith, is an act laden with profound meaning. Apostasy or *shmad* was understood as abandonment of the Jewish people. By positioning the biographies of converts and apostates within the larger history of Jewish–Christian relations, *Jewish–Christian Difference and Modern Jewish Identity* examines these abstract questions of religious identity in the context of real people in the modern world.

This chapter takes its title from a story in the pre-modern Jewish folkloric tradition. In the fifteenth century tale "Rabbi Yehiel of Paris, the Learned Bishop and the Two Demons," we read of heavenly beings who oversee conversion and apostasy. At the prospect of a Christian converting to Judaism or a Jew converting to Christianity, these demons struggle for the souls of potential converts and wager about the outcome of the process. The story tells of the unusual friendship between a rabbi and a cardinal in thirteenth-century Paris. Two demons, hoping to wreak havoc, use their powers to try to persuade each cleric to abandon his respective religion and join the opposing faith. "One demon was on the side of the rabbi, and he wagered that he would convert the priest to Judaism. The other demon was on the side of the priest, and he wagered that he would cause the Jew to abandon his faith."[3] As this is a Jewish folktale, the rabbi's demon triumphs and the cardinal becomes a faithful member of the Jewish community. But as the tale's author and its Jewish readers knew all too well, this was merely a wishful fantasy. Cardinals of the Roman Catholic Church did not become Jews. Throughout centuries of uneasy Christian-Jewish "co-existence" during which the Church had vanquished the synagogue, thousands of Jews, including many rabbis, had been baptized. But cardinals became Jews only in folktales.

CONVERSION AND APOSTASY IN JEWISH HISTORY AND TRADITION

From its beginnings, the Jewish tradition has focused on the question of who is an insider and who is an outsider, who belongs and who doesn't. The issue, however, is differently configured in the two pillars of the Jewish textual tradition, the Hebrew Bible and post-biblical rabbinic literature. In the Hebrew Bible there is no mention of "conversion" or "apostasy," no formal way to join the Jewish people or to leave it. In biblical tales of joining the Hebrew people the emphasis is on genealogy and peoplehood. What is today taken to be the model account of conversion to Judaism, the story of Ruth, involves no statement or ritual marking the transition from one religion to another. Rather, it is a story of peoplehood, family ties and ethnic affiliation.

Ruth was a Moabite woman married to an Israelite man who died. Instead of returning to her people after her husband's death, she pledges her loyalty to her late husband's people, and to their God. She says to her mother-in-law Naomi, "Do not press me to leave you, or to turn back from following you. Where you go, I will go; where you dwell, I will dwell; your people shall be my people, and your God my God. Where you die, I will die—there I will be buried" (Ruth 1:16–17). With this confirmation of her loyalty to Naomi and the Israelites, Ruth asserts her place as a member of the Jewish people.

During the rabbinic period, following the destruction of the Temple in Jerusalem in 70 C.E., conversion was marked and formalized by ritual. Attitudes toward converts varied widely, and the Rabbis initially disagreed about the methods necessary to bring a non-Jew into the group. Eventually they established a standard practice. Commitment to joining the Jewish people required immersion in a *mikvah* (ritual bath) and additionally, for males, circumcision. But before those rituals took place the officiating rabbi would warn the candidate that membership in the Jewish people was a dangerous prospect: "For our people are now persecuted." For centuries, these ritual demands remained consistent over time and place.

In the vast corpus of the rabbinic tradition there are many stories and directives about converts to Judaism. Although the majority of these are positive, some reflect ambivalence toward proselytes. In the Talmud we read that by embarrassing or discomforting a proselyte one transgresses thirty-six or more commandments.[4] But we also read that proselytes can be problematic. In response to the rabbinic dictum that proselytes should be discouraged from joining the Jewish people, one opinion recorded in the Talmud argues that they should be discouraged because they can cause dissension in the Jewish community. "Proselytes," said Rabbi Helbo, "are as hard for Israel as a sore on the body."[5]

Maimonides (1136–1204), the great Jewish physician, philosopher, and legalist, addressed these issues in response to a query from a man who had converted from Islam to Judaism. Obadiah, as the convert was called, asked whether as a "new" Jew he was allowed to say the frequently-recited Jewish prayers that invoke the "merit of the ancestors." These prayers address God through the miracles he has performed, using the phrases, "You who have sanctified us through your commandment" and "You who have brought us out of the land of Egypt." But, Obadiah asked, what if one were not descended from the Israelites? Could a convert, a non-Israelite with no direct link to the recipients of the miracles, still recite these prayers? Maimonides' response was emphatic: "Yes, you may say all of this in the prescribed order and not change it in the least. In the same way as every Jew by birth says his blessing and prayer, you, too, shall bless and pray alike . . . because since you have 'come under the wings of the Divine Presence' (the rabbinic image for conversion to Judaism), no difference exists between you and us, and all miracles done to us have been done as it were to us and to you. . . . There is no difference between you and us."[6] In the eight hundred years since Maimonides's response to Obadiah, the great sage's understanding of the convert's place in Judaism has been deeply influential. More recently, other views that place more emphasis on what we might call a biological view of Jews and Judaism have competed with Maimonides's view for influence.

About apostasy from Judaism to another faith community, however, there was no such ambivalence. Leaving the Jewish people by joining another religion was deemed *shmad*, or "destruction," by the rabbis. The apostate was condemned and ostracized, and often placed under *herem*, or "excommunication." But as we shall see, an apostate, or *meshummad*, was for some purposes still considered a member of the Jewish people. Such is the force of the rabbinic dictum that "even if he has sinned, he remains of Israel."[7]

Medieval Jews, a religious minority in the Christian and Muslim societies in which they lived, were often forced to convert to the majority religion. Some, of course, did so of their own volition. Reasons for leaving Judaism and the Jewish people were as varied as the individuals involved. Improvement in one's social and economic condition was often a factor, as was attraction to a radically different set of beliefs and practices. But in addition to instances of voluntary apostasy, there also were forced conversions of large groups of Jews. The most extensive and dramatic of these was the series of forced baptisms in Christian Spain during the century preceding the Edict of Expulsion in 1492, which forced Jews who refused to convert to

Christianity—more than 100,000 people—to leave Spain. This event was deeply traumatic both for those expelled and for their descendants.

Until the mid-twentieth century the cases of apostasy from Judaism far outnumbered the few conversions to Judaism. During the nineteenth century tens of thousands of European Jews were baptized, while only a handful of European Christians converted to Judaism. For Jews aspiring to be part of European culture, the baptismal certificate was, as the German Jewish poet Heinrich Heine put it, the "entrance ticket." Conversion to Judaism carried no such benefits. To the contrary, it could mean isolation, ostracism, and at times dire punishment by the political or ecclesiastic authorities. The warning articulated in the Talmud that the Jewish people were a persecuted people was still relevant.

With the rise of Zionism at the end of the nineteenth century Jewish identity was newly complicated by the question of nationalism. In a similar and related manner, questions of identity and self-definition arose for members of other national and religious groups throughout Europe. As the persecution of Jewish communities in Europe increased, so did the movement to find the Jews a safe and secure national home. Secular Zionism called for a rejection of "Diaspora mentality," for the emergence of "a new Jew," for a return to biblical models, and for a rejection of rabbinic authority. But that rejection was neither complete nor categorical. Zionist thought and action incorporated aspects of the classical Jewish tradition, including the normative Jewish definition of membership: a Jew was either a person born to a Jewish mother or a person who converted to Judaism. And Jews were not the only ones raising the issue of Jewish identity. Tragically, anti-Semites soon began to raise the question of "Who is a Jew?" In the late nineteenth and early twentieth century an organized and articulate anti-Semitic movement flourished in France and Germany and the ideologues of that movement sought to define Jewishness for purposes of social exclusion.

With the Nazi assumption of power in 1933 and the subsequent passage of the Nuremberg Laws in 1935, the German state provided its own legal definition of a Jew. The Jews, according to the Nazis, were not members of a religious community; rather, they were part of a 'race.' According to the Nazi racial system, 'characteristics' could be inherited from either the mother or the father. Thus, a Jew was anyone who was "fifty percent or more Jewish."[8] This allegedly scientific definition led the Nazis to create categories to address and track partial Jews as well. "A half-Jew had two Jewish grandparents; a quarter Jew had one."[9] The implementation of this classification system was the prelude, first to the exclusion of German Jews from citizenship, and then later during World War II, to the subsequent deportation and murder not only of German Jews but of Jews throughout German-occupied Europe.

Many in the international community viewed the establishment of the State of Israel three years after the Allied victory over Germany as a response to the Nazi attempt to annihilate the Jews. With the founding of Israel in 1948, a state envisioned as refuge for those Jews who had survived the war, the question of "Who is a Jew?" would inevitably arise anew. A new term, "Israeli identity," came into use. How to define precisely that identity was of concern to both the Jewish and Arab citizens of the new state, and to Jews and non-Jews throughout the world.

SEVEN LIVES

Jewish–Christian Difference and Modern Jewish Identity tells the dramatic stories of seven twentieth-century lives. The first three sections of the book combine these stories in pairs, one of a Jew who became a Christian, and one of a Christian who became a Jew. The first pair—Madeleine Feraille and Aron Lustiger—are set in wartime France and are linked through participation in the French Resistance to the German occupation. The second pair— Donato Manduzio and Rabbi Israel Zolli—are set in Italy during the same tumultuous period. Before his apostasy to Catholicism, Zolli served as an adviser to Manduzio, a Catholic peasant who led a group of converts to Judaism. The third pair—Elisheva Bikhovsky, a Christian poet who became known as "Ruth from the banks of the Volga," and Oswald Rufeisen, a Polish Jew who became a Catholic priest after his war-time experience hiding in a Carmelite convent—are set in Eastern Europe. The final story, of Moshe Rosen, takes us to the post-war United States, where Jewish–Christian difference was being negotiated in new and startling ways. As the founder of Jews for Jesus, Rosen helped set the stage for Messianic Judaism, a phenomenon once limited to Protestant America, but now increasingly popular in Europe and Israel.

For each of these people, the move between Judaism and Christianity was a serious wager, though not one made by demons. Rather the prospective convert wagered that conversion, an act fraught with danger and possibility, would lead to a safer, richer and more fulfilling life. The negotiation and redefinition of the boundary between Jewish and Christian identity is a common theme in each story. The events of World War II and the subsequent establishment of the State of Israel directly shaped the lives of these people, and their religious journeys were intertwined with their experience of, or knowledge of, the Holocaust and its aftermath. Through these biographies we see how the question of Jewish identity touches on and illuminates the political and national realities of Europe, Israel, and the United States through a century of turmoil.

All highly articulate individuals, each of the five men and two women portrayed in *Jewish–Christian Difference and Modern Jewish Identity* left a body of written work, including extensive correspondence. Each was deeply engaged in the major philosophical, religious, and political issues of their times, and as converts to and from Judaism each struggled with the issue of Jewish nationalism in general and Zionism in particular. Some opposed Zionism; others became ardent supporters and participated in the movement. Each of them confronted the dramatic changes in Jewish–Christian relations that resulted from the aftermath of the Nazi attempt to exterminate the Jews of Europe.

In detailed and contextualized biographical portraits I tell their stories, and relate these stories one to the other. In telling our protagonists' stories I rely to a considerable degree on their own accounts of their personal and religious journeys. I have supplemented these accounts with observations gleaned from the letters, memoirs, and journalism of their contemporaries. Some of our protagonists knew of each other and some of them wrote of and to each other. In addition, I weave my own encounters with some of these fascinating people into the web of the narrative. Long before I envisioned writing this book I was fascinated by stories of conversion and apostasy. In my youth I came into contact with several of the figures in this book. Those that I did not meet, I have encountered through their writings. My personal engagement with this topic will I hope enliven these already lively narratives.

NOTES

1. Quoted in Alter, "Rewriting the Rules of Summer Fiction."
2. The case has had repercussions in other British religious communities as well. As religious schools in Britain are state-funded, many religious groups, including Muslims and Hindus, are reconsidering their own school admissions policies. Thus the British court's decision is having an impact on government policies, inter-faith relations, and intra-communal relations within the country.
3. Gaster, "R. Jehiel of Paris, the Learned Bishop and the Two Demons," 506.
4. Babylonian Talmud, Bava Metzia, 59b.
5. Babylonian Talmud, Yevamoth 47a.
6. Diamond, *Converts, Heretics, and Lepers*, 12–15.
7. Akedat Yizḥak (Venice, 1573), 258b no. 97, Ki-Teze quoted in Ben-Sasson, "Apostasy," 202–212.
8. Riggs, *Hitler's Jewish Soldiers*, 15 and 281.
9. Riggs, *Hitler's Jewish Soldiers*, 20 and 284.

Chapter One

Who Is A Jew?

In 1958, David Ben Gurion, Israel's prime minister and founding father, sent a letter to fifty-one leading Jewish intellectuals, in which he asked for their thoughts on Jewish identity. The question of "Who is a Jew?" had occupied Israel's politicians, religious authorities, and general public in one form or another since the nation's founding in 1948. Ben Gurion's current request, however, was neither general nor theoretical. Rather, he pointedly asked "how to register the 'religion' and 'nationhood' of the children of mixed marriages when the father is Jewish and the mother is not Jewish and has not converted, but both [parents] agree to have the child registered as a Jew."[1] In the ten years that he had led the Israeli government, Ben Gurion had not presented a group of scholars with a direct question of such consequence, and the responses he received, although written more than a half century ago, are still relevant today.

A parliamentary crisis had precipitated Ben Gurion's unusual letter and question. Israeli identity documents of the time recorded both one's religion and one's nationality. In early 1958, the Minister of Interior, Israel ben Yehuda of the secularist Ahdut Haavodah party, decided that children immigrating to Israel whose parents declared them Jewish would be registered as such by the authorities, regardless of any other factors. Declaration of intent would be the only criterion in determining a child's religion. This seemingly automatic recognition of Jewish status would make the child immediately eligible for Israeli citizenship under the Law of Return. The National Religious Party, however, objected to this policy. As Orthodox Jews, they recognized as Jewish only the child of a Jewish mother, or an actual convert to Judaism. The child of a non-Jewish mother would have to apply for "naturalization" and become an Israeli citizen at a later time. As a junior partner in the Israeli coalition government, the National Religious Party was threatening to withdraw from the coalition because of their disagreement with this policy and thus bring down the government.

The larger context for the crisis and Ben Gurion's letter was the Israeli Law of Return, promulgated in 1950. Written in the wake of the Holocaust, the law was formulated to be as inclusive as possible. If refugees could show they were of Jewish ancestry, they would be admitted to the recently-established State of Israel and granted citizenship. As sociologist Baruch Kimmerling has noted, "This law was considered the true embodiment of Zionism— the creation of a Jewish nation-state that would be *terre d'asile* [a territory of asylum] for any Jew in the world, whether persecuted or not."[2] Yet, this inclusivity, this broad definition of "Jewish" meant that the law was bound to clash with the more restricted meaning of the term as understood by Israel's rabbinic authorities, all of whom were Orthodox Jews. Thus, the law became a constant source of conflict. As sociologist Asher Cohen has noted, "From the founding of Israel onwards, the Law of Return was at the center of all debates about Jewish and Israeli identity."[3]

In his letter, Ben Gurion reminded his interlocutors of the details of the law. After first stating that "in Israel there is no discrimination on the basis of religion," he then went on to note, "However, Jews alone enjoy a special extra privilege afforded by the Law of Return . . . Immediately upon arrival in Israel, and after expressing a desire to settle here, they automatically and instantly become Israeli citizens."[4] This "however" clause seemed to many observers to refute the contention that "there is no discrimination" in Israel. Israel afforded no such privileges to those Palestinians who had remained in the State of Israel after the 1948 war. Nor did it permit those Arabs who had fled or been exiled during that war to return. But Ben Gurion and his respondents did not address this issue. By common consensus they seemed to agree that the Law of Return was not discriminatory. Israel was a "Jewish state" and one's "Jewishness" determined whether one would be accepted as a citizen. That a significant number of the citizens of the new state were Arabs did not at that point enter into the conversation.

Israel declared itself a "Jewish state," but what that meant was not clear; the phrase would become the locus of many points of contention. Could the Arabs of Israel, the "non-Jews" of the Jewish state, live in the state as full citizens? Were they Israelis in the same sense that Jews were? Israel's 1948 Declaration of Independence promised to "ensure complete equality of social and political rights to all its inhabitants irrespective of religion."[5] Yet, by offering automatic citizenship to all who fit a broad definition of "Jewish" (through ancestral connection), rather than the rabbinate's more narrow definition (born to a Jewish mother, or a convert), the state was working to ensure that the Arabs of Israel would remain a permanent minority. In the understanding of Israel's policy makers, increasing the Jewish population would ward off the "demographic threat" of the state's Arab population. As political scientist Gad Barzilai has noted, "One of the major national projects was to entrench Jewish domination in the state, preventing the possibility of its territory being settled by an Arab Palestinian majority."[6] For Barzilai and other astute observers of the ideological forces that have shaped Israeli identity, the Law of Return and its subsequent iterations "were supposed to entrench 'Jewishness' as the main political force in state ideology, legal ideology, and public policy."[7] But what 'Jewishness' meant was not well-defined.

Toward the end of his letter, Ben Gurion revealed his own vision of Israeli Jewish identity. "In Israel efforts must be made to increase shared and unifying properties and eliminate as far as possible those that separate and divide."[8] Ben Gurion went on to contrast the Diaspora, where mixed marriages were a threat to Jewish continuity, and the new State of Israel, where these marriages could lead to the "assimilation of non-Jews into the Jewish people, particularly in families in which the children of mixed marriages have immigrated to Israel."[9] Thus, in Ben Gurion's view, intermarriage was a positive move for Israelis. Implicit in Ben Gurion's argument is the secular Zionist view that the function of Jewish law had been to preserve Jewish "national identity" in the two millennia of exile. Now that the exile had ended and the national home been "reborn," the law was no longer necessary. Thus, the law forbidding marriage between Jews and non-Jews was no longer relevant. In fact, it could be an impediment to Jewish national rebirth. For Ben Gurion's Orthodox Jewish opponents, however, this view was heresy. In rabbinic thought the law is immutable. Revealed in all of its detail at Sinai, its function is to maintain Israel's covenant with God. Historical circumstances, including the establishment of a Jewish state, cannot alter the divine covenant and its expression in rabbinic law.

In contrast, rabbis of the Conservative Movement, identified with the Historical School of Jewish legal theory, would argue that historical circumstances have always influenced the development and implementation of Jewish law. But at the time that Ben Gurion asked for responses about Jewish identity, Conservative Judaism was not a viable denomination in Israel. Thus at the time, there was no middle ground between the assertive secularism of the new state's elites and the Orthodox Judaism of the official rabbinate.

THE RESPONDENTS AND RESPONSES TO BEN GURION'S LETTER

Who were these fifty-one intellectuals? To start, they were all men, a fact which is striking by today's standards of gender equality, particularly as the issue at hand concerned the status of the child's mother. Twenty of the scholars lived in Israel; thirty-one in Europe and the United States. They seem to have been chosen by category: one-third were Orthodox rabbis; one-third were Jewish scholars (although not rabbis) affiliated with the more liberal trends in Judaism; and one-third were secularists, among them literary and other cultural figures.[10] The majority of the responses were brief and to the point. The two most extensive and detailed letters were from Haim Cohn, the legal advisor to Ben Gurion's government, and Shlomo Goren, military chaplain and later Chief Rabbi of the Israel Defense Force (IDF), and then Chief Ashkenazi Rabbi of Israel.

Some of Ben Gurion's respondents played an active role in the particular stories I examine in this book. For example, Justices Haim Cohn and Moshe Silberg of the Israeli Supreme Court served as members of the court that decided the Brother Daniel case, a case in which a Jewish convert to Catholicism petitioned the government for Israeli citizenship. Other respondents, such as Rabbis Shlomo Goren and Menachem Mendel Schneerson, the Lubavitcher Rebbe, played a more general role as advocates for their definitions of Jewish identity. Ultimately, all of the responses to Ben Gurion's query have some bearing on the seven life-stories included here.

Ben Gurion's decision to seek responses from scholars who lived outside of Israel formulated the question of Jewish identity as one of general Jewish interest, not solely an Israeli concern. Of the fifty-one people solicited, forty-six responded. Ben Gurion no doubt carefully read these varied and fascinating letters, but in the end these scholars' learned formulations had little effect on public policy. For decades the responses remained buried in Israeli archives until Israeli scholar Eliezer Ben-Rafael published them at the beginning of the twenty-first century.[11] The wide variety of opinions that we find in these letters demonstrates the difficulty—or might we say futility—of attempting to define the term "Jew." Furthermore, the responses need to be situated in the larger context of the relationship between the State of Israel and the Jewish religion. The problem arose in large part because Israel, unlike the western democracies on which it modeled its government, keeps records of the religious affiliation of each of its citizens. Today, sixty-seven years after the establishment of the state, the definitions of Jewish and Israeli identity remain fluid and imprecise, and this lack of precision ensures that the question will return continuously to the public arena, not only in Israel, but wherever Jews reside.

The forty-six responses to Ben Gurion's letter can serve as our initial guide to the variety of definitions of Jewish and Israeli identities. As one might expect, these responses fall into three broad categories that mirror the categories of Ben Gurion's choice of respondents. For Orthodox Jews the definition was simple, precise, direct, and specific: a Jew was either a child born to a Jewish mother, or a person who converted to Judaism under the direction of an Orthodox rabbi. This standard was immutable, with no exceptions possible. Thus, one rabbi noted, addressing the question "Who is a

Jew?" did not require great erudition. Rabbi Yekhiel Weinberg (1885–1966) wrote to Ben Gurion, "This is a new question unimagined by preceding generations. A simple Jew, without philosophical predilections or newfound ideologies, would shrug his shoulders at this odd question that has arisen in the very generation of national rebirth and the return to our spiritual homeland."[12] Rabbi Weinberg's comment about "newfound ideologies" was in fact a veiled reference to secular Zionism. He, however, was not against Zionism in all of its forms, as some rabbis of the time were. The reference to "national rebirth" indicates his allegiance to religious, as opposed to secular, Zionist ideas.

For representatives of the modern Jewish religious movements that flourished in the United States, there was some willingness to broaden the borders of Judaism. For these movements the definition of "Who is a Jew?" was flexible and ambiguous. We will encounter these ideas, and their implications, in many of the stories in this book. In the United States, the Conservative and Reform movements made conversion to Judaism a less lengthy and less arduous process. It was easier, under the supervision of these movements, to become a Jew. Later in the twentieth century, during the 1980s, Reform Judaism's rabbinate made the decision to redefine who was a Jew by birth. While long-standing tradition insisted that a child's mother be Jewish, the new standard allowed that if either mother or father was Jewish, then the child was a Jew. In 1958 however, Ben Gurion did not write to the rabbis of the Reform and Conservative movements, only to scholars and Orthodox rabbis. In the 1950s these denominations had no constituencies in Israel and they would not have been relevant to Ben Gurion's quest. These liberal movements flourished in the mid-twentieth-century United States, but not in the Jewish state.

Ben Gurion's intense interest in the question of 'Who is a Jew?' had a deep personal aspect. In 1946 his son, Amos Ben Gurion, then serving in the British Army in Europe, married Mary Callow, a young Christian woman from the Isle of Man. Before the wedding, Amos had consulted with his parents. His mother Paula objected to her son's marriage to a non-Jew and asked her husband to 'talk Amos out of it.' But after meeting Mary Callow, Ben Gurion refused to pressure his son. Rather, he arranged for Mary to convert to Judaism in a relatively short time. Rabbi Joachim Prinz, an American Reform Rabbi, supervised the conversion, and the marriage went ahead as planned. But by bypassing the Israeli rabbinic authorities, Ben Gurion deepened the antipathy of the orthodox Jewish establishment toward his political leadership.

For Ben Gurion and the other secularists in the Zionist leadership "Jewishness" was *national*, rather than religious. "Jewishness" trumped Judaism, and "Israeliness" redefined Judaism. Perhaps the most explicitly secular response to Ben Gurion was that of Haim Cohn, who co-authored the Law of

Return. Cohn wrote to the Prime Minister, "There is no better way for the state to act than to indicate the religion and nationality of the child as defined by the declaration of the parents." For this legal scholar, a child's parents, not the state religious authorities, were the true arbiters of identity. "For the purposes of immigration and citizenship, the child follows his parents."[13] Aware that rabbinic law would not accept the child of a non-Jewish woman as a Jew, Cohn argued that "the meaning of 'Jew' in Knesset legislation is not identical to its meaning in religious law."[14] As we shall see, Orthodox Jewish scholars were bound to disagree with Cohn on this issue.

The issue of Jewish-Arab relations within Israel and the status of its Arab citizens did not arise in these extensive and learned deliberations, an oversight more surprising than the lack of gender diversity among the respondents. At the time roughly 15 percent of Israel's citizens were Arabs. Although citizens of the state, they did not share the full rights and privileges accorded to their Jewish fellow citizens. Suspected of disloyalty to the state and not inducted into the military, they did not achieve full integration into the Israeli social fabric.

The response from Akiva Ernst Simon, a professor at the Hebrew University and a student and colleague of the philosopher Martin Buber, proved the one exception to this oversight. Ben Gurion's contention that every Israeli citizen must be identified by both religion and nationality struck Simon as "injurious to democratic life in Israel." Citing the absence of ethnic and religious designations in a US passport, an absence which he considered "a conspicuous hallmark of active democracy," Simon argued that "the Arab citizens of Israel are entitled to rest assured that the government of Israel is doing all it can to prevent an official document from serving as a potential instrument of discrimination."[15] Unfortunately, Professor Simon's exhortation about discrimination against Israel's Arab citizens would go unheeded, as did similar warnings to Ben Gurion by Simon's mentor and colleague the philosopher Martin Buber.

CHALLENGES TO THE LAW OF RETURN

The Israeli government found a political solution to the 1958 parliamentary crisis, a solution that involved the realignment of the parties in the ruling coalition, without addressing the core question of "Who is a Jew?" A year later, another, more audacious, application for citizenship would spark a second crisis, which led to the first in a series of legal challenges to the Law of Return that would seek to expand the definition of Jewishness. In 1959 Oswald Rufeisen, a Polish Jew who had converted to Catholicism during World War II and later been ordained as a Catholic priest, arrived in Israel and asked that the Ministry of Interior recognize his status as a Jew and grant him immediate citizenship under the Law of Return.

The Ministry of Interior rejected Rufeisen's request. Two years later, in 1962, the Israeli High Court of Justice refused to hear Rufeisen's appeal of the Ministy's decision. In the court's opinion the Law of Return did not apply to Jews who had joined another religion. Paradoxically, however, the Law of Return would apply to people who professed no religious belief at all. As Israeli philosopher David Hartman noted some three decades after that 1962 decision, "Official Israeli policy regarding the Law of Return is explicit: No commitments of faith are necessary as long as no alternative faith is adopted. A Jew is accepted regardless of whether he or she is atheist, secularist, or completely uninterested in the religious meaning of Jewish life or history. In other words, a Jew wishing to return to Israel cannot seek religious meaning in any faith other than Judaism, but he or she can renounce all faiths including Judaism."[16] In the case of Rufeisen, who was known as Brother Daniel following his conversion to Catholicism, the judges argued that his apostasy rendered him "not Jewish" in the eyes of the Israeli public. In chapter 7, I examine the ramifications and reverberations of the Israeli court's historic 1962 decision in the Brother Daniel Case, a decision that is still cited in current discussions of Jewish identity.

The Shalit case of 1970 had a very different outcome. It too involved the children of a Jewish father and a non-Jewish mother, but unlike the 1958 challenge in which both parents were immigrants to Israel, Shalit was not only an Israeli citizen, but a high-ranking naval officer. While overseas Shalit had married a Scottish-Christian woman. The couple then settled in Israel, where they had two children. When Captain Shalit appealed to the government to recognize his children as Jewish, he received a more muted response than the authors of previous such appeals. In a society where military officers command the highest respect, the Israeli government could not ignore or easily reject his appeal. Shalit, a declared atheist, asked that the government register his children in a new way: their identity cards would record their nationality as *Jewish*, while recording their religion as *none*.[17] Ultimately, the court complied with this request, although it would refuse to consider similar appeals in the future. The ruling sparked yet another parliamentary crisis in which the Orthodox parties in the government coalition demanded that the Ministry of Interior be placed under their control. If Orthodox officials decided who was and was not a Jew, then the Orthodox definition of Jewishness could be preserved as the status quo in subsequent decades.[18]

In the aftermath of the Shalit case, the Orthodox rabbinate seemed to have secured the final say on Jewish identity, but the Israeli government amended the Law of Return to create a new category. One could claim the rights of a Jew, be allowed to immigrate, and become a citizen, but he or she would not be recognized as a "Jew" according to rabbinic law. According to the amendment, "These individuals included any child or grandchild of a Jew (male or female), the spouse of a Jew, the spouse of a child of a Jew, and the spouse of a grandchild of a Jew."[19] When the amendment was put into effect in 1970, it did not apply to many individuals. In the 1990s, however, after the fall of the Soviet Union, when almost a million people from the Russian Federation came to Israel, perhaps a third of them fell into the category of persons with the "right of Jew" category. They were Jews for the purposes of immigration to Israel. But they were not Jews according to the strict interpretation of Jewish law, and in the eyes of Israel's official rabbinate they could not legally marry other Jews.

Radical changes in Jewish life, both in Israel and in the Diaspora, have brought continual challenges to the Orthodox hegemony on questions of Jewish identity. The most significant of these challenges took place in the United States. In 1983 Reform Judaism embraced the "patrilineal principle": if a child's father is Jewish and the child is brought up in a Jewish home, then that child is a Jew. Reform Judaism rejected the "matrilineal principle," in which the mother's religious status determines that of the child, as too narrow and limiting. Orthodox and Conservative rabbis objected strenuously to this change; many predicted that it would result in the creation of two distinct Jewish peoples. In the thirty years that have passed since the leaders of Reform Judaism made that radical decision, a generation has grown up and is now making their own decisions about marriage and raising children. As journalist Naomi Zeveloff noted in 2012, "Patrilineal descent remains one of the most controversial decrees in American Jewish history. . . . Patrilineal Jews find themselves in limbo when they venture beyond their denominational walls."[20] In response to the rabbis of the Reform movement, the traditionalists of the Conservative and Reform denominations invoke the decisions of the Jewish legal tradition as proof of their contention that the mother's status is determinative. As historian Shaye Cohen has noted, "Rabbinic hegemony and the political setting of Jewish communities from late antiquity to early modern times jointly ensured that Jewishness would be neither elusive nor problematic."[21] Rather, it had been clearly defined within the parameters determined by the Orthodox rabbis.

A blurring of the division between Judaism and Christianity has provided an additional challenge to the Orthodox definition of Jewish identity. Although belief in the divinity of Jesus would seem to establish a firm borderline between Judaism and Christianity, the growth of "messianic Judaism" in recent decades has undermined the permanence and viability of that border. In the early-twenty-first-century United States, the loosely-organized movement includes thousands of "Jewish believers in Jesus" participating in more than three hundred congregations. In Israel as well there is a large population of such believers. There are more than one hundred messianic congregations in Israel and approximately ten thousand believers affiliated with these congregations.

In 1989 the Ministry of Interior denied citizenship to Gary and Shirley Beresford, two South African Jewish immigrants to Israel who identified themselves as messianic Jews. The Ministry considered the Beresfords' identification as messianic Jews a declaration of Christianity, and as such they forfeited the right to citizenship under the Law of Return. The Israeli Supreme Court upheld the decision to deny citizenship. Justice Menachem Elon explained the ruling in this way: "Messianic Jews attempt to reverse the wheels of history by two thousand years. But the Jewish people has decided during the two thousand years of its history that messianic Jews do not belong to the Jewish nation and have no right to force themselves on it. Those who believe in Jesus are in fact, Christians."[22] Thus, despite the Beresfords' efforts, the Israeli Supreme Court acknowledged limits to the possibility of expanding the traditional borders of "Jewishness."

THE BOUNDARIES OF JEWISH IDENTITY

These challenges to the Law of Return demonstrate both the ambiguity and the flexibility of the border that encompasses Jewish identity, but there is little doubt that such a border exists. The problems arise when determining how and where it should be drawn. As historian Shaye Cohen has pointed out, "Jewishness, the conscious affirmation of the qualities that make Jews Jews, presumes a contrast between Us and Them. . . . Between Us and Them is a line, a boundary, drawn not in sand or stone but in the mind. The line is no less real for being imaginary, since both Us and Them agree that it exists. Although there is a boundary that separates the two, it is crossable and not always distinct."[23]

During the biblical period, the border between "Jew" and "non-Jew" was not as clearly defined as it would be during the rabbinic period, following the destruction of the Second Temple. The Hebrew Bible identifies Abraham and his descendants as "Hebrews." The children of Abraham's grandson Jacob were "the children of Israel," the "Israelites" of the King James translation. During the first centuries of their dwelling in the land, the Hebrew Bible refers to them as both Hebrews and Israelites. Furthermore, there is not at this time any mention of "conversion." Rather, one joined the Israelites through marriage or proximity. "Jews" do not appear until after the Babylonian Exile of 586 B.C.E. When the Jews, or Judeans, returned from exile to rebuild the city of Jerusalem, they were asserting that, as descendants of the tribe of Judah, they were the only remnant of the people of Israel. Samaritans, or other claimants, were not, according to the biblical narrative, true Israelites.

Judaism, the successor to pre-Exilic, biblical religion developed to its fully articulated form between the second century B.C.E. and the third century C.E., a development recorded and reflected in the *Mishnah*. The rulings of the rabbis of antiquity, as recorded in the *Mishnah* and elaborated upon in the *Gemara*, defined Jewishness and codified the matrilineal principle. By creating a formal ritual that enabled gentile converts to join the Jewish people, the rabbis expanded the borders of Judaism.

The Book of Ezra provides a key moment in this transition to the rabbinic definition of Jewishness. In chapter 9 Ezra tells the exiles from Judah who are returning from the Babylonian captivity—now described as Jews, the descendants of the tribe of Judah and thus the remnant of the larger people of Israel—that they must divorce their foreign wives. These foreign wives and their children would not be considered part of the reconstituted people of Israel. The people returning from exile initially resist this command, and their officers tell Ezra that the Israelites "have not separated themselves from the peoples of the land whose abhorrent practices are the likes of the Canaanites. . . . They have taken their daughters as wives for themselves and for their sons, so that the holy seed has become intermingled with the peoples of the land" (Ezra 9:1–3). Ezra mourns on hearing this news and assembles the returnees to Zion. One of the leaders, Shecaniah, son of Jehiel of the family of Elam, "spoke up and said to Ezra, 'We have trespassed against our God by bringing into our own homes foreign women from the peoples of the land; but there is still hope for Israel despite this. Now then let us make a covenant with our God to expel all these women and those who have been born to them, in accordance with the bidding of the Lord and of all who are conceived over the commandment of our God, and let the teaching be obeyed. Take action for the responsibility is yours and we are with you. Act with resolve.' So Ezra at once put the officers of the priests and the Levites and all Israel under oath to act accordingly, and they took the oath" (Ezra 10:2–8).

Prior to the time of Ezra (c. 500 B.C.E.) the standards of inclusion in the Hebrew people were not as strict as they were later to be. As historian Michael Satlow has noted, "When Ezra arrived in Jerusalem, we are told, he was horrified to find that the Jewish families that had preceded him nearly sixty years before had intermarried. At a public meeting a committee to investigate the matter was appointed, and its report—listing the one hundred and eleven men who intermarried—closes the book of Ezra."[24] Through marriage, in fact, one could join the Israelite/Hebrew people. Thus the "foreign" wives of Joseph, Moses, and the sons of Jacob became Israelites. Ezra rejected the "foreign wives" of the Jews returning from the Babylonian Exile; he did not have a form of conversion to offer them. That form and ritual would develop only centuries later, during the rabbinic period, and it would be based on the precedent of Ezra's decision to forbid marriage to foreign wives.

The rabbinic definition of Jewishness and the stipulation that the convert must undergo a formal conversion expanded rather than contracted the border of Judaism.[25] For with a precise definition of membership came rules and rituals enabling that membership.[26] The rabbinic authorities required a declaration of intent from a prospective convert. The warning to the prospective convert is described in the Talmud: "If at the present time a man desires to become a proselyte, he is to be addressed as follows: 'What reason have you for desiring to become a proselyte? Do you not know that Israel at the present time is persecuted and oppressed, depressed, harassed, and overcome by afflictions?' If he replies, 'I know and yet I am unworthy,' he is accepted immediately and given instruction in some of the minor and some of the major commandments."[27] Commentators understood this model to apply to women converts as well, of whom there were many in antiquity.

During the Second Temple and early rabbinic periods, conversion to Judaism would have involved a long period of preparation and education, culminating in a series of ritual acts: for a man—circumcision, immersion, offering a sacrifice at the Temple. For a woman, the requirements included immersion and the sacrifice. After the destruction of the Temple in 70 C.E., the sacrifice was eliminated from the ritual. The Talmud, which contains the rabbinic teachings of the first six centuries C.E., records many accounts of conversion to Judaism. One of the Talmud's strangest tales of conversion concerns a famous Roman prostitute who witnessed the power of Jewish belief in the most compelling of ways. A young Jewish student of the Torah had travelled a great distance to avail himself of this woman's sexual services, for she was the most famous prostitute of her time. As the young man climbed up to her elaborate bed, which was on a series of raised platforms, the tassels of his *tzitzit*—the fringes on his garment worn in fulfillment of biblical law—flew in his face, reminding him of God's law. He fled the woman and returned to his teachers. This young man's change of heart so astounded the prostitute that she sought out the young man's rabbi and asked to become a Jew. The rabbi accepted her as a proselyte, and she became the mother of a number of rabbinic scholars.[28]

In the twelfth century, Maimonides codified the Talmudic legal decisions about conversion to Judaism in the *Mishneh Torah.* In this legal magnum opus, Maimonides wrote, "When a gentile wishes to enter the covenant and to be gathered under the wings of the Divine Presence, and he accepts the yoke of the Torah, he needs circumcision and immersion."[29] The reasons for these specific rituals had been explained in the *Mishnah*, a millennium before Maimonides: "Just as Israel did not enter the covenant except through three things—circumcision, immersion, and acceptance of a sacrifice—so it is the same with proselytes."[30] Thus the induction of an individual into the Jewish people is modeled on the *communal* history of that people. After the Exodus from Egypt, the children of Israel became a people in a precisely prescribed manner, through three ritual acts described in the biblical account. A person who wishes to join that people at any later point in history has to undertake the fulfillment of these same ritual requirements. Thereafter the proselyte is thought of as joined to the Jewish people, "as if they had been present at Sinai." Like the person born a Jew, the former gentile is now a full member of the covenantal community.

In rabbinic understanding, the status of "Jew," whether acquired through birth or conversion, remained immutable. One could join the community, but one could not leave it. Although a person might choose to separate from the Jewish community, the community did not have a mechanism to declare that person "not a Jew." The "deserter" or apostate could be condemned morally as a "bad Jew," but his or her status remained "Jewish." In Hebrew, the apostate is termed a *meshummad* or *mumar*. One indication that the sinning apostate Jew retains her or his essential "Jewishness" is this: if the apostate wishes to return to the Jewish fold, he or she is accepted back into the community without the full ritual required of a gentile convert to Judaism. The record of a late-fifteenth-century exchange between a Christian scholar and a Spanish rabbi provides an example of an apostate who remained a Jew, despite his conversion to Christianity. The case involved a Jewish man who had apostatized to Christianity and left his wife. In consultation with her rabbi the wife asked for the traditional *get*, or bill of divorce, which only the man can provide. A Christian scholar asked the rabbi, "Why do you want it from him? As he left his religion it would be proper for them to consider him as if he did not exist. Hence his wife should be considered a widow in every respect [i.e., and not require a *get*]." The Rabbi responded, "Apostasy cannot be of the essence but only accidental. . . . He cannot change his essence, for he is a Jew . . . This answer is true according to our religion. This is the meaning of the saying of our Sages, 'Even if he has sinned, he remains of Israel.'"[31]

The legal category of apostate applied to a Jewish woman or man who had joined another religious community. Though an apostate Jew "remains of Israel," rabbinic authorities limited the scope and possibility of their participation in the ritual and social spheres of Jewish life. The rabbis did not allow an apostate to participate in synagogue services, to serve as a witness in a rabbinic court or ritual (e.g., a marriage ceremony), or to merit burial in a cemetery consecrated as a Jewish graveyard. As one modern rabbinic authority has noted, "Far from welcoming the apostate to participate in the service, the early Jewish liturgy included *Birkat haMinim*, which explicitly cursed those Jews who abandoned their people. . . . Thus we have, on the one hand, the classic teaching that a Jew is always a Jew. On the other hand, tradition effectively shunned complete apostates, denying them an active role in the Jewish community."[32]

CONVERSION TO CHRISTIANITY

Despite these harsh strictures many Jews did convert to Christianity. In the pre-modern period of European history many conversions were the result of coercion in the form of persecution or social pressure. For many Jews, an awareness of the long history of Christian persecution strengthened their resolve to remain steadfast in their faith, a resolve that Christians tended to perceive as stubbornness. For a smaller number of Jews, awareness of persecution led to the opposite conclusion: Judaism should be abandoned, as God had abandoned his people and was no longer protecting them from their oppressors. The Spanish-Jewish physician Abner of Burgos (1270–1340) who served as a rabbi before his conversion to Christianity wrote, "I saw the poverty of the Jews, my people, from whom I am descended, who have been oppressed and broken and heavily burdened by taxes throughout their long captivity—this people that has lost its former honor . . . and there is none to sustain them. . . . When I had meditated on the matter, I went to the synagogue weeping sorely and sad at heart. And in a dream I saw the figure of a tall man who said to me, 'I say unto thee that the Jews have remained so long in captivity for their folly and wickedness and because they have no teachers of righteousness through whom they may recognize truth.'"[33]

Some fifty years after Abner of Burgos's apostasy, when at the instigation of the Catholic clergy attacks on Jews in Spain became commonplace, many Jews chose baptism rather than expulsion or death. Between 1391, when these attacks began in earnest, and 1492, when Ferdinand and Isabella issued the Edict of Expulsion which expelled all Jews from Spain, thousands of Spanish Jews converted to Catholicism. These "New Christians" were dubbed *conversos*, and despite their baptisms they were not accepted fully into the Spanish social order. As the eminent Israeli historian Haim Hillel Ben Sasson noted, the *conversos* "were accused of secretly observing Jewish practices while the Jews were blamed for providing them with the information and material that were necessary to maintain their Jewish identity. The official reason for the expulsion of 1492 was the influence Jews had on the New Christians. In 1492, the *conversos* were joined by a large group of Jews who decided to convert rather than leave the country."[34]

In Hebrew the *conversos* were known as *anusim*—those who had been forced into Christianity. Some *anusim* preserved aspects of Jewish practice, and when their descendants settled in the Low Countries in the late sixteenth and seventeenth centuries, they reverted to Judaism. From that time onward the memory of forced conversion to Christianity became a constant in Jewish communal and individual consciousnesses, and it would affect all subsequent Jewish reactions to converts and apostates. The fear of the renewal of Christian persecution and forced baptism was from then on a permanent feature of European Jewish identity.

After the French Revolution, Western European nations began to grant Jews some rights of citizenship, but conversions to Christianity continued, for social betterment, for the purpose of marriage, or occasionally for reasons of religious belief. Some converted Jews articulated a sincere belief that in Christianity they found a "fulfilled" Judaism. Estimates for baptism of Jews in nineteenth- and early-twentieth-century Europe exceed 200,000 cases.[35] Many of these Jewish converts, including those discussed in *Jewish–Christian Difference and Modern Jewish Identity*, wrote about their experiences, and as the publication figures attest, a large Christian audience proved eager to read their accounts.

A key theme in the narratives of Jewish converts to Christianity is that of uncovering the "true" meaning of the Hebrew Bible. While the Hebrew Bible was a familiar text to most Jews, they did not understand it as the Old Testament, as a precursor pointing to "the Christian Truth" of the New Testament. The classic formulation of this idea is St. Augustine's dictum that "in the Old Testament the New Testament is concealed; in the New Testament, the Old Testament is revealed." Thus for Rabbi Zolli, the Chief Rabbi of Rome in the 1930s, frequent study and meditation transformed his understanding of the deeply familiar Hebrew Bible into a prefiguration of the New Testament. We explore Rabbi Zolli's conversion in detail in chapter Five. Zolli was not the only twentieth century Orthodox Jewish scholar to convert to Christianity. In his memoirs, Philip Levertoff, a Hasidic Jew who became an Anglican priest in 1910, tells of being ten years old and finding a torn-out page from a New Testament that had been translated into Hebrew. Levertoff showed the page to his father, who flew into a rage and tore the offending page to shreds, an event which ensured the child's continuing fascination with the forbidden text. Ten years after finding that page, and after much soul-searching, Levertoff converted to Christianity. He became an Anglican priest and served as a life-long missionary to Jews. Although the Jewish community widely condemned Levertoff's apostasy, he was not completely cut off from his Jewish co-religionists. Despite his standing as a renegade Jew, a *meshummad*, Levertoff's scholarship continued to be read and respected in the Jewish community of his time.

Significantly, there were also cases in which a deep engagement with the Old Testament led Christians to convert to Judaism. The Italian Donato Manduzio, whom we meet in chapter Four, left Catholicism for Judaism in the 1920s. Missionaries from Italian Protestant denominations encouraged Manduzio to explore the Old Testament. Once he had studied it deeply, he accepted the Jewish interpretation of its message, rejecting Christianity and its appropriation of the Hebrew Bible. Moses rather than Jesus became Manduzio's model of leadership, as he led a large group of Italian peasants into Judaism in the 1930s and 1940s.

CONVERSION, JUDAISM, AND ZIONISM

In each account of conversion to Judaism or apostasy to Christianity included in *Jewish–Christian Difference and Modern Jewish Identity*, the Holocaust, Zionism, and the State of Israel play pivotal roles. Whether one was a Christian who chose to join the Jewish people or a Jew who chose to become a Christian, one could not escape engagement with these issues: After the Holocaust and the establishment of Israel, what is the meaning of Jewish identity? Is the Jewish future inextricably linked to Israel? Does conversion to Judaism require one to become a Zionist? Does becoming a Jew obligate one to live in or show allegiance to the self-described Jewish state? If so, how does one understand the political and religious nature of that state? When a Jew becomes a Christian, must he or she sever ties to the State of Israel? What responsibility if any do today's Christians, whether of Jewish origin or not, have toward Israel?

A wide variety of answers presented themselves. Donato Manduzio, having seen his small neo-Jewish community in San Nicandro survive World War II, wanted his followers to stay in Italy and bring even more Italian Catholics into the Jewish faith. His followers, however, scarred by their wartime experiences and inspired by their encounters with Jews from Palestine, saw *aliyah* to Israel as the fulfillment of their turn to Judaism. Manduzio, always somewhat skeptical about Zionism, died soon after his formal conversion to Judaism and was buried in San Nicandro. His wife Antonia remained in the village and carried on his missionary work, but most of his followers emigrated from Italy to Israel soon after 1948, settling in an agricultural community near the city of Safed. Like the San Nicandro Jews, each of our converts to Judaism wanted to be associated with the new Jewish experiment in Israel, but each understood that experiment in a different way.

In 1925 the poet Elisheva, born into a Russian Christian family, moved to British Palestine with her husband, the Zionist functionary Shimon Bikhovsky. Although Elisheva shared her husband's love of the Hebrew language and hope for its rebirth, her choice to remain a Christian rather than formally convert to Judaism alienated many of her colleagues in the Hebrew literary and artistic community of 1930s Jewish Palestine. When Bikhovsky died suddenly at the age of fifty, Elisheva and her infant daughter were left destitute and isolated. If Elisheva had converted to Judaism, perhaps a better living situation would have presented itself. As it was, she died in abject poverty in 1949, with her literary genius acknowledged only years later. We explore her story in chapter 6.

Ruth Ben David, another of our converts to Judaism, whom we meet in chapter 2, was a single parent when she and her son, Uriel, moved to Israel in 1954. Her work in the French Resistance during World War II led to an interest in and sympathy toward the Jewish people. After the war she con-

verted to Judaism. Although Ruth began life in Israel as an ardent supporter
of the Israeli government and its policies, she soon became disillusioned.
Eventually she became an ardent anti-Zionist, and a leading voice in the
ultra-Orthodox community of Meah Shearim.

Our four Jewish converts to Christianity also engaged with Zionism,
though to a lesser degree than our three converts to Judaism. For conversion
to Christianity represented a turn away from the particular and toward the
universal. In Judaism's self-understanding, Jews are in a special covenantal
relationship with God. The founders of Christianity, Jews themselves, reima-
gined this covenant as extended to all of humanity. Zionism, however, with
its focus on a national homeland for the Jews, represented a continued affirmation of the particular, not the universal. Despite this particularity, Zionism's core idea—"the return of the Jews to their land"—retained its hold on
these converts' imaginations. Rabbi Israel Zolli, one of our Jewish converts
to Christianity, visited Palestine in the mid-1930s and engaged in a series of
conversations with Chief Rabbi Abraham Isaac Kook. His decision to join
the Catholic Church was a rejection of the Zionist idea, which he considered
a political rather than a religious solution. Despite his decision to fulfill his
Jewish past in a Christian future, Zolli read widely in Modern Hebrew and
followed events in Palestine closely.

Moshe Rosen, the founder of Jews for Jesus, created strong bonds between that Christian missionary movement and the State of Israel. Rosen,
whom we meet in chapter 8, was an American Jew who chose to join the
Baptist church and then worked to bring other Jews to Christianity.

The young Aaron Lustiger of Paris, whom we meet in chapter 3, joined
the church during his adolescence. His parents' attempts to dissuade him
failed. He attended seminary, served as a parish priest, and rose to the top of
the French Catholic hierarchy. Paradoxically, Lustiger's conversion to Christianity brought him closer to Zionism. Lustiger made pilgrimages to Israel
beginning in 1951 and continuing into to the 1990s. He supported the establishment of the Hebrew Vicarate in Israel, the community of Hebrew-speaking Catholics that today numbers in the thousands.

BEN GURION'S QUESTION, REDUX

Among the respondents to David Ben Gurion's letter of 1958 was Alexander
Altmann, professor of philosophy at Brandeis University. Though ordained
as an Orthodox rabbi Altmann did not serve as a congregational rabbi, but as
a university professor. Altmann proved more philosophical and pragmatic in
his response than the Orthodox rabbis on Ben Gurion's roster. He framed the
issues underlying the children of a mixed marriage problem astutely, even
prophetically, noting, "Presumably, in these cases the parents do not wish

their children to undergo a rite of conversion. . . . The parents themselves are not observant and see no need for their child to be accepted as a convert, as they are satisfied with his being Jewish solely in the national sense of the term. . . . In effect, the questions is . . . is there a category of Jews whose Judaism is limited to national affiliation alone."[36]

After a long and thoughtful consideration of this question, Altmann answered in the negative. A purely national identity for Jews was for him untenable. "The whole of the national effort of the Jewish people stems from unity between religious faith and the desire to ensure the survival of the nation. . . . It is clear, therefore, that there can be no recognition of Jewish nationality as separate from religion."[37] Despite this conclusion, which seemed to place the definition of Jewishness in the hands of the Orthodox rabbis, Altmann called for a conversion policy that was flexible and compassionate. He hoped that "at the crossroads at which we find ourselves at this time, when the different diasporas are coming together in Israel . . . the rabbis will approach the issue of converts charitably and will ease the acceptance into Judaism of those children whose parents have arrived in Israel as a place of refuge and freedom. . . . I pray that the rabbis in the State of Israel will do everything in their power to further the full integration of these children."[38] Alexander Altmann's advice fell on deaf ears. Over the subsequent decades the Israeli Rabbinate has become ever stricter in policing the borders of Judaism.

Israeli secularists have attempted to counter this tendency by advocating the expansion of the borders of Jewish identity. In 2000 Yossi Beilin, then serving as the Israeli Minister of Justice, published a book calling for a more liberal approach to the question of Israeli Jewish identity, especially in relation to the identity issues that confront American Jews. Noting that the Israeli Rabbinate refused to acknowledge the validity of conversions to Judaism performed by Conservative or Reform rabbis, Beilin called for the Israeli government to institute "secular conversion."[39] A number of American Jewish intellectuals had called for a similar process. The 1983 Reform movement's decision to accept 'patrilineal descent' was very much on their minds. By the 2010s when the children of Jewish fathers and non-Jewish mothers, who were now considered Jewish according to Reform Judaism, were reaching adulthood, there was a public clamor for a new definition of Jewishness that would be highly inclusive.[40] In Israel, where the definitions of Jewish/non-Jewish are a matter of practical concern and intrude on the conduct of daily life, the struggles over Jewish identity continue to play out in dramatic fashion.

The Palestinian suicide bombings in Jerusalem in the mid-1990s resulted in one of the most dramatic expressions of the conflict over Jewish identity. Among the many victims of the bombings were Russian immigrants to Israel who fell into that category of people who had the rights of Israeli Jews, but were not Jews according to the rabbinate. Thus, they could not be buried with full rites in a Jewish cemetery. Secular Israelis, who saw the victims of the bombings as Israelis who had given their lives for the Jewish state, were outraged by the refusal to bury them as Jews. But many Orthodox Jews defended the rabbinate's decision.

Decades earlier, in 1965 J. L. Talmon, one of Israel's leading intellectuals, suggested that "the Jewish religion may paradoxically be facing its supreme test precisely in the Jewish state, and the problem of Jewish identity may prove even more intractable there than in the countries of dispersion."[41] In the second decade of the twenty-first century, both Jewish identity and Israeli identity continue to resist precise definition, and Talmon's observation seems more timely than ever.

The first of our seven accounts of conversion and apostasy, the story of Madeleine Feraille of Calais, France, approaches the issue of Jewish identity from the point of view of the outsider. Madeleine, who took the name of Ruth, the model convert of the Hebrew Bible, sought a form of Judaism that was authentic and all-encompassing. Along with the biblical Ruth, Madeleine wanted to be able to say in the most unequivocal fashion, "your people shall be my people, and your God my God" (Ruth 1:17).

NOTES

1. Quoted in Ben-Rafael, *Jewish Identities*, 145. See also Cohen and Susser, "Jews and Others," 65. In Israeli identity documents of the time both "religion" and "nationality" were listed. In the past decade the "religion" designation has been eliminated from Israeli identity cards. But in documents kept in government files of *mirsham hatoshavim* ("registration of inhabitants"), the religion of every citizen is recorded. One consequence of this is that individuals from different religions cannot marry one another within Israel. For according to Israeli law, in which there is no civil marriage or divorce, couples can only be wed by the clergy of their own respective religion. One way around this restriction is the so-called "Cyprus Marriage": the couple travels to Cyprus or another European site, is married there by the civil authorities, and returns to Israel with a marriage license. Today, only "nationality" is listed on Israeli identity cards. But that designation, too, is highly problematic. And as we shall see later in this book, that designation is often challenged.
2. Kimmerling, *The Invention and Decline of Israeliness*, 41.
3. Cohen and Susser, "Jews and Others," 61.
4. Quoted in Ben-Rafael, *Jewish Identities*, 145.
5. "Declaration of Israel's Independence 1948."
6. Barzilai, "Who is a Jew?," 29.
7. Ibid.
8. Quoted in Ben-Rafael, *Jewish Identities*, 146.
9. Ibid.
10. Ben-Rafael, *Jewish Identities*, 34–35.
11. Ibid.
12. Ibid., 333.
13. Ibid., 183.
14. Ibid., 181.
15. Ibid., 310.
16. Hartman, *Israelis and the Jewish Tradition*, 15–16.

17. See Anti-Defamation League, "The Conversion Crises." Also see Alter, "The Shalit Case."

18. Barzilai, "Who is a Jew?," 30.

19. See the section "Testing the Principals" in Anti-Defamation League, "The Conversion Crisis."

20. See Zeveloff, "Patrilineal Jews Still Find Resistance."

21. S. Cohen, *The Beginnings of Jewishness*, 343.

22. Associated Press, "Israeli Court Rules Jews for Jesus Cannot Automatically be Citizens."

23. S. Cohen, *The Beginnings of Jewishness*, 341.

24. Satlow, *Jewish Marriage in Antiquity*, 136. Also see S. Cohen, *The Beginnings of Jewishness*, 261, on "the process of limited choices."

25. For more on Ezra and "conversion" see Ellenson and Gordis, *Pledges of Jewish Allegiance*, 19, 173.

26. See Halbertal and Hartman, *Judaism and the Challenges of Modern Life*, 120–133.

27. Babalonian Talmud, Yevamot 47a.

28. Babalonian Talmud, Menahot 44a.

29. *Mishneh Torah, Isurei Bi'ah*, 13:4 quoted in Ellenson and Gordis, *Pledges of Jewish Allegiance*, 30.

30. *Sifre Numbers* 108 quoted in Segal, *Paul the Convert*, 98.

31. *Akedat Yizhak* (Venice, 1573), 258b no. 97, Ki-Teze quoted in Ben-Sasson, "Apostasy," 202–212.

32. Central Conference of American Rabbis, "Apostate in the Synagogue."

33. Quoted in Ben Sasson, "Apostasy," 203.

34. Ben Sasson, "Anuism."

35. Endelman, *Jewish Apostasy in the Modern World*, 18.

36. Quoted in Ben-Rafael, *Jewish Identities*, 153–154.

37. Ibid., 155.

38. Ibid., 157.

39. See Fishman, *Double or Nothing?*, 130–31.

40. Fein, "Open a Secular Door to Judaism"; Wilensky, "What would you call me?"

41. Talmon, "Who is a Jew," 36.

Chapter Two

The Conversions of Ruth Ben David: (Madeleine Feraille, 1920–2000)

CONVERSION AND APOSTASY IN WARTIME FRANCE

The extraordinary lives of our two French converts, Madeleine Feraille (1920–2000) and Aaron Lustiger (1926–2007), were shaped by their youthful experiences of World War II. The fall of France to the German army in the summer of 1940 radically altered the lives of all French citizens. The subsequent German occupation of France as well as the deportation and murder of France's Jews deeply affected these two young people in a unique manner, leading each to change religious affiliation. Feraille's family was Catholic and Lustiger's was Jewish. Feraille, disillusioned by the wartime behavior of her countrymen and co-religionists, left the Catholic Church after the war and set out on a long religious quest that would lead her to the most rigorous form of ultra-Orthodox Judaism. There is no doubt that Feraille's awareness of the fate of France's Jews under the Vichy regime encouraged her to identify with a persecuted people. In the early 1960s Feraille, then known as Ruth Ben David, would become a protagonist in the Yossele Affair, one of Israel's great political controversies. From her role in that political affair she would emerge as a public figure in Israel, assuming a leadership position in one of Jerusalem's ultra-Orthodox communities during the 1970s and 1980s.

Our second French convert, Aaron Lustiger, who, like Feraille, was beset and burdened by religious questions from childhood, abandoned the Jewish milieu in which he had been raised and was baptized into the Roman Catholic Church in 1940, at the age of fourteen. The moral failure of France's political and intellectual elite during the war left a deep impression on Lustiger. After the war, he attended seminary and was ordained a priest. Father

21

Lustiger rose quickly through the ranks of the French Catholic hierarchy. For a decade he served as a clergyman to the students and faculty of the Sorbonne. In 1981 Lustiger was appointed Archbishop of Paris and in 1983 Pope John Paul II named him a Cardinal of the Church.

Neither Feraille's nor Lustiger's parents were particularly devout, but they identified strongly with the religious communities in which they had been born and raised. The future Ruth Ben David wrote of her parents, "Neither of them were church-goers; my father had agnostic and anti-clerical tendencies, but I myself had always had strong religious emotions."[1] Only in ultra-Orthodox Judaism would Madeleine Feraille find the full expression of those religious emotions. Similarly, Cardinal Lustiger in a 1986 interview recalled, "As a child I perceived my Judaism only as a social identity, since all the education I had received was essentially secular."[2] It was in the Catholic Church that the young Aaron Lustiger would find his religious identity. Yet, throughout his long life he would maintain an active relationship with Jews and the State of Israel.

Was it the secularism of their respective upbringings that led each of these two converts to seek religious authenticity and authority in a radically different tradition? Did the cowardice and collaboration that they had witnessed in World War II France energize their search for ultimate truths? To what extent did Feraille and Lustiger find it necessary, as they embarked on their respective religious searches, to reject the religion and culture into which they had been born? How did each attempt to maintain some continuity with their familial and cultural pasts? The answers to these questions illuminate the modern conversion process in general and these two remarkable twentieth-century lives in particular.

Like Aaron Lustiger, who had converted to Catholicism a few months before the German invasion of France in June 1940, Madeleine Feraille responded to the fall of France by embarking on a search for authentic religious experience and a strict moral code. For both Madeleine Feraille and Aaron Lustiger, the German invasion and subsequent French collaboration generated a moral dilemma which required much more than a philosophical response. Each sought meaning and structure in an established faith community, one that would enable them to confront the problem of evil and take moral action. Once they found their respective communities, each would take a leadership position in them.

Feraille's and Lustiger's experiences of World War II and their understandings of its meaning in history were at the core of their religious and cultural transformations. As Feraille/Ruth Ben David, wrote in the early-1960s, "The recent tragic war with its enormous impact changed many lives, and mine among them."[3] The challenge generated by the moral "fall of France" was the great crisis of her youth. Lustiger too was explicit about the war's effect on his spiritual development. His conversion to Catholicism and his life as a priest, bishop and cardinal, were linked to his understanding and interpretation of his wartime experiences. The deportation to Auschwitz and subsequent murder of his mother and other family members were of course formative experiences for him. French complicity in this betrayal of his family troubled him deeply, and as a Catholic priest and leader of French Catholicism he was always in the grip of these issues.

FROM MADELEINE FERAILLE TO RUTH BEN DAVID

Let us turn first to the story of Madeleine Feraille, the future Ruth Ben David of Jerusalem's ultra-Orthodox enclave, Meah Shearim. As a child growing up in a middle-class Catholic family in the northern French port of Calais, Feraille had no idea that there were Jews in France. Much later she would write, "I must have thought that the Jews were an ancient people like the Romans who had long disappeared and whose language was a classical one like Latin."[4] Her mother's exotic appearance encouraged Madeleine's childhood fantasy that the family was of Spanish rather than French ancestry. Madeleine described her mother's family as being "of the Spanish type—dark haired with deep moldering eyes." When as a teenager she learned that there were Jews in France, young Madeleine Feraille wondered aloud if she had secret Jewish ancestors in her French Catholic family. Madeleine suggested this to her mother and grandmother, but they rejected such a possibility, despite the family's declared aversion to eating pork and its insistence on soaking meat to rid it of as much blood as possible before cooking.

In her Calais lycée, Madeleine was an enthusiastic student of ancient history. The curriculum included a short section on Jewish history, a subject she found very compelling. She asked her parents for a Bible, a book not commonly found in French Catholic homes of the time. Like other converts from Catholicism whose stories we shall explore in *Jewish–Christian Difference and Modern Jewish Identity*, Madeleine Feraille acquired a Bible from Protestant missionaries, in her case from the Salvation Army in Calais. Like Donato Manduzio in 1930s Apulia, whom we shall meet in chapter four, Madeleine Feraille found that her Catholic co-religionists were appalled that she was not only reading the Bible, but reading it in a Protestant translation. One of her classmates said to her, "You are a Catholic and not allowed to read the Old Testament. It is a book written by the Devil." Madeleine replied, "No, you are possessed by the Devil."[5] The Catholic Priest of San Nicandro had told Donato Manduzio something similar only a few years earlier: "The Protestant Bible is the devil's book. It should be burned, not studied." It is important to note that reading a Protestant Bible did not lead Madeleine Feraille and Donato Manduzio to a Protestant denomination. Rather, they embarked on religious quests that led them to examine and reject Protestant belief, and later convert to Judaism. Reading the Hebrew Bible/Old Testament had a powerful effect on each of them, although not the result that either had anticipated. Jews, they discovered, had a glorious past, and they also had a place in the present.

The first reading of a previously unknown sacred text strongly affected many converts, as we shall see in several stories included in the following chapters. Many Jewish converts to Christianity tell of first reading the New Testament and being moved by its narratives, with the objections of fellow Jews often serving only to increase the allure. For Aaron Lustiger, reading the Old and New Testaments as a single unit inspired his conversion to Christianity. Other sacred texts could have an equally powerful effect. For the German-Jewish philosopher Edith Stein, raised in a German Orthodox Jewish home, reading Teresa of Avila's autobiography would convince her of the truth of Catholicism. Stein spent the night reading the book, and in the morning declared, "This is the truth."

With Hitler's rise to power in 1933 and the subsequent enactment of the Nuremburg Laws in 1935, Madeleine Feraille and her lycée classmates became aware of German anti-Jewish propaganda and legislation. They soon learned that some of their classmates were Jews. As Feraille said of her understanding at the time, "Jews meant to me the Old Testament and nothing more, and I am sure that there were many more children, and I supposed adults too, who thought the same. Because of anti-Semitism . . . I became aware of the great tragedy of the Jewish people, whose history I had so much admired but presumed to have come to an end long, long ago."[6]

Feraille was twenty years old when Germany invaded France in 1940. Moving with startling speed, the Wehrmacht rapidly overwhelmed the French army. Over 100,000 French soldiers were killed, twice as many were wounded, and perhaps five times the number of wounded were captured. The news that a million French soldiers had been captured and taken to prisoner of war camps in Germany and Austria thoroughly demoralized the French public. The Germans divided the country into two zones: a northern occupied zone and a southern zone indirectly under their control. A collaborationist French government seated in the city of Vichy administered the southern zone, where there was slightly more freedom than in the north. Calais, the Feraille's hometown, was in the northern occupied zone. Madeleine's father joined the ranks of the Resistance and she soon followed. For the duration of the Nazi occupation she would serve as a courier between Resistance groups and on many occasions guide refugees to safety.

In September 1939 just after the outbreak of war, Madeleine married a young man from Nice who had recently been drafted into the French Army. Only after her husband was called to the front did she realize that she was pregnant. Her son Claude was born in October of 1940, after a difficult pregnancy. Soon after, Madeleine enrolled in courses at the University of

Toulouse, with a concentration in the study of literature and religion. Separated from her husband who was at the front, Madeleine began to reevaluate her marriage. "About this time doubts began to enter my mind about any real understanding between my husband and myself."[7] The marriage fell apart, ending in divorce. As Feraille recalled insightfully, "He still loved me, but as there was nothing intellectual or spiritual to bind us, I felt it could not last nor survive the time when my looks and youth would inevitably fade."[8]

The conduct of her countrymen during the German occupation, especially the Vichy regime's complicity in the deportation and murder of France's Jews, was deeply disillusioning to Madeleine Feraille. As she said, "The experiences of human beings descending to such levels of conduct had a deep effect on my mind. In my despair I came to doubt man's capacity for genuine progress."[9] At the time of the German invasion in 1940, there were approximately 300,000 Jews in France, among a total population of roughly 40 million people. About one-half of the resident Jews were French citizens; the rest were foreign Jews with various forms of temporary or permanent papers. During the course of the war, the Germans and their French collaborators deported 75,000 French Jews to death camps in the East, where very few survived.[10]

This disillusionment, as well as the influence of her fellow university students and her father, led Madeleine to make contact with the Resistance in Toulouse and offer to serve in its ranks. "It was part of my duties in the Resistance to help Jews within the very limited possibilities that existed for these unfortunate people . . . This was my first contact with Jews and their tragedy of these days—hunted by the mighty Nazi hounds, captured and slaughtered."[11] She successfully smuggled documents and people through occupied zones and across borders. Madeleine was by numerous accounts a beautiful young woman, and she seems to have used her appearance to advantage. She was able to convince German and Vichy officers that she was an innocent traveler and that her border crossings had no political import. As one observer has noted, "The Germans were far less prone to stop women who looked pretty and well turned out."[12] It would be easy today to level a feminist critique at this emphasis on Ferraille's appearance, but that would run the risk of overlooking her bravery and her heroic efforts. Madeleine Ferraille, regardless of tactics, was an intelligent, efficient, successful member of the French Resistance who saved lives by smuggling Jews and information past German lines. After the war, Madeleine moved to Geneva where she worked in the insurance business, brought up her son, and continued her graduate studies. Later she set up an import-export business based in Geneva and Paris. As she continued her studies toward a doctorate in religion, Madeleine realized that her attachment to the Catholic Church had grown even weaker. "Catholicism did not satisfy me, neither appealing to my logic or my heart."[13] She befriended a group of Seventh Day Adventists who invited her to their weekly Bible discussion group. Attracted to their way of life and tradition of study, Madeleine considered joining an Adventist Church, but soon found that she could not accept the Adventists' rejection of medical intervention. Later, after her conversion to Judaism, she realized that "what attracted me to the Adventists was what they had selected from Judaism, but it was only later, when I went back directly to the source, that I fully realized this."[14] Madeleine's quest, and Lustiger's as well, emphasized "getting back directly to the source" of religious truth. She began to look to the Jewish students and business people whom she met to enlighten her about Judaism, but she soon found that "my Jewish friends in Geneva knew nothing about their religion, or any other."[15]

A FIRST JOURNEY/PILGRIMAGE TO ISRAEL

In France and Switzerland, Madeleine Feraille's search for an authentic form of religion only led her to greater frustration. Increasingly, she felt estranged from her Catholic past. "I had lived until the age of thirty with people among whom, in spite of intellectual contacts and ties of affection and friendship, I had always been different, a stranger in search of truth, in search of a path."[16] She knew of Jewish communities that had survived the Nazi onslaught and been revived after the War, but these communities seemed anything but welcoming to her. As a young Catholic woman, she had no way of encountering "authentic" (her term) Jews. "In despair of a practical solution to my all-absorbing dilemma my attention was drawn to Palestine which was the height of interest at that time. . . . The State of Israel, still a sensation, was but two years old. There, I thought, the real Jews must be, Jews whose way of life corresponded with the sanctity of the soil."[17]

In that same year, 1950, Father Aaron Lustiger, serving as a parish priest in Paris, also began to take an active interest in the new State of Israel, particularly in its Catholic monastic and lay communities. The Carmelite order, with which he was affiliated, had monasteries in Haifa in the north and Bethlehem in the south (then in the Kingdom of Jordan). The Catholic Church also controlled a number of holy sites and institutions in Jerusalem, including the Ecole Biblique in the Jordanian sector and the Ratisbonne Monastery in the Israeli sector. In 1951, Lustiger, like Madeleine Feraille, would make the first of many visits to Israel.

In the early 1950s, Madeleine Feraille met a young Israeli man visiting Paris, whom she identified as "Simon S." Simon quickly became infatuated with her, and soon invited Madeleine to visit him in Israel during the summer vacation. He hoped to marry her, adopt her son Claude, and live with them in Israel. Considering this idea, Madeleine Feraille, accompanied by Claude, traveled to Israel that summer, where she met Simon's friends and family.

"They were all very pleasant, full of energy and enthusiasm, but none of them was a believer. To them, as to my friends in Geneva, religion seemed to be something that belonged to the past. The only important task in their eyes was to build up their country so that Jews might have a refuge where anti-Semitism could no longer affect them."[18]

If Madeleine Feraille had at that point chosen to remain in Israel and convert to Judaism, her story would have been unusual, but not extraordinary. In the 1950s, thousands of Christians moved to Israel with Jewish spouses. Many, but not all, converted to Judaism. During that early period in Israeli history, it was easier to become an Israeli citizen than today, when the state-sanctioned Chief Rabbinate asserts more control over questions of religious identity, and demands that candidates for citizenship under the Law of Return prove their Jewish bona fides.

Madeleine's first journey to Israel did not satisfy her religious needs. The Jews she met were secular rather than religious, and thus not the "real Jews" of her expectations and imagination. She could not envision a life for herself and her son Claude with a man like Simon who "in spite of living in the Holy Land, was not religious." Such a marriage, she felt, "would be wracked by some kind of mental incompatibility. . . . My imagination had envisaged Jews who were altogether different from Simon. Men with long prophetic beards, austere and devout."[19] This image of the devout Jewish man and woman, though somewhat stereotypical, was the image that Madeleine would seek and eventually encounter.

Though impressed by the energy and industriousness of the young Israelis that she met, Madeleine Feraille realized that she did not want to be one of them. As she described it over a decade later, "It was Judaism, not Zionism, that I wanted to embrace. . . . I wanted to come and live among Jews in order to worship God and serve Him, not to sing *Hatikvah*, though I was not unmoved when this Israeli anthem was sung."[20]

CONVERSION

On her return to France, Madeleine Feraille decided to seek out a rabbi and convert to Judaism. A friend recommended Rabbi Elbez of Paris, the head of Liberal or Reform Judaism in France, who agreed to supervise her conversion. Madeleine studied with him for a few months. In post-War Europe, conversion to Judaism for reasons other than marriage was a rare event. Making Madeleine Feraille's conversion even more unusual was the fact that her son Claude, now ten years old, also wished to become a Jew. The only objections to their conversions came from Jewish acquaintances, both personal friends and business associates. As Madeleine later recalled, "They were not in the least religious. They thought I was mad, and particularly objected to my dragging my son into 'that adventure'."[21] Claude had been circumcised by a French physician a year earlier. Thus both he and his mother expected him to convert. At the conversion ceremony in 1953, Madeleine took the given name of Ruth, the paradigmatic convert of the Bible, and as a surname, Ben David. Claude took the name Uriel, one of the guardian angels in the Jewish tradition.

On her path to Judaism, constructing arguments against remaining a Christian, the young Madeleine Feraille seemed to intuit long-standing Jewish critiques of Christianity. Like others considering conversion, she examined the religious tradition in which she had been raised, in her case Catholicism, against the tenets of a new faith, Judaism. Christianity positions the New Testament as the fulfillment of the Old Testament, which in the Jewish tradition stands alone as the whole of sacred scriptures. Feraille turned this classical Christian understanding of Judaism on its head. In her developing view, Christianity became not the fulfillment of Judaism, but a distortion of it. She saw sharp differences between the Christian and Jewish approaches to scripture and the regulation of human behavior: "Even as a young girl I had been struck by the gulf between what was required by the Gospels and the capacity of flesh and blood to perform. Later, I came to suspect the dangers inherent in teachings that, I felt, could only lead human beings to hypocrisy or revolt. Perhaps that was why the genuine humanity of the Pentateuch and the Psalms had such appeal to me."[22] Feraille's intuition echoes the arguments against Christianity presented in medieval Jewish polemics, where Christian ideals are presented as ideals impossible to realize, and as such, lead to the abandonment of all moral imperatives. Judaism's demands, though more detailed and rigorous, are—Jewish polemicists argued—more realistic.

For Madeleine Feraille/Ruth Ben David, conversion to Judaism was not the end of a process, but rather the beginning of one. She soon questioned whether a Reform Jewish life would satisfy her, either spiritually or intellectually. Her doubts concerning the authenticity of Reform Judaism grew with her attendance at the Paris temple. The Reform Jewish liturgy, which she found "church-like," combined with the few ritual obligations expected of the members of the Paris Reform congregation, convinced her that Reform Judaism was weak and watered down. She told Rabbi Elbez that the Confirmation ceremony for the girls of the Temple reminded her of the Catholic rituals of her youth. The ceremony "took me back twenty years to the time of my first communion." Leaving the Temple building that day, Ruth reflected, "Jesus must also have been a Reformed Rabbi in his time."[23] While this idea might have pleased other converts, it repelled Ruth Ben David. She wished to reject completely the essential beliefs of Catholicism. In search of a more traditional Jewish path Madeleine Feraille/Ruth Ben David began to attend lectures at one of Paris's Orthodox congregations, at a synagogue whose rabbis and members followed the ideology of Religious Zionism.[24]

In the mid-1960s, Madeleine/Ruth, reflecting on her conversion to Judaism a dozen years earlier, described a feeling similarly expressed by other converts whose stories are told in this book, a feeling that only with conversion does one begin to feel at peace. For Madeleine Feraille, it was her former life and not her new Jewish life that now struck her as alien. Madeleine's search for truth, however, was to be a life-long search. It did not stop at age thirty, when she chose to become a Jew. The more Ruth learned of traditional Jewish life, both in the synagogue and in homes she was invited to visit, the more she was attracted to it. Orthodox traditions of study and learning, particularly reports of the Yeshiva world, fascinated her. As she said, "I continued with renewed fervor my study of Torah and the Holy Tongue. I was coming to realize that Reform Judaism failed to satisfy my spiritual need."[25]

As an introduction to Orthodox Judaism, Ruth attended the lectures of Rabbi Klein of Paris. The rabbi soon fell in love with her and wanted to marry her. Taken aback by this unexpected development, Ruth did not reciprocate his feelings. Furthermore, the congregation reacted negatively to the idea of a rabbi marrying a convert to Judaism, an objection that would haunt her again years later.

The thirty-one-year-old businesswoman and single mother would suffer a much greater shock several months later. While Madeleine was busy with her graduate studies and her exploration of Judaism, her Jewish partner in the import-export textile business had attempted to defraud the French government of taxes. Because Madeleine Feraille was the managing partner of the company, the customs officials held her responsible. She spent two months in a Paris prison, where she became quite ill. Her attempt to keep Kosher while in prison did not help matters. This ordeal, which frightened her son Claude, only deepened her religious commitment. Soon after her release from prison she began a course of study with Rabbi Rubinstein of one of the Orthodox Jewish communities of Paris.[26] Madeleine Feraille/Ruth Ben David, independent as she was, did not bridle against rabbinic supervision; she welcomed it. After two years of rabbinical supervision, she underwent a second conversion ritual, this time under Orthodox auspices. Unlike her earlier Reform conversion, this second conversion required comprehensive study and careful scrutiny of her personal life and habits. In keeping with the rabbinic dictum that a candidate for conversion to Judaism who declares, "I will keep all mitzvoth but one," is to be rejected, Madeleine/Ruth fulfilled all religious obligations, with no exceptions.

Madeleine/Ruth arranged for her son Claude, now renamed Uriel, to travel to Israel and enroll in a school at Kibbutz Yavneh, which was affiliated with Mizrahi, the Religious Zionist Movement. She expected the school to prepare Uriel for his Bar Mitzvah. Madeleine stayed in Paris, where she worked to put her business back together and to associate herself with Orthodox Jewish synagogues and Talmudic academies. When she visited an ultra-Orthodox yeshiva in Aix Les Bains, she was captivated by the students' devotion to Torah study. The yeshiva was affiliated with the Satmar Hasidim, whose rabbi, Yoel Teitelbaum, was the most explicit and articulate Orthodox opponent of Zionism. For the Satmar Rabbi, Jewish nationalism, whether in its secular or religious form, was incompatible with Jewish thought and practice.

Ruth Ben David would remain in France for another six years. During that time she made additional trips to Israel. With each journey she became increasingly disillusioned with the State of Israel, though not with the Land of Israel and its ultra-Orthodox Jewish inhabitants—then a small minority. Madeleine's understanding of Israel's "meaning in history" became increasingly oppositional. She wrote, "Zionism in general, even the religious Zionism of the Mizrahi, lost its appeal for me." Invited to attend the 1954 Independence Day celebrations, Ruth found the military display clearly at odds with her personal history as a veteran of the French Resistance. "By virtue of my past I could not look upon this with much excitement and emotion. Military parades with uniformed participants could not evoke in me an elevation of the spirit. . . . What could marching soldiers mean to me? . . . Could I not see this all in the Champs Elysees?"[27] The notion that Israel's military victories were miracles repelled her. In her eyes Israeli victories were triumphs of sheer force, and not of the spirit.

Ruth's rejection of Zionism, but not of Orthodox Jewish life in Israel, led her into a conundrum, one that might have defeated a less determined convert. Her conversion to Orthodoxy, and her subsequent turn to ultra-Orthodoxy, was in part a rejection of European modernity. In Israel she witnessed most Jews embracing enthusiastically that very modernity. She herself was a thoroughly modern woman—independent, successful and assertive. Yet, she sought something else, a deepening of religious experience, not a rejection of it. But despite her objections to political Zionism, she felt drawn to live in Israel, among her newly adopted people.

Ruth Ben David settled in Israel in 1960. Yet within a few years, she became convinced that the political and cultural ideas dominant among Israeli Jews were a betrayal of the Jewish tradition. She described Zionism as "the thesis that nationalism should replace the Torah as the basis of the Jewish people" and condemned the Zionist movement as "a calamitous mistake."[28] Israel, in her eyes, was becoming "a mundane, materialistic, secular culture."[29] Having decided to live in Jerusalem, Ruth was dismayed to find that the state's presentation of Jewish Jerusalem was decidedly secular in character. She wrote that "for the purpose of tourism, the government of Israel does not refrain from calling their part of Jerusalem 'the Holy City,' though they do not themselves believe in any holiness."[30]

ULTRA-ORTHODOXY AND ZIONISM

The final stage of Ruth Ben David's religious journey led her to what she considered the most authentic of Jewish communities, the ultra-Orthodox or Haredi Jews. She found this community well represented in both France and Israel. As historian of Jewish ultra-Orthodoxy Menachem Friedman has noted, "The relationship between Zionism and Jewish Orthodoxy presents one of the most interesting and complicated questions in the history of the Jewish people. . . . For the believing Jew, the idea of the Return to Zion is bound up with the idea of messianic redemption, and the establishment of a Jewish society in the Land of Israel is justified only to the extent that this society preserves religious tradition."[31] It was to the preservation of the most rigorous interpretation of Jewish religious tradition that Ruth Ben David intended to devote herself.

Orthodox Jewish opposition to Zionism is as old as the Zionist movement. When Theodor Herzl convened the First Zionist Congress in 1897, the majority of Orthodox rabbis—some estimate as many as ninety percent—opposed participation in a movement organized by secular Jews. So how and when did Orthodoxy become Zionist? The answer is sometime during the second half of the twentieth century. The Holocaust and the establishment of the State of Israel convinced Jews of the viability and necessity of Zionism. Today, only a small group of Orthodox rabbis are anti-Zionist, although many might be described as "non-Zionist."[32]

Opposition to political Zionism expressed ultra-Orthodox opposition to modernity. The Hasidic "courts" and "dynasties" of Eastern Europe viewed Zionism as heresy. Hasidut emphasized the mystical and the redemptive; it shied away from activist movements that sought to hasten the redemption through political and social means.[33] In particular, the ultra-Orthodox argued that Zionism promoted a false messianism. Like Christianity, Zionism presumed that Rabbinic Judaism, and the Law it understands as central to Jewish life, had been superseded. Like Christianity, Zionism presented itself as the fulfillment of biblical prophecy. Just as Christians saw the Passion and the Resurrection as the culmination and fulfillment of Old Testament history, so the Zionists saw the return to the Land of Israel as the culmination of Jewish history. Ultra-Orthodox opponents of Zionism accused Zionists of being "Sabbatians," after the seventeenth century messianic leader Shabbtai Zevi (1626–76). Shabbtai Zevi's claim to be the messiah—actually, his "prophet" Nathan of Gaza made the claim for him—had caused much disruption in the Jewish world. The crisis in belief that ensued from these claims and Shabbtai's subsequent apostasy to Islam had strengthened the already long-standing rabbinic aversion to messianic fervor. To succeed, political Zionism would have to overcome this aversion.

With the emergence of political Zionism at the end of the nineteenth century, a number of Orthodox rabbis warned of a new Sabbatian crisis. In particular, they feared that the promise of imminent return to the Land of Israel led by secularists would lead to a new kind of apostasy. Unlike the apostasy of Shabbetai Zevi, which was to Islam, this apostasy would be to atheism and the abandonment of religion. As Menachem Friedman has noted, "The roots of the problem, from the standpoint of Orthodoxy, are to be found not only in the fact that Zionism is a non-religious movement which seeks to solve the problem of the Jewish people in a non-religious way; but also in the fact that the central ideas of Zionism—return to Zion, ingathering of the exiles, settlement of the Land of Israel, etc.—are deep-rooted religious concepts used in a non-religious manner."[34] By the first decades of the twentieth century, the Hasidic rabbis of Eastern Europe were expressing fierce opposition to Zionism. As the Gerer Rebbe, writing to his followers in 1901, argued, "The Holy One, blessed be He, will redeem Israel as a reward for piety and for faith in Him. Let no one imagine that the redemption and salvation of Israel will come through Zionists." As he closed his letter, the rabbi explained that a year earlier a rabbi associated with the Mizrachi movement, the religious Zionist movement, had come to visit him. "I mentioned to him the verses in the Book of Judges (about Israel going to war). Not by force does man prevail. Only sin produces the need to teach war."[35]

Many members of the traditional rabbinate continued to voice similar objections to Zionism throughout the 1920s and 1930s. From the standpoint of these ultra-Orthodox teachers, Zionism, which sought to normalize Jewish life by creating a state where Jews could live a productive modern life, was the antithesis of rabbinic concepts of separateness and holiness. The assertive secularism of political Zionism's leadership repelled these rabbis and their followers. But changes in historical circumstances would soon challenge these perceptions. Although the Zionist leadership was secular, its aim—to establish a Jewish state—seemed increasingly necessary in light of growing European anti-Semitism.

In 1936, several prominent Agudat Israel rabbis settled in Palestine and called for active cooperation between their followers and the secular leaders of the Yishuv. Previously, the rabbis of Agudat Israel, a political organization that represented Orthodox Jews, opposed cooperation with the predominantly secular Zionists. But because of the growing hostility of the Palestinian Arabs toward the Zionists (and by extension, toward all the Jews of Palestine) these rabbis changed their minds and their policies. When the Arab Revolt against the British and the Jews broke out later that same year, the Agudah movement agreed to participate in fund raising for the Haganah, the

Jewish defense force, which was defending Jewish areas from Arab attacks. In response to these accommodations with secular Zionism, a group of anti-Zionist rabbis left the Agudah organization and formed a new group, the Neturei Karta (Guardians of the City). They took their name from a Talmudic dictum that the true guardians of a city are not the warriors but the students of the Law, the Torah.[36]

As a small but highly visible and vocal oppositional group, the various factions of the Neturei Karta made their opposition to Zionism widely known. Sharp differences of opinion about the relationship of Judaism and Zionism often cut across family lines and caused deep rifts in the ultra-Orthodox communities of Jerusalem. The best known case is that of the Blau brothers, Moses and his younger brother Amram. Moses approved of accommodation with the Zionists and became a leader of the Agudat Israel political party. Amram was against any compromise and became an effective proponent of the Neturei Karta ideology. The brothers and their divisive disagreement will play a substantive role later in our story.

The Israeli government published a pamphlet in 1964 which was titled, "A Study in Fanaticism: The Neturei Karta Extremist Group." Anticipating the argument that the Neturei Karta's opposition to the State of Israel was based on religious principles, the pamphlet stated that "the decisive and overwhelming majority of observant Jews in Israel dissociate themselves entirely from the excesses and doctrines of this small extremist fringe group."[37] This was no doubt true, but the assertion that they were "extremists" only bolstered the Neturei Karta's view that they in fact represented a saving remnant loyal to "Torah-true Judaism."

GUARDIANS OF THE CITY

Only when Ruth Ben David had adopted the ideas and practices of the ultra-Orthodox opponents of Zionism did she feel that she had arrived at the final destination on her religious journey. Neither Reform Judaism nor Religious Zionism had provided the full break with the past that she sought. But in ultra-Orthodoxy she found a school of thought that emphasized Jewish separation not only from the non-Jewish world but also from Jewish secularism. It was only after studying with Rabbi Maizes at the ultra-Orthodox Seminary at Aix Les Bains that Ruth found "that true Torah enclosure which was to be my final destination."[38] In that community she found both a spiritual and a physical safety.

Under the influence of that separatist ideology Ruth Ben David returned to Israel in 1960 and settled in Jerusalem. Hoping to work as a translator and teacher she was eager to master Israeli Hebrew. Her rabbi, however, explained to her that "Zionist Hebrew is a complete substitution for 'Loshon

Kodesh,' the Holy Tongue, spoken by the prophets and the sages. It is a
different language, with a strange un-Jewish idiom." Her experiences in Israel led her to similar conclusions. "After the immense deception I had felt at
the spiritual and moral abasement in Eretz Israel, I felt that he was right."[39] A
half-century earlier, many Orthodox rabbis had denounced Eliezer Ben
Yehuda (Eliezer Perlman), described by Zionists as "the Reviver of the Hebrew language," when he arrived in Jerusalem. Ben Yehuda was a prolific
journalist as well as a lexicographer, and he was assertively secular. His
campaigns to make Hebrew a spoken language of daily use gained many
followers, but also generated great opposition.

The Neturei Karta were quick to vilify Ben Yehuda for his secularization
of the Hebrew language. In an anti-Zionist tract, they reported the legend of
his demise: "It is perhaps worth mentioning that Ben Yehuda, the chief
architect of Zionist Hebrew, died suddenly on the Sabbath, holding his pen in
hand and writing in Hebrew."[40] For the ultra-Orthodox reader, the implication was clear—Ben Yehuda died as the result of his deliberate and provoca-
tive desecration of the Sabbath. His "revival" of Hebrew was not to be
emulated by "Torah-true" Jews. Yiddish would remain the ultra-Orthodox
daily language, not Hebrew.

With no employment prospects before her, and with her son Uriel to
support, Ruth was dependent on her new religious community. In France she
had been an independent woman. At twenty she had served in the French
Resistance. She had raised her son on her own, had managed an import-
export firm, and had attended graduate schools in both France and Switzerland. Now Ruth was joining a community in which women had little agency,
power, or influence. Her new community's ideology was one of resistance to
modernity, including resistance to the emancipation of women. How would
that community assimilate a thoroughly modern woman? Her teacher, Rabbi
Maizes, must have been aware of Ruth's dilemma—and of the ultra-Orthodox community's dilemma, if they were to accept her in their midst. He
summoned her to his study in Jerusalem and asked her to engage in a conspiracy, something that seemed tailor made for her. Ruth was immediately
brought into the community's highest level of power and authority. In a
word, she was treated like a man, and a worldly, capable man at that.

Ruth wrote that while sitting in Rabbi Maizes's office and waiting for him
to describe her task, she "became progressively more convinced that something of the greatest importance, something fateful, was under way."[41] The
rabbi appealed to Ruth's sense of destiny, telling her that "there is a great
mitzvah [good deed] before you, and as I see it, only you can carry this
through." As the task was explained to her, Ruth was at first shocked and
then exhilarated. She knew that before her arrival in Israel a young boy,
Yossele Schumacher, had been abducted by his Orthodox grandparents and
hidden from his secular parents and the Israeli authorities. In fact, all Israelis

knew of the case. Not only had the press widely publicized the incident, but the Knesset, the Israeli parliament, had debated its implications. The Israeli police were now seeking Yossele Schumacher, the eight-year-old boy who had disappeared, and they were searching for him in Orthodox communities throughout Israel.

Yossele's grandparents were friends of Rabbi Maizes. They were recent immigrants to Israel from the town of Uman in the Soviet Union, and unlike the vast majority of their Russian Jewish co-religionists, they had kept alive the Hasidic traditions of their forebears. Members of the Breslav sect of Hasidim, they were determined to bring their grandson up in that Hasidic tradition. The boy's parents, however, had settled in a secular kibbutz, and they strenuously objected to the grandparents' plans for their son. The grandfather, Rabbi Nachman Shtarkes, asked his ultra-Orthodox associates to hide Yossele, his daughter's son. This they had managed to do for a few months by moving him from place to place within Israel's Orthodox enclaves. Now with the Israeli police frantically searching for Yossele, Rabbi Shtarkes and his supporters sought to smuggle the boy out of Israel.

For both the ultra-Orthodox factions and the Israeli government, the stakes were high. The ultra-Orthodox were convinced that returning Yossele to his parents was part of a nefarious Zionist plot to secularize as many Orthodox children as possible. Orthodox leaders had made similar accusations about the children of Yemenite and Moroccan immigrants. The Israeli government saw the abduction of Yossele as a direct challenge to its authority to govern all factions of the state's complex religious mosaic, a mosaic in which Jews were only part, and a fractious part at that.

During the interview, Rabbi Maizes told Ruth Ben David that she, with her experience in the French Resistance, her knowledge of European languages and cultures, and her commitment to ultra-Orthodox Judaism, was the person to smuggle Yossele out of Israel and save him, and hence many other children, from secularism. Only through her actions could "Torah-true Judaism" resist the secular power of the state. When Ruth spoke of the logistical difficulties she foresaw, Rabbi Maizes invoked destiny and the will of God. "I do not know which means you will find, but I know that you are the one destined to do this. God has led you up till now on your long way. He will lead you and the child. You act, and we all shall pray for you."[42]

As the result of this conversation, Ruth Ben David became embroiled in the "Yossele Affair" of 1960 to 1962. Rabbi Maizes, who had survived both the Nazi and Communist regimes with his religious faith intact, saw Israeli secularism as yet another historical threat to the Jewish tradition. In his view, Israeli government threats to Jewish religious life had to be resisted with zeal and subterfuge. A Jewish government that persecuted Orthodox Jews was no different from a Fascist or a Communist government. It was in fact worse. According to ultra-Orthodox opponents of Zionism, the Jewish people were not to rebel or take action toward their own political independence. They based this idea on rabbinic teachings about the Jewish role in history subsequent to the destruction of the Temple. Jews were to remain passive and submit to the rule of "the nations." They were not to rebel against them. The Israeli authorities saw the refusal to hand over Yossele Schumacher as a serious challenge to the authority of the state; thus, they were determined to find him. In 1960 Israel's Supreme Court decided in favor of Yossele's parents and ordered Rabbi Shtarkes to hand over the boy. He refused and was jailed.

Ruth Ben David soon found herself pitted against Israel's much-vaunted security and intelligence services. The Shin Bet, the internal security services, searched for Yossele in Orthodox neighborhoods, villages, and Kibbutzim. Not only did they search in vain, but Shin Bet's operatives were mocked by the occupants whose houses they searched. Groups of children taunted the police and army, singing the words "Where is Yossele?" set to a popular Hasidic *niggun* or melody. Yossele, it was soon assumed, must have been smuggled out of the country; he was nowhere to be found. Prime Minister Ben Gurion then turned to the Mossad, Israel's overseas intelligence agency. In 1960 its operatives had captured Adolph Eichmann and brought him to Jerusalem. In 1962, after Eichmann had been brought to trial, Israel's Prime Minister reasoned that it was a small matter for the Mossad to find a missing Jewish child. How difficult a task could that be? There were a limited number of ultra-Orthodox communities throughout the world. Surely Israel's spies could infiltrate one of them and find where Yossele was hidden.

Ruth Ben David also involved her son Uriel in the plot to smuggle Yossele out of Israel. He too became part of the conspiracy. Twenty years old at the time and having spent years at Orthodox yeshivot, he was eager to help his mother smuggle the boy out of the country. Furthermore, according to Ruth Ben David's account of the case, Yossele himself was eager to cooperate in his own disappearance. "This eight year old boy was already a little man, gifted with intelligence and a will above his age. He understood very well what was going on, and he knowingly participated in the fight for his faith."[43] As Yossele told Ruth, "I don't want to be with my parents, who don't want to let me stay with them anymore. They don't want me to be a proper Jew."[44] The plan was for Ruth Ben David "to bring Yossele unnoticed out of Israel by having ostensibly brought with me a daughter when entering the country with whom I would then quite naturally and quite obviously be taking out when I left."[45]

Ruth Ben David took Yossele out of Israel in June of 1960. In the meantime, the Israeli police continued to search for him. A year later, the boy was still missing. Rabbi Nachman Shtarkes, his grandfather, had been released from jail, and the government of Israel seemed impotent in the face of ultra-Orthodox defiance. The Prime Minister voiced fears that a rebellion by religious fanatics was a distinct possibility. In February 1962, Ben Gurion ordered Mossad Chief Isser Harel to take over the search for the missing boy, a search previously conducted by the police and the Shin Bet, the internal security services. Harel, who has been described as "Israel's J. Edgar Hoover," renewed the search within Israel proper and when that failed, extended the search overseas. But his agents, some of whom had participated in the kidnapping of Eichmann two years earlier, were unable to infiltrate those ultra-Orthodox communities suspected of harboring the boy. The Mossad had no agents who had mastered the intricacies and nuances of Orthodox Jewish law and custom. When Mossad agents attended religious services in these communities they were quickly identified. Once discovered, they were summarily and angrily ejected from the synagogues and study halls.

Where was Yossele while the Mossad was searching for him? Ruth had disguised Yossele as a girl, taken him to Switzerland, and then enrolled him in a *yeshiva* there. As she saw it, Yossele's best chance for concealment was among other young ultra-Orthodox boys. And his best disguise when traveling was as a girl, her daughter "Claudine," named, of course, after her own son Claude (now Uriel). Enrolling the boy in a yeshiva had the added benefit of continuing his religious education and strengthening his ultra-Orthodox identity. When word came that the Mossad was looking for Yossele in Switzerland, Ruth Ben David spirited the boy to Brussels and then to Paris. Each time she traveled, she presented the child as her daughter "Claudine." When the Mossad focused its search on the Haredi community of Paris, assembling forty agents there, Ruth Ben David took Yossele to New York, hiding the boy with a family of Satmar Hasidim in Williamsburg, Brooklyn. She then returned to France.

The Mossad, anticipating this move to hide the boy in the United States, had asked the FBI to cooperate in the search for Yossele. In the summer of 1961, FBI agents searched the summer camps run by New York's ultra-Orthodox Jewish communities in the Catskill Mountains. I was a camper in one of those camps, Camp Agudah in Ferndale, New York, that summer. I vividly remember the agents searching our camp grounds and our rustic cabins. It was a boys-only camp, and while the search was going on, we sang loudly, but not in prayer or in greeting. Rather, we were singing, "Where is Yossele?," the mocking song from Israel's ultra-Orthodox communities, which our camp counselors had taught us a few days earlier. In Israel, the song was used to taunt the police searching for the boy. But that cultural reference was lost on the strapping federal agents who seemed pleased that we accepted their visit with equanimity, and perhaps even with celebration.

Ruth Ben David and the other conspirators who hid Yossele Schumacher and spirited him from country to country managed to keep the boy hidden for almost three years. Fascination with the Yossele case was widespread throughout Israel and Jewish communities worldwide. As Ruth later said,

"The Yossele affair had become an everyday topic throughout the country, and indeed, throughout the Jewish world." Ben Gurion was losing patience with the Mossad and its head of operations, Isser Harel. According to Ruth, "The affair dominated the minds of the Israeli public. It became a matter of prestige for the police, the government, and for Ben Gurion himself."[46] The tensions raised by the Yossele affair were exacerbating secular-religious tensions within Israel and many of the more moderate Orthodox Jewish religious leaders called on his kidnappers to release him. Ruth began to feel isolated and condemned. "Loneliness joined my helplessness and together surrounded me, gripping me even tighter."[47]

In mid-1962 the Mossad caught up with Ruth Ben David in Paris. By that time Yossele was living with his adopted family in the Satmar community in Williamsburg, Brooklyn. Ruth, interrogated by the team that first questioned Adolf Eichmann, initially denied any connection to Yossele. When presented with evidence that she had smuggled Yossele out of Israel disguised as her daughter, Ruth proudly admitted her complicity, but refused to divulge the boy's whereabouts. She relented, however, when Harel, head of the Mossad, told her that her son Uriel, now serving in the Israeli Army, had divulged his mother's involvement in the case. She felt betrayed and realized that the kidnapping had failed.[48]

When Ruth told Harel that Yossele was living with a Hasidic family in Williamsburg, Brooklyn, he relayed this information to the United States Attorney General, Robert Kennedy. Kennedy instructed the FBI to give Mossad their full cooperation. In September 1962, FBI agents, accompanied by Mossad operatives, took Yossele into custody and flew him back to his parents in Israel. Ben Gurion was relieved; some would say triumphant. The ultra-Orthodox opponents of Zionism had been defeated, at least temporarily.

THE RABBI AND THE CONVERT

Despite her efforts on behalf of the ultra-Orthodox community, Ruth Ben David still found acceptance within that community difficult. In *The Guardians of the City*, she writes, "After the Yossele affair I was accepted by the residents of Meah Shearim as a member of the community. I had earned my place among them by fighting in the battle for Judaism. But their admiration for me was mixed with misunderstanding. I was different. No woman in Meah Shearim spoke many languages; none had attended university. It didn't matter to them that I had accomplished these things before I had discovered the Torah. And I was the first convert they had encountered. Therefore, despite their admiration of me, they were open to gossip about my past, some of it spread by the Israeli security services."[49] The insular, separatist and anti-Zionist communities of Jerusalem's Meah Shearim neighborhood could not fully embrace a woman as unusual as Ruth Ben David. But her will to be accepted would change their minds.

In September 1965, three years after Yossele's whereabouts were discovered by the Mossad and the FBI, Ruth Ben David came to Israeli and Jewish public attention in a spectacular and unanticipated manner. Despite the fact that the Mossad had found Yossele and returned him to his parents, Ruth's participation in the kidnapping made her a heroine among ultra-Orthodox Jews and drew her closer to the leadership of anti-Zionist Orthodoxy. So close, in fact, that several of the leading rabbis of the movement sought her hand in marriage. Though she was a convert, competition for her hand was vigorous. That she was a very attractive woman in her mid-forties did not hurt. In 1963 Ruth agreed to marry the leader of the Neturei Karta, Rabbi Amram Blau, a sixty-eight-year-old widower with ten adult children. A legal betrothal agreement was drawn up, but the marriage was delayed for two years. In rabbinic tradition, a couple may be betrothed—by a betrothal agreement signed before a court of rabbis—for years before the actual wedding. Rabbi Blau's children objected to the marriage. Also among the objectors, it seems, were some of Blau's rabbinic colleagues who had sought Ruth's hand and been turned down by "the righteous convert."

In 1965 in a small private ceremony held in the predominantly Orthodox city of Bnei Brak, Ruth married Rabbi Amram Blau. He was seventy years old; Ruth was forty-five. He was the spiritual leader of the most rigorously Orthodox, anti-Zionist and separatist Jewish group in Jerusalem; she was a convert from Catholicism and an independent and forceful woman who had fought in the French Resistance and later defied the agents of the Mossad. Rabbi Blau too had been defying the Israeli authorities, in his case since 1948. Like Ruth, he had positioned himself at the ideological and political extreme of Israeli Jewish life. In 1938, a decade before the establishment of Israel, Blau broke with his brother Moshe, chairman of the Agudat Israel movement, which sought a *modus vivendi* with the Yishav's secular Zionist leadership. Blau contended that accommodation with the Zionist movement would weaken "Torah-true Judaism."

Would Rabbi Amram Blau's rabbinic colleagues and their followers approve of this unprecedented betrothal? Within Meah Shearim most marriages were endogamous. The community summarily rejected potential spouses from Jewish families outside of Meah Shearim and its counterparts in Europe and the United States. So how would a convert from Catholicism fare? Obviously, not very well. There was legal opposition to the marriage, as well as gossip and innuendo. The Rabbinic Court of the Edah ha-Haredit, the ultra-Orthodox community, responding to a petition, nullified Rabbi Blau's formal betrothal to Ruth Ben David. Although Ruth was no longer legally obligated to marry Rabbi Blau, she chose to do so anyway.

Ruth wrote, "I was to become the partner and consort of a great and kind man, a leader of the remnant of the struggling selfless Torah Jewry. This marriage, of which I never thought myself worthy, created a storm, the stormiest of my life."[50] The storm was so great that Rabbi Blau and his prospective bride found it impossible to continue their lives within Jerusalem's ultra-Orthodox enclave. They were shunned by friends, including Amram Blau's children and his rabbinical colleagues. On the advice of the Satmar Rebbe, who lived in Brooklyn, both Ruth and Rabbi Amram moved to the city of Bnei Brak, near Tel Aviv. And it was in Bnei Brak in September 1965, three years after Yossele was found by the FBI, that our unlikely couple finally wed.

But it was not only among Israel's Orthodox population that the scandal of their marriage reverberated. Israel's largest circulation newspapers, *Maariv* and *Yediot Aharonot* had been covering the story for weeks. *Yediot Aharonot* published the news of the wedding in a banner headline: "Rabbi Amram Marries the Convert in a Midnight Wedding Ceremony."[51]

For the year following their wedding, the couple lived in Bnei Brak, then they returned quietly to Meah Shearim. But Rabbi Amram Blau never regained the leadership of the Neturei Karta. The scandal surrounding his marriage to "the convert" had undermined his authority. Most of his own children had turned against him. Decades earlier his radical anti-Zionism had estranged him from his elder brother Moshe. Now, in the mid-1960s, more and more ultra-Orthodox Jews were making some sort of accommodation with the Israeli government, and Blau would be further isolated. Blau's uncompromising attitude toward the Israeli authorities seemed unreasonable and anachronistic to many in his ultra-Orthodox community; he refused to use Israeli money, pay Israeli utility bills, or use government subsidized public transportation. Some younger Haredim of the Neturei Karta learned and used Modern Israeli Hebrew; this profanation of "Loshen Kodesh," the sacred language, scandalized their elders, Blau among them. Members of the younger generation argued that without knowledge of Hebrew, life in Israel was becoming increasingly difficult, even for ultra-Orthodox Jews living in separate, and separatist, communities.

In the summer of 1971 Ruth had been married to Rabbi Blau for six years, but the couple was no longer living together. One morning a young man from France appeared at her Jerusalem apartment, asking to convert to Judaism. He did not want to deal with the Israeli authorities—the official rabbinate—but rather, with a rabbi who was fully "authentic." He had read of Ruth's religious journey and was now asking her to help him find a rabbi who could supervise his conversion.

Ruth must have recognized in this young man some of the same impulses that drove her to her first conversion some fifteen years earlier and then later drove her to seek the most "authentic" of Jewish communities.[52] The Blaus tutored the young man and facilitated his conversion to Judaism. Within a year of his conversion they found him a wife from a Haredi family and enabled them to join the Meah Shearim community.

In her memoir Ruth reflects on how fortunate this convert was to be born into an era when information concerning Orthodox Judaism was so widely disseminated. But she mourned the fact that unlike this French convert, who came directly to her, most potential converts to Judaism approached Zionist rabbis. "These converts learn Hebrew in 'the Jewish state,' are taught about the religion, and are received as Jews on the condition that they become Israelis. And of course, these people are later drafted into the Israeli army."[53]

Beginning in 1967, Ruth would make an annual journey overseas. She would raise funds for ultra-Orthodox charitable work and engage in "private diplomacy" throughout the Mideast. "As I am fluent in six languages, and can communicate in a few other languages, I was able to travel effectively."[54] As her husband Rabbi Amram refused to apply for an Israeli passport, he never left Israel. Ruth, with multiple passports, served as his emissary and ambassador.

Rabbi Amram Blau died in 1974 at the age of eighty. Since his marriage to Ruth in 1965 his influence among his rabbinic peers had declined considerably. His reputation did not survive the "scandal" of his marriage to the much younger woman who was a convert from Catholicism. When Rabbi Amram died, Ruth was fifty-four years old; she would survive him by twenty-six years.

From the late 1960s to the mid-1980s, Ruth Ben David traveled widely in the Arab and wider Muslim worlds, serving as the Neturei Karta link to the remaining Jewish communities of the Muslim world. She was rumored to have met with Ayatollah Khomeini in 1980, the year after his triumphant return to Teheran. With Khomeini or one of his associates, Ruth made the case for the new regime's responsibility to protect the Jewish community of Tehran, then numbering 25,000 people.

When Ruth Ben David died in 2000 she was an honored member of an ever more factionalized segment of Jerusalem's ultra-Orthodox community. Her remarkable life had been shaped by her experience of World War II in France, and particularly by the fate of France's Jews at the hands of the Vichy regime and its collaborators. Her participation in Yossele Schumacher's kidnapping was, in her mind, a continuation of her work in the French Resistance. She was fighting the forces of darkness, in whatever guise they took. Many of the same forces shaped our next protagonist, Aaron Lustiger of Paris, but the trajectory of his religious experience was a mirror opposite of Ruth Ben David's. As Ruth Ben David moved from a Catholic upbringing to an intense Jewish life, Aaron Lustiger would move from a Jewish upbringing to the pinnacle of Catholic ecclesiastical power and prestige.

NOTES

1. Ben David, Typescript, 7.
2. Lustiger, *Dare to Believe*, 76.
3. Ben David, Typescript, 7.
4. Ibid., 19.
5. Ibid., 20.
6. Ibid., 22–23.
7. Ibid., 28.
8. Ibid., 29.
9. Ibid., 44.
10. On women in the French Resistance see Moorehead, *A Train in Winter*, 54.
11. Ibid., 30.
12. Ibid., 49.
13. Ben David, Typescript, 49.
14. Ibid., 51.
15. Ibid., 74.
16. Ibid.
17. Ibid., 75.
18. Ibid., 76.
19. Ibid., 77.
20. Ibid., 78.
21. Ibid., 81.
22. Ibid., 56.
23. Ibid.
24. Today we might describe this group as Modern Orthodox and Religious Zionist.
25. Ben David, Typescript, 83.
26. Ibid., 103.
27. Ibid., 115.
28. Ibid., 174.
29. Ibid., 180.
30. Ibid., 177.
31. Friedman, "The First Confrontation Between the Zionist Movement and Jerusalem Orthodoxy," 103.
32. See Rabkin, *A Threat From Within*, 54–55 on non-Zionist Agudah.
33. On this paradox see Krauss, "Judaism and Zionism."
34. Friedman, "The First Confrontation Between the Zionist Movement and Jerusalem Orthodoxy," 103.
35. Selzer, *Zionism Reconsidered*, 22.
36. Jerusalem Talmud, Hagigah, 1.7.
37. Israeli Prime Minister's Office, *A Study in Fanaticism*, 7.
38. Ben David, Typescript, 192.
39. Ibid., 199.
40. Weiner, *The Wild Goats of Ein Gedi*, 151.
41. Ben David, Typescript, 200.
42. Ibid., 202.
43. Ibid., 207.
44. Ibid., 288–89.
45. Ibid., 221.
46. Ibid., 306.
47. Ibid., 356.
48. See Ben David, Typescript, 430; Eisenberg, Dan, and Landau, *The Mossad*, 44–46.
49. Ginsberg, "Guardian of the City: The Secret Life of Ruth Blau," 178.
50. Ben David, Typescript, 475.
51. Ettinger, "Notes on Scandal."
52. Blau, *Shomrei Ha'Ir*, 218–220.

53. Blau, *Shomrei Ha'Ir, 219.*
54. Blau, *Shomrei Ha'Ir*, 222.

Chapter Three

Jean-Marie Lustiger, the "Jewish Cardinal" (1926–2007)

Madeleine Feraille, twenty years old when the Germans conquered France in the summer of 1940, understood that a calamity had befallen her country and that her life would be radically altered. But it was not until she joined the Resistance that she realized her life was in danger. And only when her tasks in the Resistance included smuggling Jews across borders did she understand that the German occupation mortally threatened an entire population, the Jews of France.

That same fateful year Aaron Lustiger, the child of Polish Jews who had immigrated to France after World War I, was fourteen. From his parents and grandparents he had heard often of the Russian pogroms of the late-nineteenth and early-twentieth centuries. As he later recalled, "From the moment that I was conscious of existing, I learned about the threat of pogroms and persecution."[1] Thus Lustiger's reaction to the fall of France was sharper and more immediate than Feraille's. "When I saw the Germans moving in, I knew that Jews were going to be killed. I knew it better than my parents. It was clear that that would happen."[2]

The German invasion of France and the horrors that followed strongly shaped both Madeleine Feraille and Aaron Lustiger. Feraille's search for religious authenticity led her from Catholicism to Protestant Christianity, liberal Judaism, and finally to ultra-Orthodoxy. Lustiger's discovery of the Protestant Bible would lead him from secular Judaism to a religious quest that could be answered only by conversion to Catholicism.

CHILDHOOD, YOUTH, CONVERSION

Like Madeline Feraille's Catholic family in Calais, Aaron Lustiger's Jewish parents were not particularly religious. Charles and Gisèle Lustiger had come to Paris from Poland in the early 1920s. Their attachment to Jewish culture was through Yiddish language and literature, rather than through religious thought and ritual. Aaron's father, like thousands of other European Jews born to Orthodox families, had rebelled against the restrictive world in which he had grown up. Thus when young Aaron's developing religious sensibilities sought expression in his parent's secular Jewish home, they found none. He wrote, "As a child, I perceived my Judaism only as a social identity, since all the education I had received was essentially secular. I was the son of immigrants who knew that he was a Jew and belonged to a community persecuted for no other reason than the evil of human beings. . . . It is in Christianity that I discovered the biblical and Jewish content that had not been imparted to me as a Jewish child."[3] Like many twentieth-century Jewish converts to Christianity, Lustiger's Jewish identity was based on ethnic identification and a sense of a shared Jewish culture, not on a commitment to religious practice. For these converts, their Jewish identity, often based on Yiddish secularism, was devoid of religious significance. For Lustiger, Christianity represented religion. "Yiddishkeit," in contrast, was an expression of secularism in a distinctly Jewish form.

In his memoirs Lustiger recalled his discovery of the Bible: "My parents had a bookcase, which was locked, and I was not supposed to read any of the books in it. It contained all sorts of books, which my parents had bought. They had great respect for books and bought more or less anything. The key was kept on top of the bookcase, so it wasn't very difficult for me to stand on a chair and find it. I opened the bookcase and read all sorts of things: I read Zola, I read Abel Hermant, I read all those boring novels that came out between the wars; but I also found the Bible, the Protestant Bible, and I read it right through. It had the Old and New Testaments. I read the Bible passionately, and I didn't say a word to anybody. I can't remember if I was eleven or twelve at the time, but from then onward, I began to think about these things and to mull over them."[4]

This secret discovery of the Protestant Bible deeply moved the young Lustiger. For Madeleine Feraille, reared in a Catholic French family, the Old Testament with its stories of the Jews was her door into Judaism. For Lustiger, however, it was the New Testament that proved to be the source of excitement. "What particularly impressed me was that there was a continuity between the Old Testament and the New one. I read them straight through."[5] Like the other converts to Christianity portrayed in this book, Lustiger's initial reading of the New Testament was pivotal in convincing him that Christianity was the fulfillment of Judaism. "From that time on, the reading of the New Testament took a place in my Jewish consciousness. For me, it dealt with the same spiritual subject, the same benedictions, the same stakes: the salvation of men, the love of God, the knowledge of God. I am persuaded that the identification between the suffering Messiah and persecuted Israel was something intuitive and immediate for me."[6]

When an interviewer asked Lustiger if he considered what he had experienced as a teenager a real conversion, he answered, "It was more like crystallization than a conversion. Through the circumstances I had mentioned, I had found that when I first really confronted Christians, I knew their beliefs, better than they did themselves. When I reread the Gospels at that stage, I already knew them. I say at that stage, because it was then, that my parents absolutely refused to accept that I was convinced; they thought it was disgusting."[7] For the Lustigers, conversion to Christianity was apostasy and Christian doctrine was repellent. In their secularism they rejected all religious belief, but none more than Christian belief.

When war broke out in 1939, the Lustigers had the foresight to leave Paris and move to Orléans, although Aaron's mother, Gisèle, soon returned to Paris to mind the family business. The young Aaron began to attend in secret the Orléans Cathedral. "It was during this period that I received a Christian initiation, that I made my entry into Christianity."[8] In the summer of 1940, after his baptism and first communion, Lustiger was admitted to a lycée in Orléans, which he attended from 1940 to mid-1942. As he later recalled, "So it was in those years that I began to draw near to Christianity by thinking, by reading, those were the only influences on me: books and the culture I was imbibing at the lycée from different teachers. Later on, I found out about the beliefs of those teachers, some were Jewish, some were committed Catholics, some were unbelievers, others were agnostics; but I had a long, interior path to follow, and fundamentally it was Christ who gave me the key to my searchings; Christ as Messiah, an image of the Jewish people. At the same time I knew that persecution had been the lot of the Jews in history, and that it had been the source of their dignity."[9] Lustiger here echoes the sentiments of many of his Jewish contemporaries who saw persecution not as punishment or the consequence of engagement with the divine will, but as the inexplicable central experience of Jewish history.

But when fourteen-year-old Aaron Lustiger attempted to explain his religious experience to his parents, parents who were distant from any sort of religious or spiritual experience, he encountered fierce opposition. They were incredulous that he sought baptism in the Catholic Church. Despite Lustiger's attempts to explain that he saw baptism not as abandoning Judaism but as fulfilling his destiny as a Jew, his parents were scandalized. "For my parents, this reasoning was thoroughly incomprehensible, insane, and insufferable; the worst of things, the worst of misfortunes that could befall them. I was acutely aware that I was causing them unendurable pain. I was torn apart by their suffering. And I truly took the step only because of an interior necessity."[10]

Lustiger's parents asked him to speak with a local rabbi about his decision. This request must have seemed hypocritical to the young Aaron, whose secular parents rarely if ever consulted a rabbi. As Lustiger described the meeting, he and his parents met with the rabbi; the discussion went on for several hours. Aaron felt that he had "demonstrated to the rabbi that Jesus is the Messiah, as predicted in the Hebrew Bible." Acknowledging the depth of the young man's convictions, the rabbi told the Lustigers, "There is nothing you can do; let him go ahead."[11] Deeply respectful of his parents, Aaron secured their consent for his baptism by arguing that becoming a Christian at the time of the fall of France to the Germans would protect him from German actions against the Jews. "I think that it was for that reason that they finally conceded."[12]

In response to their disgust and dismay, he explained, "I am not leaving you, I am not going over to the enemy, I am becoming what I am, I am not ceasing to be a Jew; on the contrary, I am discovering another way of being a Jew."[13] Recalling this period in his life, Lustiger went on to say, "I know, and knew then, that Jewish people think that's a scandalous way to talk. But that's what I experienced, when I chose my Christian names, I chose three Jewish names: Jean, Aaron, Marie. It's obvious if you look at the Hebrew forms. I kept the name that I received at birth."[14] At no point subsequent to his conversion did Lustiger ever deny his Jewishness. Rather, he would emphasize his Jewish origins throughout his long career in the Catholic Church.

As an adult thinking back to his adolescence, Lustiger remembered that he made the decision to become a Catholic priest at the time of his baptism. Thus, his decision to convert was not a decision simply to join the Church but a decision to become a servant of the Church. His initial idea of service to humanity had been to pursue a career as a physician. When asked why he could not have served humankind from within Judaism, Lustiger replied, "For me at the time, the contents of Judaism were no different from what I was discovering in Christianity. I saw Judaism then as a historical condition marked by persecution. I did not think for one moment of leaving it, but it found its fulfillment in welcoming the person of Jesus the Messiah of Israel, it was in recognizing him, and it was only in that recognition, that Judaism found its meaning."[15] For Lustiger, Christianity was a form of "fulfilled" Judaism. And Judaism was "a historical condition," not a way of life.

Lustiger may have seen his parents as assimilated and secular, but it is clear from his description of them that they retained a great deal of their Jewish cultural identity. They continued to speak Yiddish to each other, although they spoke French to Aaron. They occasionally went to synagogue, and Charles attended Yom Kippur services. Decades later, when Lustiger was serving as a parish priest and then as a bishop in Paris, he would quietly attend the *Yizkor* (memorial) services on Yom Kippur at the Chief Rabbi's synagogue. Indeed as we shall see throughout this book, Yom Kippur, the Day of Atonement and the most sacred date on the Jewish calendar, continued to hold an important place in the spiritual lives of apostates, converts, and doubters. Yom Kippur is a day when all Jews, no matter how far they are from traditional observance, are expected to come together in worship. The rituals observed on that day, including fasting, prayer, and confession, evoke the memory of ancient rituals and memorialize worship in the Temple in Jerusalem.

Despite his parents' secularism, Lustiger developed a religious sensibility at an early age. As he told an interviewer, "In the end, my religious sensibility was probably richer than might be supposed, given my parents indecisive position and their detachment from a Judaism that was, as they described it, superstitious, archaic, and prevented the liberation of the Jews. These are the words I heard at home."[16] From his parents however, Lustiger did become familiar with a rich body of Jewish folklore and storytelling. They told him about their ancestors, and often emphasized to their son that he, Aaron, was named for Aaron, the brother of Moses, and that they, the Lustigers, were Levites. In Jewish tradition, the Levites, or descendants of the Hebrew tribe of Levi, were the priests' assistants in the Temple. Later when he was the Cardinal of Paris, Lustiger would write, "This was a lesson I have never forgotten. I, like my ancestors, was a Levite."[17] Certainly as a Catholic priest, Lustiger would have been acutely aware of the Church's assertion of continuity between the Levitical rituals of the Hebrew Bible and the rites of a Catholic priest.

Young Aaron Lustiger, although unfamiliar with the text of the Bible, was familiar with biblical stories, and these stories helped lay the groundwork for his discovery of the Bible itself and his subsequent conversion to Christianity. His parents' story about Aaron, brother of Moses, is but one example. These tales, however, often fashioned for children, had not prepared the young Lustiger for the power of the original text. By the time he was eleven or twelve years old and first came across the Bible in his parents' library he had already developed what he called "a taste for serious reading."[18] His encounter with the actual words of the Bible proved a great revelation. "I really had the impression that I had known about it [the Bible] already, because I did know—I knew about Abraham, I knew about Moses, and Aaron is my name. My mother told me about Aaron, he was Moses brother. Thus it was not like reading the Upanishads; I was much more surprised by Greek mythology. With the Bible I was exploring a world whose existence I had heard about, I was entering a familiar world, one to which I belonged, but of which I had only fragmentary knowledge."[19]

Soon Lustiger was more biblically literate than his parents, and more politically aware. He was more astute about Germany and the intent of the

Nazis than his parents. He spent two summers in the late 1930s studying in Germany, and he had seen Nazism at first hand. In 1937 during his second summer in Germany, Lustiger met a boy who was a member of the *Hitlerju-gend* (Hitler Youth). This German boy did not realize that Lustiger was Jewish. Lustiger recalled that the boy would "show me his Hitlerjugend knife and boast 'We are going to kill all the Jews.' It was a brutal, crude Nazism as experienced by a thirteen-year-old, unconscious of what he was repeating, but it was clear to me that Nazism represented a mortal danger and that it was the resurgence of the pagan, and the idolatries of the goyim."[20] Here, Lustiger the theologian, reflecting on his adolescence, claims to have recognized in his pre-war encounter with Nazism a hatred of Jews that stemmed, not from Christian antipathy, but from pagan anti-monotheistic atavism. In the Hebrew Bible, the idolatry of the "goyim" (the pagans) is the signifier of paganism, and in Lustiger's understanding that was the catalyst for hatred of the Jews, which is a hatred of monotheism. Thus Nazi claims to Christian loyalty had to be false as well. Pagans would hate all forms of monotheism, and Judaism, the original monotheism, most of all.

On his return from Germany, Lustiger told his parents about the repression and discrimination he had witnessed, but they were skeptical that Hitler could have any plans for France. As he recalled, "My father particularly was not at all worried about the Germans. Hitler did not frighten him; he was Germany's problem. My parents thought that France was strong, that it would defend freedom; they had an indestructible confidence in France."[21] Lustiger's parents were confident that France could withstand a German onslaught and that if it did fall, the French people would protect the Jews.

When the Germans finally conquered France, Lustiger was not as shocked as his parents, but he was nevertheless fearful of the consequences. "It was an unheard of blow, a wound, a humiliation. . . . I was aware of everything that adults were discussing and that filled the newspapers. . . . The 'Jewish problem' was at the heart of the political situation, because in Germany there was Nazism and anti-Semitism; in France there was anti-Semitism that was taking Léon Blum as a target. Thus, the Jewish issue was mixed with the political one."[22] Blum, the Prime Minister of France, was a Jewish socialist and the target of considerable resentment and rage from the French Right.

Lustiger drew a clear distinction between Christianity and anti-Semitism. "It is true that I had absorbed the paternal and maternal accounts of persecutions perpetrated by Christians, but I felt that their stories concerned anti-Semites—not the Christians spoken about in the New Testament: that is Jesus and His disciples."[23] Lustiger would maintain this distinction—between anti-Semitism, an ideology tinged with paganism, and Christianity, a faith which flowed out of Judaism—throughout his long scholarly and ecclesiastical career. As a priest, and later as a cardinal of the Church, Lustiger confronted the legacy of French Christians who had collaborated either with the Nazis in the occupied zone, or with the Vichy government in the south. When, in the decades after the war, accusations were made that the Catholic Church, its hierarchy, and particularly the Pope did not do enough to save Jews, Lustiger went on the offensive. He pointed out that many Catholics, particularly priests in France and elsewhere, did help save Jews. For Lustiger, the Christians who collaborated with the fascists, and particularly those who aided the Nazi extermination of the Jews, were not "true Christians, but rather pagans."[24] To explain both the complicity of many Christians in the murder of the Jews and the silence of Pope Pius XII during the war, Lustiger argued that Nazism was anti-Christian; hence Christianity could not be held responsible for the Nazis' crimes. Rather, the Nazi crimes represented "the resurgence of the pagan." If Pope Pius did not speak out more forcefully, it was only because of the limits of his power and his fear that any criticism of Hitler's policies would bring harm to the church.

Although Lustiger and other apologists for the Catholic Church have made these arguments many times in the decades since the end of World War II, most historians of anti-Semitism do not find them convincing and do not accept them. In their opinion, the Christian-influenced anti-Judaism of the centuries preceding World War II did much to prepare the way for the genocide of the Jews. The Nazi hierarchy may have harbored pagan ideas, but an admixture of Christian anti-Judaism and nineteenth-century racism proved to be the driving influence supporting the perpetrators of the Holocaust. In this analysis, the European churches, including the Catholic Church, bear some responsibility for the fate of Europe's Jews during the Second World War.

THE FALL OF FRANCE AND THE DEPORTATIONS OF FRANCE'S JEWS

In June of 1940, the German army quickly defeated the French army and occupied the country, dividing it into two zones. The German military maintained direct control of the northern two-thirds of France, while a collaborationist regime, based in the town of Vichy and headed by World War I hero Marshal Pétain, administered the southern third of the country. During the first year of the occupation, from the summer of 1940 to the summer of 1941, the population of the southern zone fared better than those in the occupied zone. But with the beginning of Operation Barbarossa in 1941, when two million German soldiers invaded Russia in an attempt to conquer the Soviet Union, the situation in France changed radically. The German army—and later the Gestapo—moved into what had been up until then Vichy France. The Jews were among the first victims of the German entry into the area. The

Vichy government had required the registration of the Jews but did not begin deporting them until after the start of Operation Barbarossa.

Evaluating the behavior of the French under German occupation is an extremely contentious issue, both among the French public and among French politicians. As the British historian Robert Gildea noted in the 1990s, "More than fifty years after the event, the German occupation is still a subject of heated debate—and a debate that is far from being resolved. This is explained in part by the shame and guilt felt by the French people about the occupation. . . . The explanation of the debate, however, also lies in the fact that the French have never faced up to their war-time past in any sustained and systematic way."[25]

Both Madeleine Feraille and Aaron Lustiger were ashamed of their countrymen's collaboration with the Nazis during the occupation. Influenced by her father and her schoolmates, Feraille joined the Resistance and fought against the occupation. Lustiger, in school at the time, first in a lycée, and then in a Catholic seminary, was a French Jew in hiding. His opportunities for resistance were limited. He supported the Resistance as best he could—by handing out leaflets and joining protests. The debate about the behavior of the French during the occupation turns on the question of French complicity in the fate of the Jews of France. In 1939, there were roughly 300,000 Jews in France. During the course of the war, the Germans and their French collaborators rounded up some 75,000, or about one-fourth, of these French Jews, and handed them over to the Gestapo, who sent them to Auschwitz, where virtually all of them were murdered. Among the 300,000 Jews living in France in 1939, approximately 70 percent—including Aaron Lustiger's parents, who had emigrated from Poland—were foreign born. Many of these immigrants had made their home in France, as the Lustigers had, since World War I. They had come not only from Poland, but also from Russia, Hungry, Romania, and other countries. Even before the German invasion of France, these "foreign Jews" had been the target of French anti-Semitic propaganda. Tragically, there were French citizens who were eager to collaborate with the Vichy authorities in rounding up these foreign Jews for deportation to Auschwitz.

Who was a Jew in occupied France? How did one define Jewishness? There was the classical rabbinic Jewish self-definition: a Jew is someone either born of a Jewish mother, or a convert to Judaism. But in Germany and Nazi occupied Europe, the definition of who was a Jew differed from country to country—the Nazi authorities had their definitions; the occupied countries often used different ones. Within the first three months of the occupation, the German authorities demanded that the French conduct a census of all of the Jews in France. In the summer of 1940, the Vichy government approved a "denaturalization law" which reviewed the cases of some half a million naturalized citizens and deprived many Jewish immigrants of their French citizenship. The *Statuts des juifs*, a series of discriminatory statutes that the Vichy regime enacted in 1940 and 1941, included their own unique and specific definition of who was a Jew: a Jew was "someone with three Jewish grandparents or, alternatively, two Jewish grandparents, if his or her spouse was Jewish."[26] In Germany, and throughout German-controlled areas of Europe, which by 1944 was virtually all of Europe, there were many Jews who had converted to Christianity, or whose parents or grandparents had converted to Christianity. The German authorities, however, rarely took these baptisms into consideration. In France, a high-ranking German official told his French subordinate that everyone of Jewish ancestry must have the word "Juif" stamped on his or her identity card. "Baptism," the official said, "has no effect."[27]

With the imposition of the September 1940 racial laws in France, the Vichy government required all Jews to register with the authorities. Lustiger, describing his parents' quandary, remembered their uncertainty: "My parents had hesitated to declare themselves. All French Jews were asking themselves whether they should register or not."[28] A high-ranking Church official, who was mentoring Lustiger, sent a letter to the authorities asking, "Must the Lustigers declare themselves? They are French citizens and are honorable people whom I know."[29] A Vichy official replied, "As French citizens they have nothing to fear, tell them to go ahead and declare themselves, there is no need to worry."[30] As Lustiger noted later, "If you look at the dates on the letters and what was already taken place at the time, you know that this reassurance was an outright lie. My parents ended up by registering as Jews; they wore the yellow star. I never did, I should have been registered in Paris, since my parents were; to avoid arrest, my mother used to hide the yellow star as she made trips between Paris and Orléans."[31]

According to the *Statuts des Juifs*, Jews could not work in the public sector, and the laws severely limited their participation in the professions as well. Emulating Nazi Germany, the Vichy government closed many Jewish businesses, and then placed them in the hands of "Aryan administrators." The legal fiction was that while the Jewish proprietor retained ownership of the business, it was now to be run by a non-Jew. Many Frenchmen took advantage of these Ayranization policies and stole homes and businesses from their French fellow citizens who were Jewish. As Robert Gildea notes, "The relentless persecution, which gradually closed down opportunities for Jews to make an honest living, drove them into poverty, clandestine activity, and despair."[32] French officials widely enforced the *Statuts de Juifs*, but betrayal of the Jews of France went well beyond mere legal statutes. As Gildea noted, "The French public could be a good deal more anti-Semitic and mercenary than the French administration."[33] Aaron Lustiger saw this happen many times. The Lustigers ran a millinery shop in Paris which the authorities turned over to an "Aryan administrator." As the Nazis began to round up Jews, Gisèle Lustiger went into hiding in Paris. A year later a neighbor denounced her in order to curry favor with the French authorities. Gisèle Lustiger was sent to the Nazi deportation camp at Drancy, and from there was deported to Auschwitz, where she was murdered.

The actions of his countrymen deeply disillusioned the young Lustiger. As he recalled, "France was Petainist. Which is not to say that it was Nazi; it foundered and passed through a dreadful ordeal."[34] Aaron's mother remained at the deportation camp in Drancy for over a year before being deported to Auschwitz at the beginning of 1943. She wrote short letters to her son from Drancy, and in his memoirs, Lustiger quotes one of them: "*Mes enfants*, it is a fatal illness, above all, protect yourself from it."[35] Did she mean Jewish identity? Did she mean French collaboration with the Germans? We don't know, and neither, it seems, did her son.

Asked to explain why his parents did not go into hiding as early as possible, Lustiger cited their confidence in France. "They continued to hope that France would not abandon the Jews; that it would not give in to the Nazis. That is why they did not protect themselves in time. What eventually happened had been inconceivable to them and they resigned themselves to the idea only when forced to do so by circumstances."[36] "My family," said Lustiger, "belonged to that generation that had invested its hopes in the liberalization of the early-twentieth century in Central and Eastern Europe. My young father, my young mother, rejected the religious world, as if it had been made of absurd constraints, antique curios, in order to enter into the modern era, without denying anything of their identity and their social or familial boundaries."[37] While Lustiger's parents clung to their Jewish ethnic identity—an identity marked by Yiddish language and Jewish folkways, they rejected the rituals and prohibitions of Orthodox Judaism. Lustiger's search for a "religious world" would end in the Catholic Church, a choice which his parents found incomprehensible.

BECOMING A PRIEST AND VISITING THE HOLY LAND

Aaron Lustiger, now known as Jean-Marie Lustiger, studied literature during his two years at the Catholic lycée in Orléans, and it was here that he decided to become a priest. "I discovered a Christian life of rigor and beauty. Before leaving Orléans, I had been going to mass almost every day, or as often as seemed possible for someone for whom such a practice meant getting up early in the morning. Thus I discovered a regularly organized Christian life. Every day there was the mass and prayer service and also time for personal meditation. Each week, some elements for enriching our religious life were proposed to us. What for some of my fellow students had become a routine, of which they were possibly weary, struck me as an extraordinary novelty."[38]

Following his tenure at the lycée in Orléans, Lustiger moved to Paris where he attended Catholic seminary, before his ordination fourteen years later. As he recalled, "In 1946 I entered the university seminary, the Séminaire des Carmes, at the Institut Catholique in Paris—and in 1954 I was ordained a priest."

The organized structure of Christian practice deeply inspired the young Lustiger, who as a convert from a secular form of Judaism did not have the experience of following a regular disciplined set of religious obligations. His fellow students, who were brought up Catholic, may have found these structures limiting and uninspiring, but for Lustiger they opened up a whole new world of religious experience. "It is in Christianity that I discovered this biblical and Jewish content that had not been imparted to me as a Jewish child. Thus it happened that in the course of my life that I thought that I became a Jew because, by embracing Christianity, I finally discovered the values of Judaism, not denying them in the least."[39]

The "beginner's mind," to borrow a Zen phrase, that Lustiger brought to his experience of Christian ritual, was the product of the newness and strangeness of the Catholic rites. He recalled being "stupefied to discover that there are believers, steeped in Christianity since childhood, who do not understand this mystery."[40] Asked to give an example of the mysteries that he discovered in Catholicism, he replied, "Foremost would be the Eucharist, the Mass. Even though I had not had a Jewish education I knew enough to recognize the ritual of the Passover in the Eucharist. It is the sacrifice of the Lamb, it is deliverance and salvation: the grace of God. When I discover Christians who have lost this reverence, and no longer understand the Eucharist, I say to myself, 'they are pagans.' They do not know what they are saying, or doing, or how much they are in contradiction with what they are supposed to believe."[41]

In the early 1950s, while Lustiger was studying for the priesthood, the abbot of his seminary asked him to organize a trip to the Holy Land. The trip began in Beirut. From Lebanon the seminarians crossed into Syria and Jordan and then into Jerusalem. Lustiger recorded his response upon his arrival in Israel:

> I had an extraordinary shock, both emotional and spiritual, on seeing the land of Israel, the promised land of Abraham, the Holy Land. When you are studying the Bible at your desk, you can ponder indefinitely about what is said, or not said, by avoiding too many questions about the reality of a particular event and the way it touches you. But there in the Holy Land, I could not put anything having to do with the truth of such events between parentheses. The question presented itself in an historical way and history, with a brutal and indisputable objectivity presented itself geographically. The soil itself, the Holy Land, and its inhabitants became so eloquent that a decision became

urgent. I could no longer dodge the question of whether I would decide to adhere unreservedly to the reality of God's gift.[42]

During his seminary training, Lustiger had to put aside his growing doubts about the historicity of the Bible's narratives and the divine origin of the biblical texts. As long as he did not have to confront the actual landscape of those narratives he could rely on an abstract ideal of faith. He did not have to answer the question, "Did all of this actually happen?" But seeing the 'holy places' and relating to them as a Jew, a descendant of the biblical Hebrews, forced him to confront his doubts, to abandon them, and to choose absolute certainty.

In Jerusalem's Church of the Holy Sepulcher, Lustiger prayed at the marble slab upon which, according to Catholic believers, Jesus's body lay before its resurrection. Convinced that he was in the actual historical spot, the young seminarian experienced something of a spiritual crisis. As he later recalled, "The light given to me at that precise instant in a word, the interior experience, can be translated in this way: What determines everything is my personal relationship to the one in whom I recognize myself created, called, saved, loved and capable by the gift he makes to me of being a witness to what has been granted to me. Such, with a question, and a decision, I lived through the remainder of that month in a mixture of joy and distress. And I discovered with pride, the land of my ancestors, and also the State of Israel."[43]

After he became a priest, Lustiger referred to his first visit to the Holy Land and the crisis of faith he underwent as a pivotal moment in his spiritual development. As he described that visit, "I saw myself with my back to the wall during a trip to the Holy Land. . . . In the reality of the country of Christ, I perceived a kind of physical brutality of landscape and facts, which did not of course give me proof, but compelled me to take a position with regard to the Word. The struggle with the angel had lasted long enough, I had to get away from indecision, there was a need for a victor and a vanquished."[44] Thus for Lustiger, as for many other pilgrims and travelers to the Holy Land, the physical reality of the land of Israel served as a type of "fifth Gospel"— or "third Testament"—an experience that validated and strengthened faith. Like the biblical Jacob, who was transformed into Israel, Lustiger had wrestled the angel of doubt and won. And like Jacob, he would be forever marked by the experience.

This pilgrimage was the first of many that Lustiger would make to the Holy Land. At one point in the late 1970s he considered moving permanently to Israel, where he hoped to serve as a priest in the local Catholic community. In preparation, Lustiger studied Modern Israeli Hebrew speech and pronunciation, listening to numerous Hebrew instructional audiotapes.[45] But before his Israeli plans developed any farther, his Church superiors decided to promote him to a position of leadership in the French Church.

His Church superiors had chosen wisely, as Lustiger proved to have remarkable leadership skills. Much later, Lustiger would recall his rise through ranks of the Catholic Church. "My responsibility was the chaplaincy of the Sorbonne and other universities in Paris. I met a lot of people in the intellectual world of Paris at the time. Then, for ten years, I was parish priest of a place on the edge of Paris, near Boulogne—and then to my great surprise, I was appointed Bishop of Orleans by the Pope, but I was even more surprised when I was appointed Archbishop of Paris."[46]

THE AUSCHWITZ CONVENT CONTROVERSY

Throughout his career in the Church, the Catholic hierarchy often called on Lustiger, as a high ranking clergyman of Jewish origin, to mediate, and, if possible, to adjudicate problematic situations involving Jewish-Catholic relations. Perhaps the most prominent conflict where he served as the Church's lead negotiator grew out of the presence of a Catholic convent at Auschwitz. In 1984 in Communist Poland, a group of nuns from the Carmelite order asked permission to open a convent near the site of the Auschwitz Concentration Camp. Under the Polish government, the camp had become a memorial to Polish victims of World War II, and the nuns saw it as a place where they could pray for the souls of the victims. The building that they intended to occupy stood next to the camp. Known as the Old Theater, it had served as the warehouse where the Nazis stored the poison gas used to murder the inmates. There was little publicity when the convent first opened; it did not seem to disturb the local remnant of the Polish-Jewish community. Doctor Stanislaw Krajewski, one of the leaders of that community, said in 1985, "I saw that the convent was in an abandoned building, just outside the Camp base. I was, and would have been satisfied with it [the convent], had I been sure that it wouldn't have grown."[47] But as tourism to Auschwitz grew, with increasing numbers of both Polish nationals and international visitors touring the camp, the Carmelite convent became a focal point of international interest. In fact, it became part of the tour of the camp, especially for Catholics, who wanted to memorialize the Catholic martyrs who had died there.

Rumblings of general dissatisfaction with the Polish Auschwitz memorial predated the opening of the convent. Many Jewish observers thought that the Polish Communist regime obscured the fact that the vast majority of the people murdered at Auschwitz had been Jews. The regime described the dead of World War II as 'victims of fascism,' rather than as victims of anti-Semitism. They organized the names on monuments by nationality, rather than by religious affiliation. Thus, the Polish Communists memorialized the dead as French, or German, or of other nationalities, but they did not recognize any of the victims as Jews.

A fundraising campaign started by friends of the Carmelite order to renovate the building where the nuns were living brought the new convent to the attention of Jewish organizations in Europe. In 1985, the World Jewish Congress asked for a meeting with the Polish Catholic clergy in order to protest the establishment of the convent on a site which had assumed a kind of sanctity for Jews. As one scholar described these developments, "After protests from Jewish groups (mostly outside Poland) objecting to the presence of the nuns at the site, in 1987 an agreement was reached and ratified in Geneva between representatives of the Roman Catholic Church and European Jewish leaders. The accord stipulated that the convent would be moved from the vicinity of Auschwitz by 1989."[48]

At the 1987 meeting in Geneva between representatives of the World Jewish Congress and the Catholic Church, Cardinal Lustiger played a major part in negotiating the agreement. He was one of three western European Cardinals who met with Cardinal Macharski of Kraków and a group of Jewish leaders in order to resolve the issue. In a statement issued after the meeting, the participants announced that because of the "uncontested realities of the symbolic character of the extermination camp of Auschwitz, monument and memory of the Holocaust," they would continue their discussions until the problems occasioned by the opening of the convent were solved.[49]

At a second Geneva meeting, which was held the following year, the participants agreed to the construction of a visitor's center which they hoped would become a meeting place for Christians and Jews. The Church agreed to relocate the convent to this new center, which would be clearly outside the camp. But the complicated relationship between the nuns of the Carmelite order and the Catholic Church in Poland made the agreement difficult to expedite. As Genevieve Zubrzcki noted in the *Crosses of Auschwitz*, "The deadline by which the nuns were supposed to relocate was, by all accounts, unrealizable. . . . There was also clear resistance and some ill will on the part of the sisters, whose vows were made to that specific convent, at that specific site, and who stubbornly refused to leave. Finally, the affair was further complicated by the fact that as a monastic order, the Carmelites are not under the jurisdiction of the diocesan bishop but under the Head of the Carmelite order in Rome. Although Polish, the nuns refused to submit to an agreement ratified by representatives of the Polish Roman Catholic Church."[50]

Lustiger was an ideal interlocutor for these Geneva talks. He was not only a cardinal of the Church, but a converted Jew, and respected by many Jewish leaders. Unlike other converted Jews, Lustiger had maintained the trust and confidence of many in the Jewish community. Thus, it was Lustiger, more so than any of the other participants, who managed to cool the tempers of the parties involved in the Geneva meetings. He helped draft the "Auschwitz Declaration" which begins with the Hebrew word *zakhor* (remember). In a balanced and inclusive fashion this document speaks of Auschwitz, of the Nazi attempt to exterminate the Jews of Europe, and of the Nazi conquest of Poland. It commemorates the Jews as well as the other groups who were victims of the Nazis. As Jewish theologian Richard Rubenstein noted, "The painful controversy over the location of the Carmelite convent within a building a few yards from Auschwitz brought to the surface many of the persistent wounds of the still un-mastered trauma of World War II. Some of the most difficult aspects of Jewish-Christian and Jewish-Polish relations were once again made manifest."[51]

Two years after the Geneva agreements were concluded, the nuns had yet to vacate the Old Theater building. Hoping that the agreements would still be honored and that the convent would soon move, Rabbi Marc Tanenbaum of New York, one of the foremost Jewish proponents of dialogue with Catholic communities, described the strong feelings of many in the Jewish community: "Most Jews understand the appropriateness of the Carmelites honoring Polish-Catholic victims of Nazism. However, since Auschwitz was built for the primary purpose of exterminating European Jews, it had become a gesture of appropriation, rather than an act of reconciliation."[52]

In 1989 two startling developments took place that severely complicated the controversy, turning it into an international incident with powerful implications for both Polish nationalism and Jewish activism. On the date that the nuns were supposed to leave the Old Theater building and move the convent elsewhere, a group of Polish-Catholic activists erected a twenty-foot high cross near the site. It was the same cross that had been used at Pope John Paul II's 1979 mass at the nearby camp of Birkenau. The presence of the cross raised the stakes for all of the parties. Catholic groups saw the cross as an assertion of Christian religiosity in Communist Poland. Jewish groups in Europe, the United States, and Israel, saw it as an insult. In their opinion the Polish Communist regime had for decades obscured the fate of the Jewish victims in the camps, choosing, in Soviet fashion, to lump all of the victims together as the 'victims of fascism.' Jewish groups wanted the Nazi death camps remembered specifically as sites of Jewish suffering and destruction, not as sites of a universal calamity. They protested the presence of the cross as well as the fact that the nuns had not yet moved from the disputed location.

Then in July 1989 American rabbi Avi Weiss and six colleagues staged a protest at the convent. They entered the Old Theater building on a Friday afternoon, before the Sabbath, and proceeded to "welcome the Sabbath" by lighting candles and praying. According to Rabbi Weiss's account of the event, a Polish construction crew, egged on by a priest, assaulted the protestors, with the leader of the crew yelling "Heil Hitler!" while the nuns quietly stood by and watched.[53] Rabbi Weiss's demonstration, and the powerful reactions to it, became an international news item, with *The New York Times* covering the story on its front page. The Cardinal of Kraków, Cardinal Macharski, found the *Times'* coverage outrageous and he accused "some western Jewish centers of a violent campaign of accusations and slander and outrageous aggression. The nuns, their human and Christian dignity, were not respected; the peace to which they are entitled was disturbed. The Christian faith as well as symbols and piety were not respected."[54]

In April 1989, before the Rabbi Weiss protest, *The Jerusalem Post* had published an interview with Cardinal Lustiger. In that interview Lustiger expressed hope that the controversy over the convent could be solved expeditiously by agreeing to a delay in the implementation of the Geneva agreements. Within perhaps the next six months or so, he conjectured, the nuns would agree to move. In the following years, he hoped, the visitor center would be built and the convent re-established nearby. Lustiger went on to explain that there were important symbolic issues behind what seemed on its face to be a controversy over real estate:

> The problem is not only a practical one, it is also a symbolic issue—I don't want us to be at the origin of a rash of anti-Semitism that would serve the Polish internal political interests. We shouldn't press too hard on the Carmelites and turn them into martyrs for a mere six months—it would be stupid. It is perfectly legitimate for the Carmelite nuns to pray and express in their faith, their link with the massacre of millions of Poles and their compassion for all of the other victims. This is not disrespectful or intolerable. It would be so if it appeared as a gesture of appropriation or of a negation of the *Shoah*. Since there is no such risk of that, I don't see why these women couldn't do it at a certain distance from the Auschwitz concentration camp. Progress has been made in Poland; it would be foolish on behalf of the Jewish organizations not to see that we now have a gate to penetrate the Polish-Soviet universe, which is deeply anti-Semitic.[55]

Michel Zlotowski, the interviewer from *The Jerusalem Post*, noted that Lustiger referred to himself as a fellow Jew throughout the interview. "During our conversation he often spoke of 'we.' When asked to whom the 'we' referred, he said: 'We, the Jews, of course.'"[56]

Zlotowski also asked Lustiger why he avoided the use of the word *holocaust*, and referred instead to the German murder of the Jews of Europe as the *Shoah*. Lustiger explained, "I never use the word *holocaust*, its meaning is very precise. It's a sacrifice wished, or requested, by God to glorify Him or to expiate a sin. The genocide was a catastrophe, a crime."[57] Lustiger, unlike many Jews and Christians of his generation, was careful to avoid theologizing the Nazi murders. As the English word *holocaust*, derived from the

Greek, refers to sacrifices consumed by fire, applying that word to the victims of the Nazis implies that they were sacrifices on the altar of history.[58]

Because of Lustiger's intervention, Pope John Paul II made the decision that the Carmelite convent at Auschwitz should be moved to a nearby site. But the Polish Catholic hierarchy resisted this decision, and the move took more than four years to implement.

What enabled Cardinal Lustiger to succeed as a negotiator in the controversy over the convent at Auschwitz, and in other controversies in Jewish-Christian relations? One would not have expected a convert from Judaism, an apostate, a *meshummad* in Jewish terms, to be acceptable to Jewish interlocutors. But for the most part, the Jewish community, particularly in Europe, welcomed Lustiger as a trusted negotiating partner. Few if any traditional Jews, however, would have accepted Lustiger's claim that he was still a faithful Jew. The implication that a Catholic cardinal could still be a Jew constituted a blurring of the lines between religions, a situation unacceptable to the leadership and membership of the organized Jewish community. The key to Lustiger's acceptability is that the leadership of the Jewish community perceived him, in the terms of historian Shulamit Magnus, as a "good bad Jew." Magnus describes "good bad Jews" as "Jews who converted to Christianity opportunistically or for personal reasons and who use their positions as both former Jews and current members of the majority religion to help Jews and Judaism in situations of extreme duress."[59] For her primary example, Magnus cites the story of the nineteenth-century scholar Daniel Khwolson, a converted Jew who served as Professor of Semitic Languages at the University of St. Petersburg. Khwolson used his knowledge of Hebrew and the Jewish tradition to refute allegations that Russian Jews used the blood of Christian children in their Passover rituals. Khwolson's book-length refutation of this accusation influenced the Russian court to free Jews accused in "Blood Libel" trials. For his efforts, Khwolson became a hero to many Russian Jews.

Perhaps Lustiger's most concise articulation of his understanding of his role in Jewish-Christian relations came from a conversation with another Polish Jewish convert to Catholicism. In 1984 Cardinal Lustiger met with Brother Daniel, the former Oswald Rufeisen, whom we shall meet in chapter seven. Brother Daniel, a converted Jew who lived as a Catholic monk in the Carmelite Monastery in Haifa, had come to Paris from Rome, where he had had a private audience with Pope John Paul II. Lustiger and Brother Daniel held their conversation in Yiddish, the language of their childhood. According to Brother Daniel, Lustiger said to him, "Jews have been crucified by us Christians for many centuries. We failed to see in them the brothers of Christ. Jews were condemned to follow the same path that Jesus did. Christians did to the Jews what was done to Christ without realizing that they were continuing to crucify Christ. We, the Jews in the church, have an obligation to make the Christians aware of what they have done to the Jews."[60] In 2005, Pope John Paul II asked Lustiger to represent the Vatican at the sixtieth year commemoration of the liberation of Auschwitz. A year later, in 2006, Lustiger would accompany the new Pope, Benedict XVI, to a commemoration at the concentration camp at Birkenau.[61]

LUSTIGER AND CHRISTIAN-JEWISH RELATIONS

Lustiger served as archbishop of Paris for twenty-four years, from 1981 until 2005. He was an activist and an assertive administrator; his opponents often referred to him as "the bulldozer." His theological and political views were conservative. He worked to prevent the appointment of left-leaning clergy, had many progressive clergy removed from their positions, and generally upheld the teachings of the Vatican. At the same time Lustiger opposed the radical right, especially the racist tendencies of Le Pen and his National Front party. He also cultivated contacts with Jews in France and elsewhere. In turn, European Jewish public figures often sought out Lustiger as an interlocutor. Although these Jewish leaders were aware that Lustiger was a convert, they still sought his help when necessary. In 2001, at the age of seventy-five, Lustiger tendered his resignation, as required by Church law. The Pope, however, would not accept it; he served another four years as archbishop, before retiring in 2005. He was ill at the time and would live another two years, dying in August of 2007.

In these last years of his life, Lustiger was even more engaged with Jewish issues; he thought that the Church in France had something to learn on an organizational and communal level from Jewish life in the United States. He was especially impressed with Jewish school networks and institutions of higher learning. In the Jewish day schools, Talmudic academies, and rabbinic seminaries of the more traditional Jewish denominations (both Conservative and Modern Orthodox), Lustiger saw models and methods that French Catholic education could emulate. While the Chief Rabbi of France and the communal leadership of French Jewry had a warm relationship with Lustiger, American and Israeli Jewish leaders were suspicious and wary of him. In France, Lustiger was one of a number of young Jews who had converted to Catholicism in the mid-twentieth century, many while in hiding with Catholic families or Catholic institutions during the German occupation. Although Lustiger was not actually one of these children—he had chosen to convert for personal reasons at age fourteen and then been baptized over his parents' objections—he was often thought of as a Jew forced to convert in order to save his life. There was, in fact, a certain sympathy and understanding of the plight of these French Jews who had become faithful Catholics.

But these factors were not as relevant for American and Israeli Jews as they were for European Jews.

Among Israeli Jews, the memory of Polish Catholic hostility to Jews was very much alive. Polish Jewish survivors of World War II were aging and dying, but their children, grandchildren, and many of their associates harbored a great antipathy to European Catholicism in general and to Polish Catholicism in particular. Lustiger sought to overcome this antipathy, hostility, and suspicion by reaching out to Jewish individuals and organizations, and attempting to be an advocate for Jewish causes. The case of the convent at Auschwitz was one such case. Another was his attempt to engage Jewish thinkers on a theological level. From 2004 to 2007, during the last three years of his life, Lustiger became an active participant in Catholic-Jewish conversations about law, theology, and community.

These public conversations generated both enthusiasm and criticism. The United States served as the venue for most of these dialogues, as it does for most Jewish-Christian inter-religious interaction. In 2004, Lustiger and twenty European Catholic clergy traveled to the United States to visit centers of Jewish learning and Jewish communal life. Well publicized, these visits received praise from liberals and drew fire from religious conservatives—both Catholic and Jewish. Lustiger was the organizer of and catalyst for these meetings.[62] With his fellow Church officials, Lustiger visited Yeshiva University, an Orthodox institution in upper Manhattan, where he attended a study session with rabbis and students. As *The New York Times* reported, "The Catholic delegation, which included Cardinal Francis George of Chicago, was assembled by Cardinal Lustiger, who converted from Judaism as a youngster and speaks Yiddish. Exposing his fellow cardinals to the Yeshiva world was, he said, 'a way of showing them how to be men of faith in the modern world.'"[63]

Yeshiva faculty member Rabbi Hershel Reichman, perhaps the most eloquent of those who disapproved of the clergymen's visit to Yeshiva University, argued that the meetings were contrary to the teachings of Rabbi Soloveitchik, the late rabbinic authority of Yeshiva University. Reichman wrote, "It is no accident that the *meshummad*, Cardinal Lustiger, led the delegation to Yeshiva University. Lustiger himself explained this when he previously said, 'I was born Jewish and so I remain, even if that's unacceptable for many. For me the vocation of Israel is bringing light to the goyim, that's my hope, and I believe Christianity is the means of achieving this.'" Strongly disagreeing with Lustiger, Reichman continued, "The message of the Church is crystal clear: *shmad*, or apostasy, is acceptable—a Jew can become Christian and say *kaddish* and do a *kiddush ha-shem* as a Jewish-Christian. Lustiger is a Jew for Jesus and is quite acceptable to Jews—so then, are all Jews for Jesus acceptable? Heaven forbid! Let us not allow the Church to manipulate us." Reichman then quoted his teacher, Rabbi Soloveitchik, who wrote in

1964 in the wake of Vatican II, "Religious dialogue between Jews and Christians is prohibited. Social dialogue concerning human and social issues, particularly, anti-Semitism, is permitted." Reichman, forty years after Soloveitchik published that legal decision, concluded, "Thus, the only *halachic* issue for us to decide today is whether or not any particular event is 'religious' or 'social.' To my mind, priests listening to Yeshiva students learning Torah in a *beit midrash* is a 'religious event.' I would also say the same if rabbis went into churches to listen in on Christian religious classes."[64]

Two years after the 2004 visit to Yeshiva University, in March 2006, Lustiger and a group of Cardinals paid a similar visit to Yeshivat Chovevei Torah in New York City. At the time Chovevei Torah was a recently-established rabbinical seminary that positioned itself to the political and social left of Yeshiva University. The World Jewish Congress organized the visit. Thirty bishops and two cardinals participated. The churchmen and the Yeshiva students broke up into small groups to study Talmudic passages together. Reporting on this meeting, the Israeli Orthodox journal, *Yated Neeman*, singled out Lustiger and the new seminary for derision. In the article entitled "Yeshivat Chovevei Torah: Is It Orthodox?" the anonymous author again invoked Rabbi Soloveitchik's dictum that theological conversations between Orthodox rabbis and Christian scholars are beyond the pale.[65] The *Yated* article went on to ask how the leaders of Yeshiva University and Yeshivat Chovevei Torah, "both of whom have frequently called themselves students of Rabbi Soloveitchik," could reconcile the Catholic cardinals' visit with their mentor's opinion: "Would Rav Soloveitchik let a Cardinal, let alone a *meshummad*, speak to his students?"[66]

For many religious conservatives, the problem stemmed from Lustiger's refusal to define himself as either Christian or Jew. Lustiger sought to redefine these categories, to blur the boundaries between the two religions. He sought to be both Jew *and* Christian, claiming that his Judaism found full expression in his Christianity. When Pope John Paul II made Lustiger the Archbishop of Paris in 1981, Marcel Lefebvre, the founder of the Society of St. Pius X, a traditionalist Catholic group, complained, in the language of coded anti-Semitism, that the position should not be given "to someone who was not truly of French origin."[67] Similarly, traditional Jewish leaders, among them the Chief Rabbis of Israel, objected to Lustiger's engagement with Jews and visits to Israel. He was an apostate Jew, they claimed, and not worthy of the respect due a fellow clergyman.

In his sermons and lectures, Lustiger often made reference to his Jewish origins, to rabbinic ideas, and to rabbinic texts. At a lecture titled, "How Can We Believe in God Today," which Lustiger delivered at the École Polytechnique in December 1982, a student asked the cardinal about the relationship with other cultures. He replied, "I will remain within the biblical tradition. Of course other cultures can be considered from the historical standpoint. The confrontation between revelation and paganism is something that is absolutely universal. It took place in the conscience of Abraham, first in Israel, then in all of the Mediterranean world, and the neighboring cultures where confrontation took place between revelation and spontaneous religion. That confrontation is the very fabric of our entire holy history, between God who reveals himself through his envoys and witnesses, and paganism which is a constant factor in everyone—there is a pagan in every one of us."[68] In the lecture, he explained his concept of revelation: "Revelation is that which gives access to one who is 'other'—different from anything humans can imagine—the only God is God. The word 'God' leads to confusion; we made up this word in our Western languages—as a generic term—'the god who,' 'the god of.' We make a genus of it: 'the gods of the Hindus,' 'the gods of archaic civilizations,' thus one could put labels on the various species of gods, just as one sticks labels on the various species of one genus. But prophetic biblical revelation is the affirmation that there is only one God, that he does not belong to a genus, that he cannot be put into a class; he can only name himself and his very name is mystery."[69]

LUSTIGER AND THE STATE OF ISRAEL

Starting when he was in seminary and continuing through his tenure as the priest of Sainte-Jeanne-de-Chantal and chaplain of the Sorbonne, roughly the period from 1951 until 1969, Lustiger made annual pilgrimages to Israel. After 1969, and particularly after his 1981 accession to the Archbishopric of Paris, Lustiger made fewer trips to the Holy Land. These later journeys were no longer in the nature of a personal pilgrimage; he was now a spokesperson for the Church. Lustiger accompanied the Pope on several trips to Israel—including Pope John Paul II's 2000 visit to Jerusalem. On these trips Lustiger was in contact with Israel's small Hebrew Catholic community. In addition to the well-established Palestinian Arabic Catholic community whose origins were centuries old, there was also a small community of Catholic immigrants—typically Catholic men and women married to Jewish spouses—who were known as Hebrew Catholics because their liturgy was said in Hebrew. On his first visit to Israel in 1951, Lustiger had met Father Jean Roger Henné, an Assumptionist Father who introduced Lustiger to the problems that this group encountered living in the Jewish state, particularly the challenge of sustaining a vibrant religious culture in a Jewish state dominated by secularism. Lustiger sought to be an interlocutor and advocate for these Hebrew Catholics. Over the years, he gave many sermons to this Israeli Catholic group, joining them in worship at the Catholic Church in Abu Ghosh, an Arab village near Jerusalem.

In tandem with these visits, Lustiger developed a theological position concerning the State of Israel. Speaking to the congregation at Abu Ghosh in 1979 he explained, "Contemporary history has placed before us another para-doxical event: the rebirth of the State of Israel. This state was politically inspired by the secularized West and its culture. Even if this is still the object of vigorous internal debates, Israel introduced the idea of a secular state granting equal rights to its citizens, regardless of their religion, into the Middle East. The paradox is, that the people of Israel while claiming its specificity as such, intends to make its entry among other nations on the Western model, which is becoming universal."[70] Here Lustiger returns to a theme he often spoke of: the State of Israel, as the fulfillment of Jewish history (following his model of Christianity as the fulfillment of Judaism) needs to have a religious underpinning, and that its citizens are in historical and religious error if they promote secularism. In this, paradoxically, he was very similar to fellow French-born convert Madeleine Feraille/Ruth Ben Da-vid, who also decried the secularist practices and ideologies of Israeli Jews.

While Lustiger expressed a general concern about secularism among Is-raeli Jews, he was more interested in developing an ideology for Israeli Catholics. He speculated that the Hebrew-speaking community of Catholics, a group which since 1957 had been permitted to say the Mass in Hebrew, had great historical significance; that this community was a positive sign of the future of Christian-Jewish relations. He thought that this Israeli-Catholic community could fulfill "in association with the Arab-Christian commu-nities, the mission entrusted by Jesus to his disciples. Between Judaism and Islam, between the Arab and Western cultures, among all the contradictory political claims being made in that region, who else could be called on to live this beatitude? Blessed are the peacemakers for they shall be called Sons of God. It is this witness that the torn and divided Middle East awaits from Christians."[71] We shall see in chapter seven that Brother Daniel (Oswald Rufeisen), another Polish covert, also thought that the Israeli Catholics had a significant role to play in interfaith and international relations.

In "Israel and the Gentiles," a 1995 lecture at Tel Aviv University, Lusti-ger further developed his ideas about religion and the destiny of Israel, the people, and the state:

The particular history of this people has been arranged for the salvation of all peoples. But this people's history has evolved not according to the ambition of empires and nations who seek to dominate all others. It is God alone, the unique God, who reigns over all peoples and through all peoples discover their equal dignity. Here then we come face-to-face with the paradox of the destiny that is 'all of Israel.' The children of Israel have now been gathered together in a state like others—neither more nor less—and that is legitimate and neces-sary. The state was founded by the descendants of the people that God has called to be his People 'not like others,' but 'for others'—because of his plan for universal salvation. And what is true for this nation of Jews, living in the recently created State of Israel, is also true for members of the Jewish people, dispersed among the nations of which they are citizens. Yet their vocation of bearing witness depends not on human power, but on God.[72]

Lustiger presented "Israel and the Gentiles" on the eve of *Yom HaShoah,* Holocaust Memorial Day. He noted in his introductory comments, "I am here to take part in the ceremony to be held at *Yad Vashem* Holocaust Museum, commemorating the fiftieth anniversary of the liberation of the concentration camps."[73] Though Lustiger's Tel Aviv audience may have been confused by his theological speculations, many seemed to respect and appreciate his comments about commemoration. Other Israeli Jews, however, were quite upset by his presence at the event. As *The New York Times* reporter covering the event put it, "Instead of touching an ecumenical chord, the visit pierced old religious wounds and rubbed them raw."[74]

The Ashkenazi Chief Rabbi of Israel, Meir Lau, objected to Lustiger's participation in the *Yom HaShoah* ceremonies. A child survivor of the Buchenwald concentration camp who was appointed Chief Rabbi in 1993, Lau declined the invitation to share the Tel Aviv University podium with Lustiger. He told journalists that Cardinal Lustiger should not have been invited to Israel to commemorate *Yom HaShoah.* "Lustiger betrayed his people and his faith during the most difficult and darkest of periods," said the Chief Rabbi. As the *Times* reporter explained, "The issue was the fact that Lustiger had chosen to be baptized in 1940. It was a decision he has explained born of spiritual awakening—not an attempt to save himself from the Nazis—while he attended a Catholic school to which his Jewish parents had sent him at the outbreak of World War II." For Rabbi Lau, and for many other Orthodox Jewish Israelis, Lustiger, despite his prominence, his ideological and political sympathies with the State of Israel, and his participation in attempts to improve Catholic-Jewish relations, remained a *meshummad,* an apostate. In his 2005 autobiography, Lau recalled, "As a resident of Tel Aviv, a citizen of Israel, and a Jew, I protested with all my being against the idea of inviting Cardinal Lustiger on that evening!"[75] The word *meshummad,* apostate, was to remain prominent in the Israeli lexicon when referring to Lustiger. In 2007, when Lustiger died in Paris, the right-leaning newspaper, *The Jerusalem Post,* in its headline about the cardinal's death, would refer to Lustiger as a *meshummad.*[76]

A similar conflict concerning Lustiger's participation in Jewish events occurred in 2005, two years before his death. In October of 2005 there was a celebration marking the fortieth anniversary of *nostra aetate,* the document issued at Vatican II that sought to redefine the relationship between Catholicism and other religions, and particularly between Catholics and Jews. Hebrew University held a conference to examine the legacy of *nostra aetate,* while the Vatican held a ceremony in Rome to mark the occasion. The *nostra aetate* document "condemned anti-Semitism, repudiated the charge that blamed the Jews for Christ's death, and recognized the Jewish people's right to return to the land of Israel and to live there as a sovereign nation. The document recognized the Jewish roots of Christianity and ended the 'teaching of contempt' which had long been the approach of Christianity to the Jews."[77] Honored at the event were many of the people who had been involved in the creation of the papal document and others who had carried on the subsequent work of Catholic-Jewish reconciliation, foremost among them Rabbi David Rosen of the American-Jewish Committee. But an embarrassing problem arose. As *The Jerusalem Post* reported, "Notably absent from the Vatican ceremony was Rabbi Riccardo Di Segni, the Chief Rabbi of Rome, who refused to attend in protest against the fact that Cardinal Lustiger, a Jewish convert to Catholicism, was also asked to speak. Di Segni felt that the choice of Lustiger contradicts the fact that any dialogue necessarily demands respect for the belief of others and a repudiation of attempts to convert them."[78] Although Rabbi Rosen and the other speakers had agreed to the presence of Cardinal Lustiger, the Chief Rabbi of Rome's complaint unsettled them. Rabbi Rosen admitted to a journalist that Lustiger's claim to be both Jew and Catholic, and his constant highlighting of his Jewish roots posed problems for Jewish-Catholic reconciliation. As Rena Rossner noted, "Rosen admits that this issue is one that needs to be resolved within the Church; it is part of the continuation of the legacy of the *nostra aetate* document." Rabbi Rosen said, "There is an ambiguity in the Church about this issue. On the one hand, Cardinal Casper, and paradoxically, Lustiger as well, say that it is wrong to encourage Jews to convert. On the other hand, there are many in the Church who believe that even if the covenant between God and the Jews is extant, the Catholic Church needs to offer Jews the opportunity to become 'complete' by converting. This tension must be resolved."[79]

Although Rabbi Di Segni, the Chief Rabbi of Rome, and Rabbi Lau, the Ashkenazi Chief Rabbi of Israel, objected to Lustiger's participation in these Jewish ceremonies, the Chief Rabbi of France, Samuel Sirat, refrained from criticizing the cardinal. According to Rabbi Sirat, Father Lustiger attended a Paris synagogue annually on the *yahrzeit* of his mother, and recited the *Kaddish*.[80] On these occasions, Lustiger would remove his cardinal's robes and attend in civilian clothes. But Rabbi Sirat's affection for the Cardinal could not override his objection to Lustiger's insistence on being both a Christian and a Jew. As Sirat told interviewer Daniel Ben Simon, "Together with French rabbis, I harshly criticized the admixture he had made. One of the rabbis wrote in Le Monde that the moment they prove to him that a circle is square, he will accede to the definition that a Jew is the same as a Christian."[81]

In 1998, three years after the Tel Aviv conference and Rabbi Lau's vociferous objection to the inclusion of Lustiger in the *Yad Vashem* ceremony marking the fiftieth anniversary of the liberation of the concentration camps, there was a similar imbroglio involving Lustiger. The Center for Christian-Jewish Understanding, an American inter-faith group, awarded Lustiger the *Nostra Aetate Award* for advancing Jewish-Catholic relations. Abraham Foxman, the head of the Anti-Defamation League, protested against granting the award to Lustiger; he thought it was inappropriate to honor the cardinal. "It's fine to have him speak at a conference, or at a colloquium, but I don't think he should be honored, because he converted out, which makes him a poor example."[82] Foxman, like Lustiger, is a survivor of the war. In fact, he was hidden by Catholics who sheltered him during the war years. But Foxman did not convert to Catholicism, and he could not forget or excuse Lustiger's apostasy.

SAYING *KADDISH* AT LUSTIGER'S FUNERAL

Lustiger died in August of 2007 after a prolonged struggle with cancer. More than five thousand people attended his funeral services at Paris's Notre Dame Cathedral. Lustiger had made very specific plans for his funeral. In addition to the Catholic liturgy, Lustiger asked that Jewish texts and prayers be included. In keeping with Jewish custom, he asked to be buried with a small satchel of earth from Israel. He also wanted Jewish relatives to read one of the Psalms (112/113) and recite the *kaddish*.[83] The honor went to his cousin, novelist Arno Lustiger, who chose to read the *kaddish* standing outside the cathedral, rather than inside.

The World Jewish Congress, the organization that had sponsored the Lustiger-led visit to Yeshivat Hovevei Toah in 2006, issued a statement upon Lustiger's death that would seem to confirm his standing as a "good bad Jew":

> The World Jewish Congress (WJC) mourns the passing of Cardinal Jean-Marie Lustiger, a pioneer of Christian-Jewish dialogue. 'Cardinal Lustiger was born a Jew. His mother perished in Auschwitz. He always knew what anti-Semitism, persecution and hatred meant for the Jewish people, and he fought strenuously to overcome them. That is what he will be remembered for by many in the Jewish world,' WJC President Ronald S. Lauder said in a statement. He added: 'Together with the late Pope John Paul II, Cardinal Lustiger was instrumental in fostering dialogue and a better understanding between Catholics and Jews, both on a personal and an institutional level. His efforts are a shining example to those who want to foster mutual respect and understanding between religions and cultures.... Cardinal Lustiger's great intellect, vision and warm personality will be greatly missed. The Christian world has

lost one of its greatest personalities, France has lost a great moral and spiritual leader, and the Jewish world has lost one of its closest friends.'[84]

While he emphasized Lustiger's Jewish ancestry, Lauder made no mention of his apostasy. Lustiger, in the end, was a "friend of the Jews" rather than a betrayer of his heritage. As such he exemplified the "good-bad Jew." Like the late-nineteenth-century scholar Daniel Khwolson of Russia, the Jewish school teacher who apostatized, became an eminent professor of Semitics, and acted as an advocate for Russian Jewish causes, Lustiger had transcended his apostasy through his service to the Jewish people.

Lustiger's epitaph, which he wrote himself in 2004, reads:

> I was born Jewish.
> I received the name
> Of my paternal grandfather, Aaron
> Having become Christian
> By faith and by Baptism,
> I have remained Jewish
> As did the Apostles.
> I have as my patron saints
> Aaron the High Priest,
> Saint John the Apostle,
> Holy Mary full of grace.
> Named 139th archbishop of Paris
> by His Holiness Pope John-Paul II,
> I was enthroned in this Cathedral
> on 27 February 1981,
> And here I exercised my entire ministry.
> Passers by, pray for me.
> —Aaron Jean-Marie Cardinal Lustiger
> Archevêque de Paris[85]

NOTES

1. Lustiger, Missika, Wolton, *Choosing God, Chosen by God*, 19.
2. Ibid., 46.
3. Lustiger, *Dare to Believe*, 76.
4. Ibid.
5. Lustiger, Missika, Wolton, *Choosing God, Chosen by God*, 28.
6. Ibid.
7. Lustiger, *Dare to Believe*.
8. Lustiger, Missika, Wolton, *Choosing God, Chosen by God*, 47.
9. Lustiger, *Dare to Believe*.
10. Lustiger, Missika, Wolton, *Choosing God, Chosen by God*, 42.
11. Ibid., 44.
12. Ibid.

13. Lustiger, *Dare to Believe*, 42.
14. Ibid.
15. Ibid.
16. Lustiger, Missika, Wolton, *Choosing God, Chosen by God*, 25.
17. Lustiger, *Dare to Believe*,
18. Lustiger, Missika, Wolton, *Choosing God, Chosen by God*, 27.
19. Ibid., 27.
20. Ibid., 28.
21. Ibid., 33.
22. Ibid., 47.
23. Ibid., 28.
24. Ibid., 68.
25. Gildea, *Marianne in Chains*, 4.
26. Ibid., 218.
27. Quoted in Gildea, *Marianne in Chains*, 218.
28. Lustiger, Missika, Wolton, *Choosing God, Chosen by God*, 48.
29. Ibid., 49.
30. Ibid.
31. Ibid.
32. Gildea, *Marianne in Chains*, 223.
33. Ibid., 221.
34. Lustiger, Missika, Wolton, *Choosing God, Chosen by God*, 52.
35. Ibid., 55.
36. Lustiger, *Dare to Believe*, 55.
37. Ibid., 80.
38. Ibid., 57.
39. Ibid., 76.
40. Ibid.
41. Ibid.
42. Lustiger, Missika, Wolton, *Choosing God, Chosen by God*, 149.
43. Ibid., 150.
44. Lustiger, *Dare to Believe*, 100.
45. See Tagliabue, "Jean-Marie Lustiger, French Cardinal, Dies at 80."
46. Ibid., 53.
47. Klein, *The Battle for Auschwitz*, 12.
48. Zubrzycki, *The Crosses of Auschwitz*, 5.
49. Quoted in Klein, *The Battle for Auschwitz*, 12.
50. Zubrzycki, *The Crosses of Auschwitz*, 6, n. 9.
51. Rubenstein, *After Auschwitz*, 62.
52. Klein, *The Battle for Auschwitz*, 10.
53. Rubenstein, *After Auschwitz*, 72.
54. Tagliabue, "Polish Prelate Assails Protests By Jews at Auschwitz."
55. Zlotowski, "The Jewish archbishop speaks about the 'Shoah.'"
56. Ibid.
57. Ibid.
58. Garber and Zuckerman, "Why Do We Call The Holocaust 'The Holocaust?'" 197–211.
59. Magnus, "Good Bad Jews," 133.
60. Tec, *In the Lion's Den*, 169.
61. See Pope John Paul II, "Auschwitz: « Il n'est permis à personne de passer avec indifférence »," and Pope Benedict XVI, "Auschwitz: Benoît XVI évoque d'emblée « les victimes de la terreur nazie »."
62. Wakin and Goodstein, "In Upper Manhattan, Talmudic Scholars Look Up and Find Cardinals Among the Rabbis."
63. Ibid.
64. Reichman, "The Cardinal's Visit: Thoughts of a Rosh Yeshiva."
65. See "Yeshivat Chovevei Torah: Is It Orthodox?"

66. Ibid.
67. See Tagliabue, "Jean-Marie Lustiger, French Cardinal, Dies at 80."
68. Lustiger, "How Can We Believe in God Today?"
69. Ibid.
70. Lustiger, *The Promise*, 126.
71. Ibid., 128–29.
72. Ibid., 137–8.
73. Ibid., 133.
74. Haberman, "Jerusalem Journal: the Cardinal Visits and the Chief Rabbi is Pained."
75. Lau, *Out of the Depths?*.
76. See Staff, "Apostate French Cardinal Dies at 80."
77. Rossner, "The Rabbi, The Pope, and The Cardinal." Also see Goldman, *Zeal for Zion*, 187–88, 191, 193, 196, 201–202.
78. Rossner, "The Rabbi, The Pope, and The Cardinal."
79. Ibid.
80. Ben-Simon, "He'd say kaddish for his mother."
81. Ibid.
82. Corroler, "Jean-Marie Lustiger, mort d'un cardinal d'action."
83. See "Les obsèques du cardinal Lustiger célébrées vendredi."
84. World Jewish Congress, "Statement of the World Jewish Congress on the Death of French Cardinal Jean-Marie Lustiger."
85. See the cover of *The Hebrew Catholic*, No. 85, Winter-Spring 2008.

Chapter Four

Donato Manduzio and the Converts of San Nicandro: A Group Conversion to Judaism in 1940s Italy (Donato Manduzio, 1885–1948)

The town of San Nicandro, located on the Gargano peninsula in the Apulia region of southeast Italy, has a history of religious enthusiasms that long precedes the saga of Donato Manduzio and his circle of followers in the twentieth century. Saint Nicandro, after whom the town is named, was a Roman soldier serving in the area in the fourth century C.E. On his conversion to Christianity, Nicandro led a revolt against the pagan rulers of Apulia and was martyred in the struggle.

Better known in Italy today is Padre Pio (Pio of Pietrelcina, 1887–1968), who was born in Gargano. As an adolescent, Padre Pio joined the Capuchin order, an order "sworn to live as beggars in the world." In San Nicandro in 1910, he is said to have first developed the stigmata that would bring him so much attention. Later, he became known as a mystic visionary and miracle worker. Pope John Paul II beatified Padre Pio in 1999 and canonized him in 2002.[1]

The history of religious enthusiasms in southeastern Italy, however, is not limited to Catholicism. A Protestant presence began to develop in this part of Italy during the second-half of the nineteenth century.[2] Missionaries from groups like "the Christian Church of the Brethren" and the Pentecostals distributed Bibles and emphasized reading from the scriptures, emulating, as they understood it, the reformers of the sixteenth and seventeenth centuries. These Protestant missionaries presented the Bible and its "plain truth" as a challenge to the teachings of the Catholic Church. As Elena Cassin has noted, "The sacred book through reading which a skeptic, into whose hands it has fallen by chance, is converted is a recurring motif in stories of conversion."[3]

By the 1920s American and British missionaries began to arrive in Southern Italy in greater number. Emissaries of Anglican and Protestant denominations, they intended to bring "the Christian Truth" to the "benighted" Catholic peasants of the region. Some of these missionaries were in fact Italian born. They had immigrated to the United States or England decades earlier, converted to one of the Protestant denominations, and were now returning to their homeland, determined to bring the light of their new faith to their former compatriots and co-religionists. These missionaries distributed thousands of Bibles in Italian translation. At that time, most Italian Catholics, especially those among the peasantry, were unfamiliar with many of the biblical narratives. Access to the entire text would transform some readers, who discovered a new and electrifying religious world in the pages of these Italian Bibles.

On the theological level, the Protestant idea of an unmediated relationship with God appealed to many Catholics. Thus, the missionaries attracted a number of converts. Speaking of the Apulia region, French historian of religion Elena Cassin has noted, "Evangelical faiths could claim numerous recruits in this region, as in the whole of Gargano, between 1922 and 1930."[4] Adventists, Pentecostals, and Baptists were among the denominations that made converts in the region. At least three villages, including San Nicandro, developed communities of Sabbatarians, Christians who, influenced by the laws of the Old Testament, chose Saturday as their day of rest. In addition to Saturday Sabbath observance, these Sabbatarian communities often adopted other practices from rabbinic Judaism, including following the dietary laws and performing circumcisions.

As a result of these extensive missionary efforts, "by the third decade of the twentieth century there were no fewer than twenty-seven sects and splinter sects flourishing in Italy, despite all the efforts of the Catholic Church which jealously guarded its hard-won hegemony in this, its mother country."[5] Political factors also facilitated conversions from Catholicism. In 1922 Mussolini ascended to power. As the fascist regime began to exert control over the more remote regions of southern Italy, Apulia, known in the nineteenth century as a center of peasant revolts, tried to push back against the regime. The new Italian government quickly quashed all resistance. An older tradition of banditry and lawlessness in the area, however, coupled with ongoing resistance to governmental and ecclesiastical control, clearly played a part in the rise of Protestant sects in the region.

One factor that increased political and religious awareness in the Southern Italian towns of the 1920s was recent government legislation that made emigration from Italy much more difficult. Previous generations of Italians had gone to the United States seeking employment. Now, however, it was illegal to leave Italy, and by 1924 United States immigration laws had become much more restrictive. Thus, young Italians, faced with limited employment possibilities, often turned to local political and religious causes.

As a result of Protestant missionary efforts, some Italian Catholics, convinced that the Church had distorted and misrepresented the word of God, abandoned Christianity altogether. They gravitated toward a religion which they assumed would be more faithful to the message of the Hebrew Bible. With no Jews in the region, they were not familiar with Judaism as a living religion. Thus, imagined forms of Judaism began to spring up. In the town of San Nicandro, Donato Manduzio would reach the conclusion, after reading both the Old and the New Testaments, that the Catholic Church had distorted God's word. He also concluded, pushing his thinking to its logical conclusion, that the Protestant denominations too were similarly based on false assumptions. For Manduzio, who would become the "prophet" of the San Nicandro group, the New Testament was unfaithful to the message of the Old Testament. Only the laws and narratives of the Hebrew Bible would govern their lives. The only good life, he told his followers, was a life based on the Five Book of Moses, the Prophets, and the Writings.

EARLY YEARS: STORYTELLER, COMMUNITY ORGANIZER, HEALER

Donato Manduzio was born into a San Nicandro family of modest means during the latter part of the nineteenth century. His parents, Giuseppe Manduzio and Concetta Frascaria, owned a house and a small plot of land with some agricultural yield. At the turn of the century with the region mired in poverty, families relied on their children as a source of free labor. The young Donato worked with his brother and sister on the family land; he did not go to school and would remain illiterate into his twenties. At the age of twenty-five Donato married Antonia Vocino, a young San Nicandro woman. Like her husband, Antonia would become an important leader in the San Nicandro Sabbath group, counseling women converts, and, after Donato's death, leading the Jewish community that formed around her husband's teachings.

Drafted into the Italian army at the outbreak of World War I, Manduzio served for four years in an infantry regiment, before being wounded in the leg during an encounter with Austrian troops. While recuperating in a military hospital in Pisa, Manduzio learned to read.[6] He soon became an avid reader, ultimately working his way through all of the books in the small hospital library, including a Latin grammar. In his journal, he later recalled, "I loved reading, and diligently studied books and novels, and among them the Rotillio [almanacs] and magic, all books of false prophets."[7] The wounded soldier who taught Manduzio how to read was a socialist revolutionary. He explained that he had taken it upon himself to teach fellow soldiers to read so that they could join the revolution. The socialist revolution, however, would not be the revolution that captured Manduzio's attention. Rather, it was a religious idea that would kindle his imagination.

Poor medical care compounded the severity of Manduzio's injuries, and the young man was never to walk again. After two years of recuperation, Manduzio returned to San Nicandro and to his wife Antonia. They received a small pension from the Italian army, which, together with the income from the grapes they cultivated on their small plot of land, enabled them to live moderately well.

Upon his return to San Nicandro, Manduzio was one of the few peasants in the town who was functionally literate. He was also a natural storyteller and an avid conversationalist. He soon attracted a group of followers. They would gather in a circle around him as he sat in his wheelchair on the porch in back of his home. Manduzio transfixed his listeners with his ability to remember numerous popular Italian stories, and with his gifts of embellishment and dramatization. His impressive storytelling skills, coupled with his organizational abilities, made him a natural choice to direct the town's annual Christmas festivities, which centered on productions of stage-plays drawn from historical romances and religious epics. Manduzio would oversee these Christmas productions for the town of San Nicandro into the late 1920s.

Manduzio also soon became known in San Nicandro as a faith healer. He dispensed advice about curing illnesses and seemed to effect cures by invoking the spirit world. As an astute observer has noted, "There is nothing at all surprising about this; every little town, every village in Apulia has its healer, its medicine man, its mixer of potions, who tends and sometimes cures the sick."[8] Manduzio had a prodigious memory. His ability to remember and embellish popular Italian stories, his range of medical knowledge, and his ability to recall local medical histories deeply impressed his "followers." Thus in the decade between 1919, when he returned to San Nicandro from the military hospital, and 1930, when he had the first of his prophetic visions, Manduzio emerged as a gifted storyteller, an able community organizer, and a local healer. At some point during this period, he began to keep a record of his experiences and observations.[9] The opening sentence of the journal betrays Manduzio's confidence in his role as the guiding light of his community: "I tell here a little story, full of light, of how on a dark path a light appeared; a light which shone in the darkness and in the shadow of death."[10]

Initially Manduzio's circle included some fifty people. There were twenty adults and thirty children. Over the sixteen years between 1930 and the group's formal conversion to Judaism in 1946, these numbers would fluctuate. In addition to Manduzio, his wife Antonia, who would later take the Hebrew name Emanuela, also played an influential role, teaching the women

and children and conferring with her husband about the spiritual development of the families who were soon dubbed *Sabbatini*, or Sabbath observers,
by the villagers. Historian John Davis has noted that Manduzio's "movement
had a special attraction for women, many of whom would prove to be its
most committed members. The reasons for this are not clear, although
women also played a prominent role in many of the evangelical Protestant
communities and it may have been the opportunities to take such a role in the
religious and social lives of the community that attracted them."[11] Antonia's
prominent position within the group helped to establish a pattern. After Manduzio's death in 1948, an increasing number of women would take on leadership roles in the emerging Jewish community, and this trend would continue
among both those who settled in Israel and those who remained in San
Nicandro.

DISCOVERING THE TORAH

By 1930, Donato Manduzio, now an established healer and teacher, began to
have doubts about his practices and beliefs. In his journals of the period
Manduzio appears to be a man torn between the urge to return to the Catholicism of his youth and the impulse to embrace one of the evangelical Protestant faiths then spreading through the region. He expresses a growing dis-
comfort with the use of magic in healing. The occult sciences satisfied neither his spiritual yearnings nor his intellectual curiosity; he sought material
more substantial. On his first reading of the Hebrew Bible, and its prohibitions against magic and divination, Manduzio would jettison his occult practices completely and address his healing prayers directly to God.

Manduzio experienced his first mystical vision in the late summer of
1930, just before his discovery of the Old Testament. Manduzio did not
initially grasp the meaning of this vision. But the next day, one of his followers approached him while he was working in one of his fields. The man
brought Manduzio a Bible.

As confirmation of his vision, Manduzio claimed that when he first
picked up the Bible, he opened it to its title page, which read, "The eternal
spring of the Holy Light." The emerging Sabbatini community would mark
August 11, 1930, the date of Manduzio's "vision of revelation," as the beginning of their communal calendar. In later years they would refer to this
inaugural date when describing historical events. For example "Mussolini
took Rome and conquered Rome eight years before we saw the light."[12]

Among Donato Manduzio's followers a legend developed that their
teacher accepted the Bible proffered by the man in the field and then spent
the next two days sleeplessly immersed in its pages. His wife Antonia,
alarmed by the intensity of Donato's response to the book, sought out the

parish priest, Don Giuseppe, who warned Donato that reading the Bible could endanger his soul. "I ought to warn you, said the priest. It is not given to everyone to understand the Word of God. The Holy Bible may become a veritable pitfall in the hands of simple souls." When the priest demanded that Manduzio hand over the text, he refused. Don Giuseppe then shouted at him, "Does that mean you will not give me the book which the devil has placed in your hands?" Manduzio, incredulous, responded that he doubted the devil would be distributing Holy Bibles. "No! Not a Holy Bible," replied the priest, "but a translation by Protestant heretics which no true Christian should read. Give it to me before it's too late—and I shall burn it!"[13]

Manduzio refused to hand over his Bible to the parish priest, and for many years it was the only Bible that he and his followers had. The volume became the group's sacred ritual object from which they read and prayed each Friday night and Saturday morning. Sabbath observance was at the core of Manduzio's evolving religious practice. Based on the core belief that God had created the world in six days and then rested, Sabbath observance became one of the most consistently articulated of the Sabbatini's beliefs. In an account of his final break with Christianity, Manduzio relates a conversation with a missionary who was trying to draw him and his followers into one of the local Protestant movements. When Manduzio brought up the biblical rules about Sabbath observance, his interlocutor dismissed them as "Old Testament Laws." Manduzio immediately cited New Testament references to Sabbath observance. Silenced, the missionary ended the conversation. From that day, Manduzio would later record in his diary, "I began to make known among my friends the oneness of the Creator who in six days created all things from nothing and rested the seventh day and hallowed it."[14]

Thus the group of followers that had gathered around Donato and Antonia Manduzio began to meet at their "prophet's" house on the Sabbath and study the biblical narratives as embellished in Donato's discourses. He declared Catholicism a form of idolatry. When Manduzio asked his followers to remove all crucifixes, rosaries, and other Christian artifacts from their homes, some balked and left the group, but most did as he asked. Some burned their crucifixes in a ceremony that invoked the biblical injunction to "destroy the idols." The Protestant missionaries he met had condemned the Catholic Church as "idol worshiping Papists." Manduzio would go beyond this message and condemn all Christian beliefs as false and all Christian rituals as idolatrous. As he recorded in his journal several years later, "Immediately I proclaimed to the people the one God and the words of Sinai, and how the Creator rested the seventh day; and I confirmed the unity of the Creator who takes counsel of none other, for none other has existed besides him. And I celebrated the holiness of the Creator in the extent of the heavens." Inspired by the Psalms, Manduzio began composing his own psalms, many of which would find their way into the community's Sabbatini liturgy. This practice was an early sign that Manduzio thought of himself as a prophet on the level of the biblical prophets. He believed that he was able to extend, or continue writing, the Hebrew Bible.

DISCOVERING "OTHER JEWS"

In 1930 when Donato Manduzio and his followers first expressed their interest in Judaism, they were not aware that Jews still existed in the world. Extending their readings of the biblical narratives to their logical conclusions, they determined that the Hebrew people had disappeared from history. Isolated in San Nicandro, Manduzio and his followers had no immediate counter-evidence to challenge this understanding. Before the railroad was extended into the Apulia region in the early 1930s, the Sabbatini had limited knowledge of and little contact with the world beyond the region.

In 1930, the eighth year of Mussolini's Fascist regime, Italy had a total population of some forty million people; perhaps fifty thousand were Jews. At that time there was no official Italian governmental policy targeting this small Jewish population. Most of these Jews were concentrated in the major cities. The Apulia region, with a population of approximately 15,000 people in 1930, had no Jews to speak of. There had once been a Jewish community in the region, but it had been expelled in the sixteenth century.

How Manduzio learned that there were not only Jews in the world, but even Jews in Italy is, like much of the narrative of the group, the stuff of legend. One version of the story has it that a year after he had his first vision, "Manduzio met a traveling merchant who revealed to him that there were many representatives of the Jewish people in other Italian cities."[15] Up to the time of this encounter, Manduzio had assumed that the Hebrew people had disappeared entirely from history. He saw himself as a new Moses leading his circle of followers to recreate a God-chosen community in San Nicandro. That there might be an actual living community claiming descent from the people that the biblical Moses had led initially seemed to Manduzio highly improbable. The discovery, however, that there were in fact "other Jews" in Italy did not shake his faith in himself as prophet to his followers; he did not give up his claim of direct contact with God. As he informed Rabbi Ravenna, the rabbi who would ultimately oversee his conversion, "The one who directed Moses is the one who directed me."[16]

In 1931 when he learned that there was a Jewish community in Rome, Manduzio sent a letter to the city's Chief Rabbi, Angelo Sacerdoti. When it went unanswered, Manduzio wrote a second letter, and then a third. The rabbi later reported that he thought these initial two notes were a hoax; after all, what group would want to convert to Judaism in 1930s Europe? As he later wrote to Manduzio, "I chose in the beginning to ignore the letters because I feared someone was trying to play a joke on me. Because none of my colleagues have ever heard of a Jewish community residing anywhere in the province of Garganico."[17] But with the arrival of the third missive, reports of the Sabbatini of San Nicandro had begun to reach Rome, and the rabbi was more receptive. As he wrote to Manduzio, "When I received your third letter . . . I decided that your petition was motivated by pure reasons and that you are sincere in your desire to embrace Judaism."[18]

Manduzio begins his third letter by addressing Sacerdoti as "most sanctified and revered Excellency, the anointed Supreme Rabbi of all the Jews in Italy," and explains that "only our unshaken faith in truth and justice gives us the courage to put pen to paper."[19] He then says that he is going to "start from the beginning and introduce" his group to the rabbi:

> We are a community of unlettered workers and farmers who live in San Nicandro, which is in the province of Garganico. And we were so plagued by a thirst for knowledge and a hunger for truth that we groped around by ourselves in the darkness into which we were born. And the Almighty God, Who sees and knows all, took pity upon us. Four years ago He sent us a light. That is to say He gave us the Holy Bible, and also a man who can read it and teach it to us. That is the same man who is writing this letter on behalf of all of us.
>
> As soon as we began to study the Holy Book we understood at once that everything we had been told in the village and taught in church was a pack of lies. We learned that the only people who knew the true God were the children of Israel who once lived in the Promised Land. So we decided to separate ourselves from the heathens and idol worshippers who lived in our midst, even though they might be our own parents or brothers, and follow the teachings of Moses, the leader.[20]

In language that echoes his first vision, Manduzio's introduction emphasizes the role of prophecy in the history of his group. He and his followers are seekers who by God's light have discovered the true path and chosen to become "children of Israel"; they are not Jews by lineage. Later, Manduzio will reshape this position to suggest that he and his followers are in fact descendants of Jews, but at this point he highlights the role of discovery and the importance of the teacher or prophet in that discovery. God's light has taken the form of a Bible and "a man who can read it and teach it to us,"[21] Donato Manduzio, who through his wisdom and visions is, like Moses, leading his followers to the worship of God.

Manduzio continues the letter by explaining that "in our stupidity and conceit we have thought . . . that all the Chosen People had died and that we were the only Children of Israel alive in the world." Manduzio explains that God, through a different type of revelation, has in fact corrected this error. As he says, "But God in His mercy saw our error and yesterday he blew out the tire of a car that passed through San Nicandro, and sent us a messenger who told us about Your Excellency and gave us your address."[22]

Manduzio, having recited the brief history of his group, now gets to the point of his letter. He and his followers want to convert to Judaism:

> We are nine families: twelve males and fifteen females, and we all wish to go over to the Jewish faith if you will accept us. We are well aware that we are not worthy of this great honor, Your Excellency, but if you will tell us how to make ourselves fit, we shall gladly fulfill all the conditions you may impose upon us that we may be accepted into the Covenant of Abraham.[23]

Rabbi Sacerdoti, in his response to Manduzio, explains that it is difficult to be a Jew, difficult both because of prejudice and persecution from the outside world, and because of the demanding requirements of the faith itself. He recommends a waiting period, during which Manduzio and his followers can confirm their desire to convert.

Soon after receiving Sacerdoti's letter, Manduzio read it aloud to the community. A few weeks later, he received a telegram from Rome, a rare occurrence in 1930s San Nicandro. Rabbi Sacerdoti, in an effort to help strengthen the group, wanted to connect Manduzio and his followers to an existing Jewish community: "I have requested the Jewish community of Naples, under whose regional jurisdiction you would come, to assist you immediately."

Unfortunately, the Naples community was not interested in taking on the responsibilities of nurturing a fledgling Jewish community. In a letter to Manduzio, they mention two external factors that are currently diverting their attention: "In view of the ever increasing restrictions imposed by the government on non-Catholic communities, and as a consequence of the state of emergency engendered by the War of Liberation which our glorious army is fighting in Abyssinia, it will be most difficult, if not impossible, for us to intervene on your behalf, as requested by the Chief Rabbinate." It is worth noting that the leaders of the Naples Jewish community frame anti-Jewish sentiment and actions as "restrictions on non-Catholic communities." Furthermore, they cite the Italian invasion of Ethiopia as a second extenuating circumstance that precludes their assisting the San Nicandrans. Then, attempting to minimize the importance of their support, the Naples letter goes on to suggest, in contradiction to the Chief Rabbi's warning about the rigors of Judaism, "that every house where prayers are conducted may truly be regarded as a house of worship, and no special premises need be allocated for this purpose." Ultimately, after these attempts to dissemble, the Naples community gets to the main point of their rejection: "With all due respect, you are after all not Jews."[24]

Donato Manduzio replied with a letter chastising the Naples community for its shortsightedness, reminding them that Abraham himself was a convert. Manduzio echoes again the theme of discovering the path to true belief. This time, however, he goes further, making the stronger claim that he and his followers are in fact descendants of Jews who had to renounce their heritage.[25] Later Manduzio will elaborate on this claim to Jewish ancestry, stating that the San Nicandran converts in fact descended from Spanish Jews who had fled to Italy and then were baptized against their will.

The French Jewish scholar Jacques Faitlovich (1881–1955) visited the San Nicandro community in January 1935.[26] He was curious to know more about this group of peasants who, having learned of the existence of other Jews in Italy, were eager to join the Jewish community. Described by a contemporary as a "researcher and man of action,"[27] Faitlovich had devoted his life to the study of "lost" Jewish communities in Africa and Asia. He is best known for his "discovery" of the Falashas of Ethiopia. For Faitlovich, as a "traditional, observant Jew with an ambivalent eye on modernity,"[28] the quest for members of the "lost tribes" was linked to Zionism. Zionism would achieve the "ingathering of the exiles" through natural rather than supernatural means, including gathering in those parts of the Jewish people who had been "lost" to history. But at the time of Faitlovich's visit to San Nicandro, the Sabbatini were not yet claiming publicly to be part of the lost tribes, or to be descended from *anusim*, Jews forcibly converted to Christianity. Manduzio and his followers were "discoverers" of the Mosaic law.

More than a decade after his first vision, Manduzio would refine his claim for the group's Jewish ancestry. After studying the history of world Jewry in general and Italian Jewry in particular, he would claim that he and his followers were Levites and descendants of Apulia *anusim*—Jews forced to accept baptism. In 1943, thirteen years after his first vision, Manduzio told Pinchas Lapide, "We come of excellent Jewish stock. The very best in fact. . . . Our ancestors were Spanish Jews twelve generations ago. They were Levites all of them. The envy of the Gentiles, and jealousy within, compelled them to' disguise themselves and flee." When asked how he knew of this secret lineage, Manduzio replied, "The Lord God revealed it to me in a vision."[29]

Lineage is central to Jewish identity, and converts to Judaism often seek such an ancestral tie. In contrast converts to Christianity do not seek a Christian ancestor. Rather they seek to join a universal church. Rabbinic legends assert that those Jews who apostatize "have the soul of gentiles." That these future apostates were born into Jewish families did not, according to these legends, save these souls from becoming Christians.

In 1932 Rabbi Sacerdoti, now taking Manduzio's letters more seriously, sent an emissary, his colleague Giorgio Sessini, to San Nicandro to meet the Sabbatini. At the time the group numbered fifty people. Arriving in San Nicandro, Sessini met with members of Manduzio's circle and gave them a synopsis of the long arc of world Jewish history and of Italian Jewish history in particular. Sessini read to them from an Italian edition of Cecil Roth's *A History of the Jews*, a book he then left with Manduzio. In the mid-1930s, a few years passed in which there was little contact between Rome's Jews and San Nicandro's Sabbatini. Manduzio then sent a young San Nicandran devotee to visit the Tempio Maggiore in Rome and learn the classical synagogue ritual. That ritual would prove to be radically different from the liturgy and ritual Manduzio had developed for his followers. And conflicts would arise in San Nicandro about the implementation of the traditional liturgy.

THE "PROPHET'S" AUTHORITY: PROPHECY, THE TALMUD, AND RABBINIC TRADITION

Up to the early 1930s the Sabbatini and their "Moses" sought to live according to biblical law as understood and interpreted by Manduzio. For example, each Passover eve the group slaughtered and roasted a lamb and ate it with unleavened bread as specified in Exodus. They were not aware that with the destruction of the Second Temple in 70 C.E. rabbinic Jews had discontinued this practice. The Passover Seder had evolved as a substitute for the actual ritual of sacrifice. Until their contact with Italian Jews, Manduzio and his flock had no way of knowing this. They were, however, soon to come into contact with what Italian Rabbi Alfredo Ravenna described as "official Judaism which was separated from Manduzio by 2,500 years of religious development."[30] Manduzio was on the verge of discovering the rabbinic Jewish tradition, and that discovery would be quite unsettling.

The rabbinic tradition asserts that it is the transmitter of the revelation at Sinai, a revelation fixed and codified in the rabbinic writings. Manduzio, who "discovered" the biblical account on his own, resisted being subsumed into an already fixed tradition. This was evident from his reply to a question raised by Rabbi Sacerdoti. The rabbi had asked Manduzio how he had first heard the word of God. Manduzio replied, "I have not heard the word of God from anyone. God himself has revealed the word to me, as he did to our father Abraham."[31] Manduzio saw himself as a priest and a prophet, guided by divine intervention; that understanding of himself was central to his leadership. Rabbinic law, however, had developed over the centuries in the opposite direction—that is to say, it rejected the role of prophecy.

Manduzio was dismayed to learn that according to rabbinic teachings prophecy had ceased, and that rabbis were not in fact visionaries. How could they guide their communities without the voice of God directing them?, he asked. In 1946, fifteen years after his first encounter with the realities of Jewish life in Italy and elsewhere, Manduzio would write to the recently appointed Chief Rabbi of Rome to express disappointment and amazement that prophecy was not cultivated in the rabbinate. He went so far as to suggest to the new Chief Rabbi, "You even ought to open a school of prophecy. Thus we and you would not walk blindly."[32]

When confronted with a problem in religious law, Manduzio would seek to induce a vision. During World War II, for example, it was often difficult for the Sabbatini to gather for Sabbath and festival commemorations. With Passover 1943 fast approaching, Manduzio wondered what God would want the community to do. It was dangerous for Jews to gather. He believed that the answer would come in a dream, and he began by setting up parameters of interpretation. "If he saw men of good repute, they would keep the feast together; if he saw disreputable women, they would not keep it." Ultimately, Manduzio had a vision of a "king in his own house, in civilian clothes, in a black coat, a little dusty."[33] Manduzio interpreted this vision as a sign that the group should celebrate Passover together, which they did, despite the dangers of a group meeting to celebrate a Jewish ceremonial meal.

Manduzio stood firm on the issue of prophecy. He continued to have visions and to direct the behavior of the Sabbatini in accordance with those visions. As he worked more closely with the Italian rabbinical emissaries and the directives of "official Judaism," Manduzio was at times willing to adjust his group's religious behavior to accommodate accepted ritual practices, but he often argued with Judaism's received ideas. When in 1934 he first read a one-volume anthology of Talmudic writings, an Italian translation he had received from a traveler passing through San Nicandro, Manduzio was outraged and told his followers that it was full of "things quite unsuitable for a son of the one God."[34] He was so troubled by what he read that he asked God to send him a vision to guide him in his response. In the vision Manduzio found himself in a field full of plants and thorns, where after taking out an axe, he cut down the thorns and left the valuable plants.[35] He interpreted this vision to mean that the Talmud had both good and bad elements, and that he must choose the good and ban the bad. Overall, he judged the Talmud "a betrayal of Mosaic law" and urged his followers to disregard it. Eventually, he banned the Talmud completely.[36]

Manduzio saw himself as a priest and a prophet, and he considered his authority within his community sacrosanct. He took the Hebrew name of Levi and asserted that he and his followers were direct descendants of Levites who had been expelled from Spain in the fifteenth century and fled to Italy. He saw himself as the group's Moses (who was of the tribe of Levi), their prophet. In an illuminating exchange that took place near the end of the war, Manduzio explained his visions to Rabbi Ephraim Urbach, a member of the "Palestinian Brigade" of Jewish soldiers attached to the British Eighth Army. "I don't believe in visions," said the rabbi. Manduzio responded, "You are a rabbi because you were born into the Law and your father taught you your history. Things were not so in my case; I was blind and a prisoner of evil, and knew not the creator nor the sacred Torah. If the Lord had not taken me by the hand, as a father leads his child, how could I have come to know his ways?" As there were no "rabbis" in the Hebrew Bible, the appellation did not mean much to Manduzio, and he was dubious about Urbach's credentials. Manduzio later wrote that in a vision God told him, "He is a nobody. He is one who plies his trade."[37]

Manduzio's confidence in his own authority as a leader and prophet was evident much earlier. In 1935, Rabbi Sacerdoti of Rome died. The following year the new Chief Rabbi, David Prato, sent an emissary, Raffaele Cantoni, to San Nicandro to help Manduzio set up a small synagogue. Cantoni brought gifts including twenty-two prayer books (*siddurim*) and twenty-two prayer shawls (*talitot*), one for each of the twenty-two adult males of Manduzio's group.[38] Manduzio was less than happy with these gifts as they undercut his authority as prophet. He wished to decide when and how his followers would enter into Jewish life. After Cantoni departed, Manduzio distributed the *siddurim*, prayer books, to his male followers, but he kept the *talitot*, prayer shawls, locked in a cabinet in the prayer room, because he felt that the men were not ready to wear them.

At the time, Rabbi Prato considered the San Nicandro Sabbatini potential converts to Judaism. And he gave them to understand that within a few years he would assess their progress and if satisfied would proceed to the conversion rituals. This very well might have happened. The group took its newly defined religious rituals quite seriously, bringing them into closer conformity with rabbinic Judaism, despite Manduzio's antipathy to the Talmud. History, however, intervened. For it was in the very years that Manduzio's followers were orienting themselves towards Jewish practices and beliefs that dormant Italian anti-Semitic tendencies began to manifest themselves. With Hitler's rise to power in 1933 and Mussolini's subsequent drift towards an alliance with the Nazis, Italy's Jews found themselves the targets of propaganda attacks and later of actual physical attacks.[39]

ITALY'S RACIAL LAWS

In March 1934, a new press campaign in the government-controlled Italian newspapers spoke of "Jewish anti-Fascists in the pay of expatriates." The Mussolini government charged fourteen Jewish political figures with subversive activities. The accusations proved false, and all were acquitted. But the anti-Semitic press campaign now firmly underway only intensified with the acquittal. The situation of Italian Jewry would worsen considerably in the next few years. The Mussolini government's attitude toward Jews changed dramatically during the middle years of the 1930s. Mussolini had ruled Italy since 1922, and before 1933 his relationship with the Italian Jewish community was an ambiguous one.[40] In the late 1920s and early 1930s Mussolini condemned Nazi anti-Semitic rhetoric and attempted to differentiate Italian Fascism from its German counterpart. Racism, he claimed, had no part to play in the political and cultural life of Italy. As Il Duce stated, "Nothing will ever make me believe that biologically pure races can be shown to exist today . . . national pride has no need of the delirium of race."[41]

Most historians attribute the emergence of anti-Jewish propaganda in Italy to Mussolini's growing alliance with Hitler, who came to power in 1933. The rising tide of anti-Semitic articles in the Italian press between 1934 and 1937 worried some Italian Jewish leaders. Others, particularly those who were committed Fascists, dismissed these warning signs. The 1937 publication of *The Jews in Italy* by Palo Orano, a member of the Italian parliament, proved to be another sign of increasing problems for Italy's Jews. Orano described Jews as a "fundamentally subversive, revolutionary people who inevitable sought to control and undermine the nations in which they settled."[42] In Fascist Italy, no such book could have been published without the full approval of the government.

In June 1937 Rome's Rabbi Prato met with Count Ciano, Mussolini's son-in-law. Ciano assured the rabbi that, despite the anti-Semitic articles in the Italian press, "there was no change in the official attitude towards the Jews and that his best friends were Jews." He also stated that the Zionist movement could continue to operate in Italy.[43] Despite Ciano's official reassurances, Rabbi Prato would soon leave Rome for Jerusalem. He feared for his own safety as well as that of his family, and he was facing internal opposition from within the Jewish community, from Jews sympathetic to fascism. In September 1937 Manduzio received a letter from Rabbi Prato's emissary, Raffaele Cantoni, who had been shepherding the San Nicandro group along in the conversion process. Cantoni was leaving Italy, as was Chief Rabbi Prato. In a letter to Manduzio, Cantoni wrote, "Before leaving the country last night the Chief Rabbi instructed me to send you the following message: 'In view of the recently passed ordinances and the openly hostile attitude of the government towards its Jewish citizens, I feel called upon, although with great reluctance, to advise you to postpone the solemnization of your conversion until a more propitious time.'"[44] Manduzio, however, could not be swayed; he was determined that his followers become Jews.

With Rabbi Prato's departure to Palestine, the Jewish community in Rome appointed a new chief rabbi. He was Israel Zolli, who from 1918 to 1938 had served as rabbi of Trieste. Rabbi Zolli, whom we will meet in detail in the following chapter, would become Manduzio's contact and mentor until the end of the war. Manduzio wrote to the new Chief Rabbi soon after the implementation of the Italian Racial Laws and all but demanded that his group be considered Jews under the new laws. Zolli wrote back that the San

Nicandrans could not be considered Jews by the Italian government, because "you were neither born Jews nor has your conversion been legally completed." The irony of Zolli's reply about the San Nicandrans' Jewish identity will become clear when we examine Rabbi Zolli's story in depth.

In September 1938 the Fascist Council of Ministers issued its first decree on "the racial question." The decree excluded "all persons of the Jewish race from the teaching profession in general and barred such persons from admission to all schools and institutions of learning recognized by the State."[45] In addition to removing Jewish children from public schools and Jewish teachers from the classroom, the law terminated the employment of Jews who worked for the Italian state. A further set of anti-Jewish measures, announced in June of 1939, banned Jews from employment in all of the professions, including law, medicine, engineering, and architecture.

Unlike the 1935 Nuremburg Laws in Germany, the Italian racial laws did not apply to Jews willing to convert to Catholicism. While the German laws considered a Jew to be "any person who belongs to the Jewish nationality, irrespective of the Jew's religion,"[46] the Italian laws recognized those Jews baptized into the church as having fully jettisoned their Jewish identities and therefore not bound by the laws' restrictions. Thus in the aftermath of the imposition of the racial laws, more than five thousand Italian Jews chose to be baptized. With fewer than 50,000 Jews in Italy, this mass apostasy represented a very large proportion—approximately 10 percent—of the Jewish population.

The mass conversion to Christianity of 10 percent of Italy's Jews provides a stark backdrop to Manduzio's decision to persist in seeking conversion to Judaism for himself and his followers. Despite the warnings of Rome's Rabbis, Rabbi Prato's emissary Raffaele Cantoni, and virtually every other Jew with whom the San Nicandrans came into contact, Manduzio persisted in his campaign for the San Nicandro group to join "the children of Abraham." He remained impervious to the message that seemed obvious to all observers, no matter how sympathetic: it was not the time to convert to Judaism! Manduzio was not unaware of political developments in Italy in particular, or in Europe in general. He read newspapers, listened to the radio, and met with travelers to San Nicandro. But these were ephemeral phenomena as far as he was concerned. The Torah was eternal, as were the Jewish people. He was determined to join, or as he now understood his situation, "return" to the Jews.

LIBERATION, ZIONISM, AND PURSUIT OF THE DREAM

By the time that the Italian Racial Laws were promulgated in 1938, Manduzio was familiar with the Zionist movement. But ever insistent on the purity of the messages conveyed in his visions, he resisted the attractions of Zionism. For the prophet of San Nicandro the dream of a return to Zion was linked to biblical promise and fulfillment, not to current events. Furthermore, he had as yet to meet any Jews from Palestine. The liberation of San Nicandro by the British Eighth Army, however, would change the outlook of Manduzio and many of his followers.

In July of 1943, the Mussolini government collapsed, as pressure from the Allied Invasion drove Il Duce into exile. In September, the German Army moved into Italy in an effort to counter the Allied advance, but by October, the Allied forces—here, the British Eighth Army—had driven out the Germans and liberated the Apulia region. Among the Allied soldiers of the Eighth Army were 350 Jewish soldiers from Palestine.[47] This Palestinian Brigade would have a great influence on Manduzio and his followers. After meeting these soldiers many San Nicandrans would aspire to immigrate to Palestine.

The accounts of the initial meeting between the Sabbatini and the Jewish soldiers share a common vignette known as the "Flag Story." One of the Sabbatini, Angelo Marrochella, noticed the Star of David emblazoned on the Jeeps of the Jewish soldiers. To attract the attention of the soldiers, who had orders to stay away from the peasants, Marrochella made a blue flag with a white Star of David on it, which he hung in front of Manduzio's house. The officers and chaplain of the Jewish Brigade soon paid Manduzio a visit. When the chaplain, Rabbi Ephraim Urbach, asked Manduzio if he wanted to convert to Judaism, the prophet replied, "I wish to live by the law God gave to the Jews."[48]

To put this meeting into context, it is important to recognize that, while Manduzio had had numerous meetings with official representatives of Rome's Jewish establishment for more than a decade, it was his first meeting with a rabbi.

Meeting the soldiers of the Palestine Brigade had an overwhelming impact on Manduzio and his followers. Elena Cassin has noted, "Before meeting the Palestinian troops none of the converts would ever have thought of immigrating to Palestine." Many of the villagers realized that by going to Israel they could escape the grinding poverty of post-war Italy. Manduzio, however, was not won over by the enthusiasm and Zionist pragmatism of the soldiers. He believed firmly in the divinely ordained messianic redemption that would return the world's Jews to the Land of Israel. In a May 1944 entry in his journal Manduzio referred to the arguments raging in his community over the question of going to Palestine. "Now the breach has happened, because of the house and Palestine; but my Creator would not have it so, because the Land was not ready."[49] An additional factor was the fact that Manduzio and his wife hoped to attract more converts to Judaism from within the Catholic communities of Apulia. They did not feel that their mission to bring a pure form of monotheism to the area was complete.

One of the Jewish officers in the Palestinian Brigade played a key role in the transformation of the outlook of the San Nicandro group. He was Major Spitzer, who later changed his name to Pinchas Lapide. Elena Cassin has noted, "It was clear from the outset that Major Spitzer envisaged the emigration of these Italian peasants to Palestine."[50] Spitzer/Lapide was extremely effective in carrying out his campaign. He convinced many in the group to settle in Israel, and he aided them once they arrived there. Cassin, however, is critical of Lapide's biography of Manduzio, *The Prophet of San Nicandro*, suggesting that Lapide's account of the San Nicandran's embrace of Zionism obscures the tension within the group and Manduzio's opposition to mass emigration.

With the arrival of the Allied Jewish soldiers in San Nicandro and the news of the struggle to establish a Jewish state in Palestine, the orientation of the Sabbatini changed. Some members became more "Zionist," more focused on emigration to Palestine. This interruption from the outside was bound to cause rifts within the Sabbatini. According to Rabbi Ravenna, "The visits of the soldiers caused new disagreements in the group. Donato was jealous of them and disapproved of their plans to get the converts to immigrate to Palestine after the war. In his view, emigration should wait on the fulfillment of the messianic promise, especially since he hoped to make more converts in Gargano."[51]

Challenges from his followers and disagreements among them were not new to Manduzio. Angelo Marrochella of the flag story was in fact already somewhat of a dissident within the group. He had joined the San Nicandrans as a young man in the early 1940s. Soon after joining, Marrochella found himself more convinced by the rabbinic teachings coming from Rome than by Manduzio's "prophetic" authority. He was not alone. The more contact that the Sabbatini had with the representatives of "official" Judaism, the more the danger of schism hung over the group. Assertions that the "official rabbis" in Rome should be the group's ultimate authority angered Manduzio greatly. In 1945, a year before the group's "day of circumcision" in mid-1946, Manduzio reminded his divided followers that he was the only source of religious authority; no other authority was to be consulted or followed. As Marrochella reported in a letter to Rabbi Prato, who had returned to Rome after the war, Manduzio told his followers that "harmony could be restored only if they recognized him as a prophet and accepted his doctrine, which is better than the teachings of the rabbis who have caused Israel to sin."[52]

Manduzio was very stern with his followers and always on the lookout for "heresy" and dissension. He dubbed any opponents within the ranks, "sons of Korah." As Manduzio had declared himself and his followers "sons of Levi," he designated those who rebelled against him with the names of those Levites who rebelled against Moses. Throughout his years of leadership, from 1930 to his death in 1948, Manduzio asserted his authority to make all religious decisions for the group. Among the female followers there was a woman dubbed Debora, who also acquired prophetic authority. Her Italian name was Concetta de Leo. After Manduzio's death she would become one of the leaders of the transplanted San Nicandran community in Moshav Alma near Safed, Israel.

JOINING THE JEWISH PEOPLE

The San Nicandrans official reception into the Jewish fold did not occur until a year after the war in Europe ended. This makes their decision all the more remarkable, for by that time the extent of the Nazi murder of Europe's Jews was well known. They had decided to convert to Judaism in the early 1930s; they would not be dissuaded now, despite the murder of the Jews of Europe. Soon after the war ended, the Union of Italian Jewish Communities sent Rabbi Alfredo Ravenna to San Nicandro. The rabbi found the Sabbatini community torn by dissension, with some younger members influenced by both the official rabbinate and by Zionism, while Manduzio and the old guard held to a more biblical view of prophetic authority. Rabbi Ravenna negotiated a "peace treaty" and informed the community that the full conversion ritual could be held within the year. He would personally oversee the ritual.

In July of 1946 the first conversion ceremony, presided over by Rabbi Ravenna, took place in San Nicandro. At this ritual thirteen men and boys were circumcised by a doctor sent from Rome. Manduzio, in his sixties and in ill health, was not circumcised, but was welcomed into the faith without circumcision. Ten days later both the men and the women underwent *tvilah* (immersion ceremony) in the Adriatic Sea. Altogether seventy-four people converted to Judaism in a series of ceremonies conducted over the next year.

Donato Manduzio died on March 15, 1948, a month before the establishment of the State of Israel. The inscription on his tombstone reads, "Donato Manduzio was born in 1885 and lived in pagan ways until 1930, but on August 11 of that year, by divine inspiration, he was called by God by the name of Levi, that is priest, and he proclaimed on this misty rock the unity of God and the Sabbath day of rest. He died on March 15, 1948."[53]

Within two years of Manduzio's death most, but not all, of the converts had emigrated from Italy to Israel. Two of the San Nicandrans enlisted in the Israeli army and fought in the 1948 War. Donato Manduzio's demise eased the way to Israel for the San Nicandran converts. They would hardly have been accepted in early 1950s Israel, if the civil and religious authorities had known that they were led by a "prophet" who challenged the rabbinate.[54] But at the time, Manduzio's eccentric views of Judaism were unknown. As the group had converted to Judaism under Orthodox rabbinical supervision in Italy, the Israeli Rabbinate raised no questions about the "authenticity" of their conversion.

In Israel the Jewish Agency settled the San Nicandrans in Mosha Alma, near Safed in the northern Galilee. Already living there were Italian-speaking Jews from Libya. This Moshav, or collective farm, was on the land of the Palestinian village of Ras-al-ahmar, which the Israelis declared "abandoned" (*natush*) by its inhabitants. During their first year at the Moshav the San Nicandran converts were discovered by the Magnum photographer "Chim" David Seymour, who published wonderful photographs of the villagers. But within two years most of the San Nicandrans had left the Moshav. Some moved to Acre, others to Tel Aviv, and a small group to a moshav in the Negev near the Egyptian border.

Not all of the San Nicandro converts, however, had come to Israel. Emanuela, Manduzio's widow, and a small group of followers stayed in Italy. A decade after Donato's death Emanuella told Elena Cassin, "One night I asked myself whether it wouldn't be better for me to go to Israel with the other brothers and sisters. But if I had gone who would have opened this room [the synagogue] on Saturdays for those left behind to pray in?"[55]

Descendants of the original Sabbatini group still live in San Nicandro today. An Italian Journalist reported in 2007 that "Today's daughters of the Community feel Jewish. Only a few years ago a rabbi came and revealed to them that they were not Jewish since they had never converted."[56] But the women were neither convinced nor dissuaded. They remain faithful to their form of Judaism. They have built a small synagogue at which forty or so villagers attend weekly services. Thirty-seven of the forty attendees are descendants of the original group of San Nicandro converts, and most of them are married to Christian men.[57]

Without any preparation or experience, Donato Manduzio had negotiated the dual nature of classical Jewish identity—one component being faith in God and the Torah, and the other being the claim of direct ancestry from the people of ancient Israel, those who had received the Torah through direct revelation at Sinai. But he was not prepared to change his mind on questions of leadership and authority. Manduzio was not able to accept the claim of rabbinic Judaism that prophecy had ended with the last prophets of the Hebrew Bible, Haggai, Malachi, and Zechariah. As J. Ben David noted, "Manduzio stuck to Judaism even after he found the Jews, and in spite of his awareness that his was a different Judaism from theirs."[58]

Manduzio's Judaism was biblical, not rabbinic. He had pared the religious ideas of the Bible down to a concise message. A few months before his death, Manduzio articulated the essence of this message: "We have preached the oneness of God, the Saturday of rest, abstaining from unclean flesh, and the destruction of idols."[59]

NOTES

1. For more on Padre Pio see Cassin, *San Nicandro*, 173.
2. For details see Cassin, *San Nicandro*, 155–58; Davis, *The Jews of San Nicandro*.
3. Cassin, *San Nicandro*, 182.
4. Ibid., 20.
5. Lapide, *The Prophet of San Nicandro*, 48.
6. Ibid., 24.
7. Cassin, *San Nicandro*, 16.
8. Ibid.
9. Cassin, *San Nicandro*, 16; Lapide, *The Prophet of San Nicandro*, 25.
10. Cassin, *San Nicandro*, 19–20.
11. Davis, *The Jews of San Nicandro*, 26.
12. Lapide, *The Prophet of San Nicandro*, 198.
13. Ibid., 35.
14. Cassin, *San Nicandro*, 21; see Genesis 2:1–2 for the biblical story.
15. Semi, *Jacques Faitlovich and the Jews of Ethiopia*, 123.
16. Ravenna, "The Converts of San Nicandro," 246–247.
17. Lapide, *The Prophet of San Nicandro*, 62–63.
18. Ibid.
19. Lapide, *The Prophet of San Nicandro*, 57–58.
20. Ibid.
21. Ibid.
22. Ibid.
23. Ibid.
24. Ibid., 89.
25. Ibid., 90.
26. Ibid., 124 and 131, n. 11.
27. Semi, *Jacques Faitlovich and the Jews of Ethiopia*, 6.
28. Ibid.
29. Lapide, *The Prophet of San Nicandro*, 199.
30. Ravenna, "The Converts of San Nicandro," 249.
31. Ibid., 247.
32. Cassin, *San Nicandro*, 176.
33. Ibid., 83.
34. Cassin, *San Nicandro*, 32.
35. Ibid., 33.
36. See Cassin, *San Nicandro*, 32; Ravenna, "The Converts of San Nicandro," 247.
37. Cassin, *San Nicandro*, 57.
38. Ibid., 36.
39. Michaelis, *Mussolini and the Jews*, 59–62.
40. See Stille, *Benevolence and Betrayal*, 49.
41. Ibid., 48.
42. Ibid., 65.
43. Ibid., 136.
44. Lapide, *The Prophet of San Nicandro*, 148.
45. Ibid., 169.
46. Yahil, *The Holocaust*, 410.
47. For accounts of the meeting between the Jewish soldiers and the Sabbatini see Ravenna, "The Converts of San Nicandro," 247–8; Lapide, *The Prophet of San Nicandro*, 176–90; and Cassin, *San Nicandro*, 54–59.

48. Ravenna, "The Converts of San Nicandro," 248. For a more extensive account of that conversation see Lapide, *The Prophet of San Nicandro*, 212–15.

49. Cassin, *San Nicandro*, 59.

50. Ibid., 77.

51. Ravenna, "The Converts of San Nicandro," 248.

52. Ibid., 72.

53. Birnbaum, "Manduzio—Father of many people" (Hebrew).

54. Cassin, *San Nicandro*, 55, 77.

55. Ibid., 60.

56. Birnbaum, "Manduzio—Father of many people" (English).

57. On the Jews of San Nicandro circa 2007, see Birnbaum, "Manduzio—Father of many People" (English).

58. J. Ben-David, "San Nicandro," 254.

59. Cassin, *San Nicandro*, 76.

Chapter Five

Happy About His Conversion, Miserable About His Apostasy: The 1945 Apostasy of Rabbi Zolli Revisited (Israel Zolli, 1881–1956)

On February 13, 1945 in a private ceremony conducted in the chapel of Santa Maria degli Angeli, prominent members of the Jesuit order officiated at the baptism of Israel Zolli and his wife Emma Majonica into the Catholic Church. At the time, the sixty-four-year-old Zolli had been the Chief Rabbi of Rome for seven years. In honor of Pope Pius XII he took the first name Eugenio. He and his wife, who was several years younger, had two adult daughters. Miriam, the younger daughter, would join the church a year later.

Neither his rabbinical colleagues, nor his congregants, had any idea that Zolli was planning to convert to Catholicism—or in their terms, apostatize. Nine months before his baptism, in June of 1944, Zolli had officiated at a Sabbath ceremony held at Rome's central synagogue, the Tempio Maggiore, to commemorate the war-dead and celebrate the liberation of Rome from German occupation. Several thousand people attended this ceremony, including many of Rome's surviving Jews as well as representatives of the United States Fifth Army Group under Lieutenant General Mark Clark, the commander of the troops who had liberated the city from the Germans only a few days earlier. In his remarks, Zolli offered a message of hope and rejuvenation: "Everywhere Abel's blood comes from the earth, blood of innocent Abel slain by Cain. Nevertheless, we shall rebuild the ruins and reconstruct upon the ruins."[1] The rabbi's words that day moved many to tears. Nine months later, news of the rabbi's apostasy would again move many members of the congregation to tears, but these would be tears of sorrow, sorrow that their rabbi was an apostate.

Almost immediately after Zolli's baptism, two radically different narratives, each with its own descriptive terminology, began to emerge. For Jews, Zolli was now a *meshummad*, one who has been destroyed by his choice to apostatize. For Catholics, he was a convert to the true faith. For Jews, Zolli's radical decision seemed a capricious, inopportune betrayal, coming at a time when the surviving Jews of Italy were still reeling from the Nazi onslaught. For Catholics, however, and for Zolli himself, conversion was the culmination of a long process of deliberation and meditation.

Following their rabbi's apostasy, the congregants of Tempio Maggiore held a communal meeting at which they agreed to "sit shiva," or ritually mourn, for Zolli. More people attended this meeting than had attended the earlier service commemorating the liberation of Rome from the Nazis. Rabbi Zolli's apostasy came as a particular shock to a group of rural Catholics who were in the middle of the long process of converting to Judaism. Led by their charismatic "Prophet," Donato Manduzio, whom we met in the previous chapter, these villagers from the Apulia region of southern Italy had consulted with Rabbi Zolli about the many details of the conversion process. We can only imagine the response of these villagers, who had placed their trust in Rabbi Zolli as a Jewish authority, when they discovered that he had in fact decided to join the Catholic faith that they so recently had chosen to abandon.

Zolli's Jewish critics saw his apostasy as sudden and unexpected. They portrayed Zolli as a coward and an opportunist who left Rome's Jewish community at the moment of its greatest weakness. In the words of American Rabbi Louis I. Newman, "Conceived, as we shall see, chiefly in spitefulness and spleen against his own flock, he desired his apostasy to be given the greatest publicity. Only thus could he feed his revenge."[2]

This spitefulness and desire for revenge, according to Newman and his informants, stemmed from Zolli's frustration with the way he was treated by the leaders of Rome's Jewish community during the war. Italian Jews had faced official discrimination beginning in 1938, but they were not threatened with extermination until the German forces moved into Italy after Mussolini's fall in 1943. When the Nazis took over Rome, Zolli and his family went into hiding with a Catholic family. The presidents of the synagogue and the community, however, expected Zolli to remain in public view, and they criticized the rabbi for shirking his leadership role. Zolli responded with the assertion that the Germans certainly would have killed him as soon as they found him, just as they had systematically killed the rabbis in other Italian cities. Regardless of the dangers Zolli and his family may have faced during the war, Zolli's post-war critics considered his apostasy to be an act of retribution against a community that had criticized his behavior during the German occupation.

Zolli's decision to convert to Catholicism, however, was not sudden. It was the culmination of a process that had begun decades earlier. In 1917, when he was thirty-six years old, Zolli had the first in a series of mystical visions in which he saw Jesus. For Zolli, this vision began an extended fascination with Jesus, but it did not lead him to contemplate leaving Judaism. It would be another 28 years before he would consider converting to Catholicism. At the time of this first vision, Zolli was satisfied to keep both his vision and his interest in Jesus to himself:

> I do not seek to penetrate the mystery. What did it all mean? To me now, as then, the nearness of Jesus is sufficient. Was this experience objectively real or only subjective? I do not know; nor am I competent to analyze it. . . . I had no desire to speak of it to anyone, neither did I think of it as a conversion. What had happened concerned me, and only me. My intense love for Jesus and the experiences I had concerned no one else; nor did they seem to me at the time to involve a change of religion. Jesus had entered into my interior life as a guest, invoked and welcomed.[3]

According to Zolli's account of his conversion, the turning point came in a vision he had on Yom Kippur of 1944. He thus situated this crucial experience between the June 1944 synagogue ceremony celebrating the liberation of Rome, and the February 1945 church ceremony in which he and his wife Emma were baptized. As he recalled his experiences on that day:

> It was the Day of Atonement in the fall of 1944, and I was presiding over the religious services in the temple. The day was nearing its end, and I was all alone in the midst of a great number of persons. I began to feel as though a fog were creeping into my soul; it became denser, and I wholly lost touch with the men and things around me. A candle, almost consumed, burned on its candlestick near me. As the wax liquefied, the small flame flared into a larger one, leaping heavenward. I was fascinated by the sight of it, looked with wondering amazement at the simple spectacle. I said to myself: in this flame there is something of my own being. The tongue of fire flickered and writhed, tortured; and my soul participated, suffered.[4]

Unlike his first vision in 1917, Zolli at the time of this vision was not only in a public setting, but in the specific setting of the synagogue. According to his account of this experience, he seems to be being mystically withdrawn from, or pulled out of this setting, out of the temple and its rituals, out of Judaism:

> In the evening there was the last service, and I was there with two assistants, one on my right and the other on my left. But I felt so far withdrawn from the ritual that I let others recite the prayers and sing. I was conscious of neither joy nor sorrow; I was devoid of thought and feeling. My heart lay as though dead in my breast. And just then I saw with my mind's eye a meadow sweeping

upward, with bright grass but with no other flower. In this meadow, I saw Jesus (Christ) clad in a white mantle, and beyond His head the blue sky. I experienced the greatest interior peace. If I were to give an image of the state of my soul at that moment I should say: a crystal-clear lake amid high mountains. Within my heart, I found the words: "You are here for the last time." I considered them with the greatest serenity of soul and without any particular emotion. The reply of my heart was: so it is, so it shall be, so it must be.[5]

Zolli's life-changing Yom Kippur experience was not unprecedented in the annals of those considering conversion. Franz Rosenzweig (1886–1929), one of German Jewry's most important philosophers, had considered conversion to Christianity when he was in his mid-twenties. Rosenzweig corresponded at the time with his friend Eugene Rosenstock-Hussey, who had already converted, and their correspondence was later collected and published as *Judaism Despite Christianity*. On the verge of apostasy, Rosenzweig attended Yom Kippur prayers at a Hasidic congregation, where he had a mystical experience. Although Rosenzweig never discussed the details of this experience, it served to push him away from baptism, to reinvigorate his Jewish faith, and to send him deeper into Jewish thought and practice.

In contrast, Zolli's Yom Kippur experience led him away from Judaism. Unlike his first vision in 1917, this vision clearly resulted in a break with Judaism, and then conversion to Catholicism. A few days after his Yom Kippur experience, Zolli recalled, "I resigned my post in the Israelite Community and went to a quite unknown priest in order to receive instruction. An interval of some weeks elapsed, until the 13th of February, when I received the sacrament of baptism and was incorporated into the Catholic Church, the Mystical Body of Jesus Christ."[6]

Zolli wrote his account of these visions in 1953, some thirty-six years after he experienced the first, and nearly a decade after the last. In hindsight, he was able to present a seamless, unified narrative of his conversion process. In actuality the process was no doubt much more nuanced and complex. Zolli struggled with the inherent conflict between Judaism and Christianity throughout his life, which suggests that his conversion process was in fact not as smooth as he would have us believe.

In an interview conducted soon after his conversion Zolli said, "I was a Catholic at heart before war broke out; and I promised God in 1943 that I should become a Christian if I survived the war. No one in the world ever tried to convert me. My conversion was a slow evolution, altogether internal. I am beginning to understand that for many years I was a natural Christian."[7]

As an explanation for why he delayed his conversion for so many years, Zolli cited the example of a prominent European Jewish intellectual, the French philosopher Henri Bergson. Zolli quotes Bergson, who wrote in 1937, "My thinking has always brought me nearer to Catholicism, in which I saw the perfect complement of Judaism." But like Rosenzweig, Bergson ultimately chose *not* to convert, as he wrote, "I would have embraced it if I had not witnessed the frightful wave of anti-Semitism which for some years deluged the world. I prefer to remain with those who would be persecuted tomorrow."[8] Bergson did not want to abandon his coreligionists in their darkest hour.

Thus, for an extended period of time, Zolli, like Henri Bergson in France, saw himself as constrained by concern for his fellow Jews. Following years of increasing anti-Semitism beginning in the mid-1930s, Italian Jews now faced new and greater dangers. With the fall of the Mussolini government in 1943, the German army moved into Northern Italy and soon after, into Rome. During the German occupation, the Nazis attempted to extend the "final solution" to Italy. The Gestapo, under Himmler's direct orders—and contrary to the orders of General Reiner Stahel, the German military commander for the city of Rome, rounded up thousands of Jews and sent them to their deaths. When the Allied Forces drove the Germans out of Rome in early 1945, Zolli seems to have felt freed from his reservations about conversion. He no longer needed to stand with the persecuted, for they had been liberated from persecution.

A week after Zolli and his wife were baptized, T. S. Mathews, the Rome correspondent for *Time Magazine*, interviewed Zolli (February 26, 1945). As the correspondent pressed the new Catholic to address his renunciation of Judaism, Zolli replied, "Do you think I love the Jews less because I have become a Catholic? . . . No, I shall never stop loving the Jews. I did not compare the Jewish religion to Catholicism and abandon one for the other. This is the greatest tragedy of my life. I slowly, almost imperceptibly became a Christian and could no longer be a Jew." Mathews concluded that Zolli was "happy about his conversion, miserable about his apostasy."[9]

For earlier Jews who apostatized, baptism meant a clean break with their Jewish past. In eighteenth-century Germany, in fact, newly baptized Jews would use the abbreviation "Conv." after their names, much as lawyers would write "adv." after theirs. For both the Jewish community that was rejected, and the Christian community that was embraced, the situation was clear and the stakes were high. Embracing Christianity mean a categorical rejection of Judaism. And this situation obtained in both Protestant and Catholic churches that encouraged Jewish conversion.

In the twentieth century, however, this rigorous binary would begin to change. Some Jewish converts to Christianity sought to integrate their Jewish background into their new faith. Rather than obscure their Jewish past, they embraced and highlighted it. The Jewish converts we have met in this book, including Cardinal Lustiger in chapter 3, Israel Zolli, Brother Daniel in chapter 7, and Moishe Rosen in chapter 8, all represent their conversions as the "fulfillment of their Jewish heritage."

Immediately upon Rabbi Zolli's conversion, American Jewish leaders mounted a vigorous campaign to discredit him. The New York Board of Jewish Ministers (later the New York Board of Rabbis) sent a letter to its membership before Passover of 1945. It read in part, "The apostasy of the 'rabbi' of Rome must be made known to our people as an act of desertion and apostasy."[10] Rabbi Louis Newman's 1945 book *A 'Chief Rabbi' of Rome becomes a Catholic: A Study in Fright and Spite* further extended the campaign. The seeds of the book were planted in a sermon that Rabbi Newman preached in his synagogue, New York City's Temple Rodeph Sholom, in the spring of 1945. It is one of the many ironies of Newman's involvement in the orchestrated critique of Zolli that, as far as Zolli was concerned, Newman was not a fellow rabbi at all. Zolli, like his European Orthodox Jewish colleagues, did not considered American Reform rabbis such as Louis Newman to be true rabbis, but merely pretenders to the title.

ZOLLI BEFORE ROME

Israel Zolli was born Israel Anton Zoller in 1881 in the town of Brody in Polish Galicia, which at the time was part of the Austro-Hungarian Empire, but now is part of the Ukraine. During his early childhood Zolli's father owned a small textile mill, and his parents were well to do. The youngest of five siblings, Israel lived in a comfortable middle class home in which orthodox Jewish ritual ruled daily life. His mother, who was descended from a long line of rabbinic scholars, insisted that her youngest son study for the rabbinate, and she sacrificed a great deal in order to make sure Zolli was accepted at the Italian Rabbinical College in Florence.

The Italian Rabbinical College in Florence had been closed for decades, but Jewish scholars from Polish Galicia had reopened it in 1899. While studying there, Zolli was the protégé of Rabbi Samuel Hirsch Margulies, a renowned rabbinic scholar also from Polish Galicia. In addition to his rabbinic studies at the seminary, Zolli attended the University of Florence.[11] Zolli received a PhD in Philosophy from the University of Florence and ordination from the Italian Rabbinical College.

In 1918, Zolli became Rabbi of Trieste. With the collapse of the Austro-Hungarian Empire at the end of World War I, the city of Trieste had become Italian territory. Enthusiastic about the city's new Italian identity, Zoller Italianized his surname and became an Italian citizen. He would spend the next twenty years—from 1918 to 1938—in Trieste. During that time, Zolli would become an important and recognized cultural figure in the city. He participated in numerous debates and conversations that engaged topics from politics and culture to psychoanalysis and literature.

The Jewish community of Trieste included many influential businessmen and assimilated intellectuals. As Zolli came into contact with these cosmopolitan Jewish leaders, they became sources of new political and cultural ideas. We get a sense of Jewish life in early-twentieth-century Trieste from the journals of James Joyce and his brother Stanislaus Joyce. James Joyce taught at the Berlitz School in the city off and on from 1905 to 1915. He was surprised to find that many of the students in his English classes were Jews. Among Joyce's Jewish students and friends was the writer Aron Ettore Schmitz, who wrote under the name Italo Svevo. Svevo is perhaps best known today as the author of the novel *Confessions of Zeno* and as a model for Leopold Bloom in Joyce's *Ulysses*. Stanislaus Joyce wrote of his brother's 1908 visit to the Trieste synagogue, the pulpit that Rabbi Zolli would occupy a decade later: "In the morning [8 September 1908] he had been to a service in a Jewish synagogue and had been surprised to find many of his pupils there. He asked had the Jews any theology in the sense that Catholics have one, and was the priesthood with them a caste or a profession. He also wanted to know if they had a school of theology in which it was necessary to study, and lamented that none of his pupils ever seemed to know anything about the religions to which they were supposed to belong."[12] This charming anecdote tells us more about Joyce than about Trieste's Jews—but it does remind us that ignorance of one's religious tradition is not a new phenomenon, and not one limited to the United States.

In addition to his rabbinic service in Trieste, Zolli was also an Italian academician with an extensive publishing record, which culminated in the 1938 publication of his book *The Nazarene: Studies in New Testament Exegesis*. Throughout the 1920s and 1930s Zolli taught at the University of Padua. The importance he placed on his work as an academic can be seen in his official stationery, which read, "Professor at the University of Padua." As one of his synagogue congregants noted, "It was understood at Trieste that Zolli wished to be considered, first and foremost, as a scientist and a professor."[13] Between 1920 and 1940 Zolli published many scholarly articles, although a number of these were brief notices rather than larger, more developed arguments. Zolli ranged over many diverse topics, from articles on Modern Hebrew literature to studies in Italian Jewish history to articles comparing Jewish and Christian ritual. All of Zolli's articles fall firmly within the *Wissenschaft des Judentum* (the Science of Judaism) school of scholarship, which attempted to use scientific methods to analyze Jewish literature and culture.

Zolli yearned to be a full-time professor, but his primary job was in the rabbinate. His situation might be compared to other scholars who served as clergymen or lesser religious functionaries, and experienced considerable frustration doing so. Among the most notable of scholars in this difficult situation was Ignaz Goldziher of Budapest, the foremost Western scholar of

Islam in the late-nineteenth and early-twentieth centuries. Goldziher (1850–1921) worked for the Neolog (Reform) Synagogue of Budapest, Hungary. As a Jew in Hungary, he was not eligible for a university appointment. To support himself and his family, he was bound to his synagogue work, which he greatly resented. Despite this situation, Goldziher produced major works about Islam that are still studied today. Zolli, in contrast, had a part-time university job, but his commitment to the Trieste synagogue and the needs of its congregation demanded the majority of his time.

During the twenty years Zolli spent in the Trieste synagogue, the demands of his congregation grew steadily in intensity. Congregants in the large Italian communities of Trieste, Venice, Florence, and Rome expected their rabbis to be both interlocutors with the Catholic authorities and defenders of the Jewish faith. These congregations called on their rabbis not only to articulate Judaism's positive qualities, but also to shepherd and strengthen the Jewish community's resolve to preserve its integrity within the larger Catholic culture and to resist the Church's constant pressure to convert. The Italian Rabbinical College, where Israeli Zolli had been a student, was largely responsible for establishing this agenda and inculcating these ideas in its students.

In the history of Italian Jewry, the Church had played an aggressive and pronounced role in forced conversions, often coercing Jews into apostasy. This was in marked contrast to the situation in other parts of Europe, like Germany, France, and the Low Countries, where apostasy often appeared "voluntary," if not completely free from social pressures. But the specter of forced conversion hovered over Italian Jewish communities through the late-nineteenth and into the early-twentieth centuries. Past experiences of *mass* forced conversions, such as in the town of Brescia in the fourteenth century, haunted the Italian Jewish collective memory. Under Papal order, Church officials continued through the middle of the nineteenth century to preach sermons in Italian synagogues that emphasized conversion. At times, social pressure easily spilled over into brute force. For example, in the notorious Mortara case of 1858, when a Jewish boy was taken forcibly from his home in Bologna after being secretly baptized by a family servant.[14]

Thus Jewish communities expected their rabbis to protect their congregants from the Church's attempts to bring them to the baptismal font. The idea that a rabbi would himself become a Christian was inconceivable. If a Christian enquired about the possibility of converting to Judaism—not that many Italian Catholics did—the community rabbi's job was to discourage him or her politely but firmly. As we have seen in the previous chapter, however, that situation began to change in the 1930s, when a group of peasants in Apulia sought to convert to Judaism. From 1938 to 1945, Rabbi Zolli was one of the primary rabbis who advised Donato Manduzio's Sabbatarians in their conversion efforts. Thus, as he was slowly moving ever closer to the

Catholic Church, Rabbi Zolli was in the difficult situation of concurrently advising Catholics on how to become Jews.

In his 1967 book *Three Popes and the Jews*, Pinchas Lapide acknowledges the uproar surrounding this situation: "Needless to say, there was no lack of odious comparison and drawing of spiritual balances in the Roman press at the time." Lapide points out, however, that the attention and interest were short-lived: "Since the religious authorities of neither faith put any obstacles in the way of the converts, the story of the San Nicandro converts soon died a peaceful death."[15]

ITALY'S RACIAL POLICY AND THE JEWS

In 1936, Mussolini appointed his son-in-law, Count Ciano, as foreign minister. Ciano, who held pronounced racial views and spoke of "purifying" Italy, was a strong advocate for strengthening Italy's ties with Nazi Germany. In 1937 and 1938 as relations between the two fascist regimes solidified, the Italian government began to transform Italian racial prejudices into anti-Jewish laws and actions. The Italian dictator began to use anti-Jewish language and slogans. Following a brief visit to Germany in 1937, Mussolini adopted a "master-race" paradigm in which "the German and Italian races" would rule Europe.

Mussolini was able to tap into "a true anti-Semitic current that existed in Fascism" to formulate laws that would force the members of the Italian Jewish community "to move quickly toward a full political and national 'assimilation' in fascist Italy."[16] These new Italian Racial Laws, which deprived Jews of the right to hold government jobs, as well as attend or teach in Italian schools, differed in one important respect from the German Nuremburg Laws of 1935. While the Nazi laws were based on a racial understanding of Jewishness, the Italian laws were based on a religious classification. Thus in Italy, baptized Jews and their descendants were exempt from the newly-imposed restrictions. Therefore, in 1938–1939, more than five thousand Italian Jews—approximately one tenth of the Italian Jewish population—chose to be baptized in an effort to escape discrimination. In October 1938, Mussolini told his son-in-law, "Anti-Semitism has now been injected in the Italians' blood. It will go on circulating and developing by itself." A month later he told Ciano that he approved "of these measures unconditionally and . . . that under similar circumstances he would go even further."[17]

In Trieste, the city where Zolli had served as rabbi for twenty years, the Jewish community reacted to the new anti-Semitic legislation with "utter incredulity . . . despite the lack of a sustained history of local anti-Semitism, the city now embraced a series of anti-Semitic provisions." Among them was the prohibition against Jews teaching in Italian schools or attending those schools.[18] In 1938 Zolli, was forced to resign from his position at the University of Padua, where he had been "Professor of Arts and Jewish Literatures."

During the early years of World War II Rabbi Zolli was in touch with refugees from across Eastern Europe. As he spoke with them in Yiddish, German and Romanian, Zolli heard and believed the reports of the Nazi extermination policies. His native-born Italian Jewish colleagues, however, who had served as the leaders of the organized Roman Jewish community, tended to be skeptical of these accounts. Even if he found some aspects of these stories to be credible, Ugo Foa, President of the Jewish Community in Rome, and his associates were certain that Rome's Jews would be protected. For hadn't the fascist authorities protected Rome's Jews thus far? Hadn't there been Jews among the fascist leadership in Italy's major cities? Because Italian Fascism before 1938 was based on a purely political idea rather than a racial idea, it did not repel Jewish intellectuals and businessmen. Between Mussolini's rise to power in 1922 and the passage of the Italian Race Laws in 1938, some influential Jews in fact were attracted to Mussolini's ideas and supported their implementation.

When the Nazis occupied Rome, Rabbi Zolli urged Foa to close the Tempio Maggiore—including its synagogue, its school, and its many offices—and to encourage the members of the congregation to go into hiding. Foa responded, "Rabbi, you should be giving courage instead of spreading discouragement. I have received assurances."[19] As a magistrate in Rome's Ministry of Justice and the head of Italy's veterans association, Foa had every reason to believe those assurances.[20] Furthermore, like many Jewish community leaders in Nazi-occupied Europe, Foa based his expectations on past persecutions, during which Jewish leaders had been able to influence the authorities—often through bribes—to relent. But under no circumstances would the Nazis relent; this was a development that Foa and his associates had not previously encountered.

As historian Michele Sarfatti has noted, "Jews recognized the progressive deterioration of their position in Italian society, but they found it difficult to accept the idea of an approaching persecution. They may have been prevented from fully grasping the situation by a dulling of the senses induced by fifteen years of dictatorship, a misplaced faith in the progressive process of civilization, a deeply felt consciousness of being Italian, as well, of course, as the Fascism of some of them and the patriotism of many. In addition, there was the ambiguous public behavior of Mussolini, who not only assumed the already mentioned posture of accommodation toward the Union, but also did not take official steps against the Zionist federation."[21]

Despite the assurances of both German diplomats and Vatican officials, many of Rome's Jews would share the same fate as that of the Jews of Paris, Prague and Vienna. As Zolli had feared, the Gestapo quickly overrode the objections of the German military command and began to target the Jews of

Rome. On Saturday October 16, 1943, known thereafter to Italian Jews as "Black Saturday," Herbert Kappler, the head of the Gestapo in Rome, arrested more than one thousand Jews and imprisoned them in the city's military college, the Collegio Militaire. Out of this group of people, who were deported to Auschwitz on Monday, October 18, only sixteen survived. Overall, the Gestapo deported some two thousand Roman Jews, almost all of whom were murdered in Nazi gas chambers.

As Gestapo officers moved into the Ghetto, they searched the offices of the Rome Synagogue, where they found a list of members of the Jewish community. The Nazis now knew where Rome's Jews lived. Rabbi Zolli had urged Ugo Foa, President of the Jewish Community in Rome, and Dante Almansi, President of the Union of Italian Jewish Communities, to destroy the membership list and to recommend that members of the community go into hiding. Sadly very few Jews had gone into hiding, and with the list, the Gestapo was able to round up much of the community rather quickly. As Meir Michaelis noted, "Eichmann, for his part, had every reason to be pleased with the refusal of the Roman Jews to act until it was too late."[22]

In his autobiography *Before the Dawn*, Zolli recorded his futile attempts to convince the leaders and members of the Jewish community to go into hiding: "It was known that the German army was opposed to persecution [of Rome's Jews] on political grounds. But reason had little hold on the S.S., and the question was whether or not they could be restrained. My whole experience argued against the possibility of their being restrained more than temporarily. The contrary judgment of the two presidents was due, I think, simply to this lack of experience."[23] Rabbi Zolli and his family, however, went almost immediately into hiding. Foa and Almanasi accused the rabbi of cowardice: Why didn't the rabbi stay and provide spiritual leadership to Rome's Jewish community? they asked. But Zolli had taken to heart the many stories of Jewish refugees from the Nazi's Eastern European onslaught. As scholar Alberto Latorre noted in a 2004 interview, "Zolli knew very well the Teutonic mentality—he was the son of a German mother—as well as the persecutions directed at Jews perpetuated in Germany in the 1930s when, as Chief Rabbi of Trieste he helped many fugitives from Germany and Eastern Europe to reach Palestine."[24]

The Gestapo had ransacked Zolli's apartment some ten days before the Black Saturday roundup of October 16. Members of the Einsatzstab Rosenberg, the Nazi "research group" that focused on Hebrew books and Jewish ceremonial objects, were searching for any rare books that Zolli might have in his personal library. Founded in 1940 by Nazi party ideologist Alfred Rosenberg, the Einsatzstab was "an integral part of the dream of Nazi intellectuals to reinvigorate European thought and culture after winning the war."[25] The Einsatzstab Rosenberg pillaged Jewish libraries throughout Nazi occupied Europe, confiscating rare books and artifacts that they hoped later to display in institutes and museums that the Nazis planned to build after they won the war.[26]

Members of the Einsatzstab Rosenberg had confiscated Hebrew books from the Rome synagogue libraries the previous week, on the first day of Rosh Hashana, the Jewish New Year.[27] The Tempio Maggiore included two libraries with major collections of Hebraica and Judaica, the Biblioteca Comunale and the Biblioteca del Collegio Rabbinico. Luciano Morpugo, a Jewish publisher and writer associated with the Italian Fascist regime, who witnessed the Nazi looting of the Templo Maggiore libraries, eloquently described the scene as a Gestapo officer sifted through the rare and sacred Jewish manuscripts: "He touched, caressed, and fondled the papyri and the incunabula, turned the pages of manuscripts and rare editions and leafed through membranaceous codices and palimpsests. . . . In those refined hands, as if under keen and bloodless torture, a kind of very subtle sadism, the ancient books had spoken—later it was learnt that the officer was a distinguished student of paleography and Semitic philology."[28]

Thus, following their arrival in Rome in September 1943, the Nazis in quick succession raided the libraries of Templo Maggiore, ransacked Rabbi Zolli's home, and then deported many of the residents of the Jewish Ghetto. Although the Gestapo arrested many of the residents of the Ghetto, many other Jews in Rome managed to escape. The tragedy of the Roman Ghetto and the murder of roughly 2,000 Jews, although not in any way mitigated by the escape of other Jews, should still be understood in the context of the fate of the 7,000 Roman Jews who survived.[29] Rabbi Zolli claimed that "when the Germans took over control of all Italy, orders went out from the Pope to all monasteries and convents to hide Jews."[30] In his book *Three Popes and the Jews*, Pinchas Lapide, the Jewish theologian and Israeli historian, mentions 155 Roman Catholic monasteries and convents that sheltered Jews.[31] In France too, monasteries and convents hid Jews, particularly Jewish children. Also in Poland, Carmelite convents hid Jews.

Zolli came out of hiding after the Allied liberation of Rome in 1944, to be met yet again by hostility from survivors within the local Jewish community. Leaders of the community denounced the rabbi as a coward and worse. Little did they know that as soon as the war came to an end he would leave the synagogue for the church. Following his conversion, Zolli was free to lead a life of seclusion and scholarship, devoting all of his time to teaching and research.

PROFESSOR ZOLLI

Israel Zolli, by the last decade of his life, was no longer a rabbi, but he remained a university professor. His role in academia was the one continuity in a life radically disrupted by his decision to apostatize. According to many who knew him, he favored his university career over his clerical career and was particularly proud of his accomplishments as a scholar and teacher. In contrast, he often expressed ambivalence about his service as a rabbi. During his years in Trieste he had taught regularly at the University of Padua in the areas of Biblical Studies, Semitic Philology and Ancient Near Eastern history. After his apostasy, he would teach many of the same subjects at the University of Rome and at the Gregorian University's Pontifical Biblical Institute. But he would now do so as a full professor at a Catholic university.

In 1953 Zolli organized a conference in Rome on "The Messiah in the Old Testament." It was a return to a topic he had first addressed in his 1938 book *The Nazarene: Studies in New Testament Exegesis.* As a rabbi, Zolli had written about Jesus, but he had done so in an objective, scholarly fashion. Writing as a Catholic scholar, he now could emphasize the doctrine of the "harmony of the Old and New Testaments." According to this Christian concept, all references to the messiah in the Old Testament prefigure the coming of Jesus in the New Testament. As a Catholic scholar, Zolli now could write openly about his understanding of the pre-figuration of Jesus in the Old Testament.

As "Professor Eugenio Zolli" he continued his scholarly research and publication activities. In 1953 Zolli visited the United States, where he delivered a series of lectures at Notre Dame University.[32] As a recipient of one of the first fellowships awarded by the Fullbright Visiting Scholars Program, Zolli taught a summer course for adults on "The Hebrew and Rabbinic Background of Christian Liturgy."[33] Twenty-six students enrolled in the class. Among them were nine priests, eight nuns, and eight lay persons. An equal number of students enrolled as auditors. Thus Zolli had over fifty students attending each lecture. Father Mathis, Zolli's facilitator at Notre Dame, described student response to the course as very positive: "At first we certainly had some difficulty understanding him and even hearing him. But these were difficulties that were soon overcome and all our students, priests, seminarians, brothers, sisters and lay people had the greatest admiration and love for him."[34]

Zolli's summer course at Notre Dame, while a great success, was not free of controversy. Some in the American Jewish community, who remembered Zolli's apostasy some seven years earlier, were troubled that the State Department was making Zolli a Fulbright Fellow and that he would be teaching at Notre Dame. In a syndicated newspaper column that appeared in many local Jewish newspapers, the well-known journalist H. Ziprin penned an attack on Zolli. The article, titled "They can have him," begins with this salvo:

Is the renegade Zolli, former chief rabbi of Rome who sold his birthright for Vatican shelter, contemplating reversion to his old faith? His presence at South Bend, Ind., where he is giving a summer course in Christian precepts at the University of Notre Dame would seem to negate that thesis. His intentions were perhaps given away by his wife in Rome who is said to have told reporters that the secrecy attending her husband's trip to the U.S. was motivated by suspicion that Jewish leaders in America might seek to influence him into reconversion. Since we can't conceive of any responsible Jewish leader trying to bring that *meshummad* (apostate) back to the fold, it is reasonable to assume that Mrs. Zolli intended to kite a trial balloon if she did not in fact mean to slur Jewish intentions. It will be remembered that Zolli did not embrace Catholicism while in Vatican hiding but after returning to his rabbinic post in Rome after the liberation of Italy, and it would therefore be within his character to make or contemplate the change now that he is away from Vatican surveillance, though for our part they can have him for the rest of his life. [35]

While in the United States that summer, Zolli worked with Sheed and Ward publishers to prepare his autobiography for publication. Because of its contents, controversy again engulfed Zolli. His descriptions of his visions of Jesus and the importance that he attached to them proved problematic and disturbing to church authorities. When the publishers asked Cardinal Cicognani, the Apostolic Delegate to the United States, to write a foreword to the book, the cardinal responded by criticizing Zolli's emphasis on visionary experiences. [36] He warned that the book would not receive the Bishop's Imprimatur if the descriptions of Zolli's visions remained in the final manuscript. Cicognani wanted to tone down the visionary aspect and focus on the emotional and intellectual aspects of the rabbi's conversion.

As we saw in the previous chapter, Zolli's Italian contemporary, Donato Manduzio, who converted from Catholicism to Judaism during the same period that Zolli converted to Catholicism, also spoke of a visionary component in his conversion experience. Manduzio saw himself as a modern Moses, who would lead his Italian peasant followers into a Promised Land. His detailed descriptions of his visions and visitations from God brought him into constant conflict with the Italian Orthodox rabbis whom he encountered. Why, Manduzio asked, don't they have visions, like the Ancient Prophets of Israel? How could they lead their flocks without direct communication from the Divine? Eventually Manduzio would compromise on this issue so that his followers could undergo formal conversion to Judaism.

Zolli too compromised; he allowed the sections of his memoir describing his visions to be toned down. He also added the following disclaimer as an "author's note": "Any apparently extraordinary events which are narrated in this book are of secondary importance in the story of my conversion. This conversion was motivated by a love of Jesus Christ, a love which grew out of my meditations on the scriptures. I would like to call my reader's attention to the fact that neither the Apostolic Delegate's foreword nor the Bishop's

Imprimatur can be construed as judgment of these prelates, or of the Church, upon the nature of the events, or any other apparently extraordinary events, which might be contained in this book."[37]

Before the Dawn appeared in the United States in 1954. (It would not be published in Italy until 2004.) The introduction to the first English edition, published in 1954, represented an early salvo in what would decades later be dubbed the "Pius Wars," the debates about the role of the Vatican during the war and its response to the Nazi extermination program. In the forward, Cardinal Cicognani, wrote that Zolli had "witnessed the splendid example of . . . His Holiness Pius XII. In an astonishing and almost indescribable way, everyone was experiencing the material and moral assistance of the Supreme Pontiff during the recent war years."[38] Cicognani, by defending Pius XII before he had been widely criticized, was anticipating the political wars to come.

In *The Catholic World*, Zolli published an article titled "The Status of the State of Israel." He presents the State of Israel in a thoroughly Christian context, but his assessment is infused with a Jewish Zionist understanding of the state.[39] The essay opens with a survey of ancient Israelite history and an examination of the "fulfillment" of Israel's purpose in the life and death of Jesus. Zolli writes, "Jesus saw and forewarned the Jews of the approaching fall of the national State of Israel, and approximately forty years after his prophecy, a terrible page of history was written by Titus in letters of blood and fire."[40] This was at the time the Catholic view of Jewish destiny.

But Zolli continues, adding a Jewish perspective: "The countless victims of Nazism preceded the heroes who died to create the modern State of Israel. Now, after indescribable martyrdom under Nazism, after the terrible night of nameless misfortunes, the rosy outlines of dawn for the Hebrew state are taking shape." Most Jews today would find this part of Zolli's assessment acceptable. Zolli's reference to the Israel of Jesus's time as "the national State of Israel" implicitly establishes the connection between the ancient and the modern that is at the core of Zionist thought. In 1949, these ideas were antithetical to most Catholics. In Catholic theology, "Israel" was the church, not the descendants of biblical Israel. Zolli concludes his essay by exhorting modern Israelis to embrace Jesus: "But let not Israel's pilgrimage end now. Let not the State of Israel become the last and only objective of a suffering people, but may it go on to a more glorious destination. May Israel become God's pilgrim again."[41]

In 1956, three years after he returned from his sojourn to the United States, Zolli fell ill with pneumonia. He died in Rome in 1956 at the age of seventy-five. He had spent his last decade as an active Catholic thinker, writer, and teacher.

THE RETURN OF THE ZOLLI CASE

Rabbi Zolli might have been forgotten, or remained a curious addition to the long list of Jewish converts to Catholicism, if not for four unexpected developments. First, the controversy which erupted in the early 1960s surrounding the conduct of Pope Pius XII during World War II drew attention to Zolli. Pius XII's defenders relied heavily on Zolli's association with the Pope and widely quoted his praise of the Pope's efforts to save Jews from the Nazi terror. As Zolli wrote, "The Holy Father sent by hand a letter to the bishops instructing them to lift the enclosure from convents and monasteries, so that they could become refuges for Jews. . . . No hero in history has commanded such an army . . . in cities and small towns to provide bread for the persecuted and passports for the fugitives."[42]

The emergence of a "Hebrew-Catholic" community in Israel also drew attention to Zolli and his post-war work. In the 1950s, there were converts from Judaism who sought to retain a distinct Jewish identity within the Catholic Church. These converts fully subscribed to Church doctrines, but they often included the celebration of certain Jewish holidays within their liturgical calendar. Eventually, the Pope granted permission for the development of a Hebrew-language mass for these Catholic worshipers. Zolli became a patron saint of sorts for these Hebrew-Catholics.[43] Following the Vatican Accord of 1993, the Vatican established diplomatic relations with the State of Israel. As relations between the two institutions grew closer during the negotiations, Zolli's story influenced both the Jewish and the Catholic participants. Father David Neuhaus—an Israeli Jew who converted to Catholicism in the 1980s, was trained as a Jesuit priest, and now heads the "Hebrew Catholic Community" in Israel—facilitated the completion of the accord. Unlike Rabbi Zolli forty years earlier, Neuhaus did not remain a liminal figure, "caught" between the Jewish and Catholic worlds. Rather, he has become one of the primary facilitators of the contemporary Catholic-Israeli and Catholic-Jewish relationship.

Finally, a body of Italian scholarship emerged that focuses on Zolli's life and scholarly work. In 2004, Zolli's 1954 autobiography, *Before the Dawn*, was at last published in Italy, where it became a best seller. Subsequently in 2009, scholars from Padua, Milan and Rome published an edited volume that examined Zolli and his work. Then in 2010, Zolli's 1935 book *The Nazarene: Studies in New Testament Exegesis* was republished in Italy to critical acclaim. As historian Ana Foa wrote in her review of the book, "Zolli was . . . a liminal figure whom the Jews, understandably hurt by his defection, did not understand, and whom the Church in the postwar period, at a time still light years away from Jewish-Christian openness, preferred to leave to the side."[44] In the twenty-first century Zolli and his work had at last emerged from obscurity.In 1998 Stefano Zurio, a journalist for *Il Giornale*, interviewed Zolli's daughter Miriam, a practicing psychoanalyst in Rome who had for decades deflected questions about her parents' conversion. Now at age seventy-six, she wanted to make clear that she did not consider her parents' conversion an act of apostasy. During the interview Miriam told Zurio, "It is important that you make clear that my father never abandoned his Judaism. He felt he was a Jew who had come to believe in the Jewish Messiah. But there was no rejection of his Jewish roots or of the Jewish people. So many find that impossible to understand."[45]

NOTES

1. 1 Weisbord and Sillanpoa, *The Chief Rabbi, the Pope, and the Holocaust*, 129. For a recent reevaluation of Zolli's life and work, see Latorre, "Israel Zoller."
2. Newman, *A "Chief Rabbi" of Rome Becomes a Catholic*, 151.
3. Zolli, *Before the Dawn*, 75–76.
4. Ibid., 189–191.
5. Ibid., 189–191.
6. Ibid., 189–191.
7. Ibid., 18.
8. Ibid. 89.
9. Matthews, "Religion: Greatest Tragedy," 68.
10. Newman, *A "Chief Rabbi" of Rome Becomes a Catholic*, 80.
11. See Newman, *A "Chief Rabbi" of Rome Becomes a Catholic*, 93–102; Zolli, *Before the Dawn*, 81.
12. Davison, "Still an Idea Behind It."
13. Newman, *A "Chief Rabbi" of Rome Becomes a Catholic*, 85.
14. Kertzer, *The Kidnapping of Edgardo Mortara*.
15. Lapide, *Three Popes and the Jews*, 307.
16. Sarfatti, *The Jews in Mussolini's Italy*, 68.
17. Fermi, *Mussolini*, 369.
18. Pizzi, *A City in Search of an Author*, 171.
19. Katz, *Black Sabbath*, 20.
20. For a quite different account see Gallo, "To Halt the Dreadful Crimes," 110–135.
21. Sarfatti, *The Jews in Mussolini's Italy*, 114.
22. Michaelis, *Mussolini and the Jews*, 361.
23. Zolli, *Before the Dawn*, 152.
24. Latorre, "Eugenio Zolli: apostata o profeta?," 27.
25. Katz, *Black Sabbath*, 119.
26. P. Friedman, "The Fate of the Jewish Book During the Nazi Era."
27. See Michaelis, *Mussolini and the Jews*, 358–359; Katz, *Black Sabbath*, 118–125.
28. Michaelis, *Mussolini and the Jews*, 359.
29. Lapide, *Three Popes and the Jews*, 260–266. Lapide points out that the church, through "Papal caution and circumspection, saved close to 90 percent of Roman Jewry" (263).
30. Lapide, *Three Popes and the Jews*, 263.
31. Ibid.
32. Cabaud, *Eugenio Zolli ou Le Prophéte d'un Monde Nouveau*, 7.
33. In 2010 I was able to examine the material on Rabbi Zolli's courses, which is preserved in the Notre Dame archives.
34. Mathis to Raphael Simon.
35. Ziprin, "On The Record: They Can Have Him," 1–4.
36. Cicognani, Amleto G. to Israel Zolli.
37. Zolli, *Before the Dawn*, 25.

38. Zolli, *Before the Dawn*, 14. See also Goldman, *Zeal for Zion*, 163–208 on Cicognani's statements against Zionism.

39. Zolli, "The Status of the State of Israel."

40. Ibid., 327–328.

41. Ibid., 329.

42. Zolli, *Before the Dawn*, 152, 194, 195. Also see Lapide, *Three Popes and the Jews*, 132–133, 306.

43. See Cabaud, *Eugenio Zolli ou Le Prophéte d'un Monde Nouveau*; Schoenman, *Honey from the Rock*.

44. Foa, "The Rabbi Who Studied Jesus." For recent Italian research on Zolli see Carozzi, *Israel-Eugenio Zolli*.

45. *Inside the Vatican* Staff, "My Father Never Stopped Being a Jew."

Chapter Six

"Ruth from the Banks of the Volga": Elisheva Bikhovsky (Elizaveta Ivanova Zhirkova, 1888–1949)

Thus far our tales of conversion and apostasy have centered on the deep religious experiences of our protagonists. Each had strong ties to the traditions of their birth and childhood; each left their home faith and through long struggle joined another. The story of Elisheva Bikhovsky provides us with another tale of conversion, but her story is not one of religious conversion. Elisheva did not convert to the Jewish religion, but to Zionism, and to the emerging culture of Hebrew literature.

By the first decades of the twentieth century such an act of affiliation, one more socio-political than religious, seemed to be an emerging option for Christians seeking to join the Jewish people. Secular Jews led the Zionist movement; Orthodox rabbis, for the most part, opposed it. Might it be possible then, some Christian philo-Semites asked, to become a Zionist without formally undergoing religious conversion to Judaism? Emigration from Europe to Palestine began in earnest with the "First Aliyah," when large numbers of Jews moved to Palestine after the Russian pogroms of 1881–1882. By the turn of the century, most of the pioneers, or *halutzim*, those Eastern European and Russian Jews who participated in the "Second Aliyah" from 1904 to 1914, were assertively secular. In their youth, before they left their rabbinic academies, teachers, and seminaries, these young men and women had been brought up in Orthodox families. By going to Palestine they were rebelling against their families and religious traditions. Why then should a non-Jew, "fellow-traveler" who wanted to join them in Palestine be burdened with a new set of religious practices? Surely a non-Jewish Zionist could be equally secular?

For the female Jewish pioneers, this act of rebellion was doubly configured. These women were not only rebelling against the traditional practices that limited their activities to the home and the family business, but also asserting their gender equality by participating in the struggle to create a national home. The tensions that developed from pioneer women's expectations of social change in their new environment and the failure of those expectations to materialize completely were similar to tensions found in many early twentieth-century post-revolutionary situations. Like the women of the Russian Revolution, Jewish women in the early Zionist movement faced disappointments. They struggled for the cause as equals, but found that once the revolution had triumphed, they still had not achieved full equality.

Elizaveta Zhirkova was not one of these Jewish women pioneers, but later in life she would seek to emulate them. Born into a Moscow family with a complex cultural and religious heritage, including English, Irish, German, and Russian roots, she would struggle to create her own identity, ultimately becoming an established Hebrew writer and a citizen of the Yishuv, the pre-state Jewish community in Palestine.

Though she identified with Jews to a great extent—so much so that she settled in Palestine—Elisheva remained "a divided soul." In a 1920 letter to a European friend she wrote, "There are two souls in me—one Russian, one Hebrew." She experienced these "souls" not as complementary, but as competing. These competing souls may have served as a source of Elisheva's creativity, but they were also a source of disappointment and bitterness. Moving to Palestine would not heal this internal rupture, rather—as we shall see—it exacerbated it.[1]

EARLY YEARS

Elizaveta Zhirkova was born in Riazan, a city southeast of Moscow, in 1888. Her father was Russian and belonged to the Russian Orthodox Church. Her mother was the child of an Irish Catholic man who had settled in Russia during the Napoleonic Wars. When her mother died three years after her birth, Elizaveta was sent to live with her mother's sister in Moscow. Of her childhood, Elizaveta would later recall, "I wasn't of Jewish descent, of course, nor was I purely Russian. My mother's father was English (more precisely, Irish). He ran away from home as a young man and eventually settled in Russia. Then he married a German-born woman who had grown up in an English-speaking family. Therefore the next generation, my mother and her siblings, thought of themselves as English. My mother died when I was a child and I was brought up by my aunt, and it's with her English family, rather than my father's Russian family, that I identified."[2]

As a child, Elizaveta's awareness of her complex family history fueled her imagination. None of her childhood friends had such an "exotic" ancestry. The majority of her friends were ethnic Russians whose families belonged to the Russian Orthodox Church. Elizaveta was under tremendous pressure to conform to Russian ideas, beliefs, and traditions. Her English-German family, however, made sure to expose her to English and German as well as Russian culture. In addition, they inculcated in Elizaveta a love of the Old Testament, which she read in English. No doubt this love influenced her later attraction to Jewish culture, and to Hebrew language and literature. Elizaveta graduated from a girl's high school in Moscow and planned to train as a teacher.

During high school, Elizaveta had become friendly with a Jewish student. This Jewish friend, whose name has been lost, introduced Elizaveta to Jewish home life. The Sabbath rituals, Jewish holidays, and kosher dietary laws that she experienced in her friend's home enchanted her. Thus began her journey into Jewish life and literature. As she could read Hebrew and German, Elizaveta was soon able to decode the Yiddish newspapers she saw in the homes of her Jewish friends. She enrolled in advanced Hebrew classes and found a tutor to coach her. She quickly surpassed her Jewish friends in both Hebrew knowledge and in enthusiasm for the newest trends in Hebrew prose and poetry.

During this period, news of the Irish struggles against the English, struggles which erupted in the Irish Rebellion of 1916, made a deep impression on Elizaveta. This identification with Ireland shaped her life-long sympathy not only for the Irish but also for other oppressed peoples. In a 1923 letter to a friend, she explained, "From as far back as I remember, I had a romantic attachment to small national groups, to persecuted and oppressed peoples. First it was the Spanish, then the Poles, then the Albanians."[3] Concern for the sufferings of the Irish soon gave way to support of Zionism. When she met young Russian Zionists in her classes at Moscow University, their descriptions of the suffering of the Russian Jewish masses evoked feelings of sympathy and identification. The Jews of Russia were, in her understanding, like the Catholics of Ireland. They were living under imperial oppression and were struggling to throw off that yoke. As Elizaveta later wrote, "Strange as it might seem, the history of the Irish is the history of the Jews. The Irish were persecuted by the English because of their Catholicism and were subject to much oppression. Just like the Jews in Russia and elsewhere, the Irish were limited to certain areas and generally discriminated against."[4]

Elizaveta began writing poetry in her late teens. She had read widely in Russian and European literature, and even started a novel about the freedom struggles in the Balkans. Among the English poetry that influenced her most was Lord Byron's *Hebrew Melodies*. Byron's sympathy for the plight of the Jews, in exile from their land, stirred her. Some of her early poems invoked biblical and Jewish texts and themes, but they did so in a cultural rather than a religious manner.

In 1919, Elizaveta published two volumes of her Russian poems. In the heady post-revolutionary atmosphere of Moscow's literary circles, however, Elizaveta's romantic, modest poems received little attention from readers or critics. By the time the volumes were published, Elizaveta had been studying Hebrew for five years. In 1920 she decided to try her hand at writing in Hebrew. Her early Hebrew poems were enthusiastically received in the Hebrew reading communities of the world. They were short, lyrical and tinged with an air of melancholy. And they were not burdened with allusions to biblical and rabbinic texts, as many other Hebrew poems of the period were.

MARRIAGE, PALESTINE, AND EARLY SUCCESS AS A HEBREW POET

In 1920, the same year that she began to write in Hebrew, Elizaveta Zhirkova married Shimon Bikhovsky, her Hebrew tutor. She took the Hebrew given name Elisheva, the biblical original of the name Elizabeth, and adopted her husband's last name. The marriage was a daring move for both husband and wife. Both families disapproved of the match. Elisheva's family had expected her to marry a Russian Orthodox Christian. Bikhovsky, an ardent Zionist active in the new field of Hebrew literary publishing, was from a traditional Jewish family. His marriage to a non-Jew caused a scandal among both his relatives and his friends. For Bikhovsky's family, the problem was a religious one; the union was a "forbidden marriage." For his secular friends, the problem was cultural. Traditionally, Jews and Christians did not marry, especially in Russia. Before the Russian Revolution it was in fact illegal. Secular Jews considered "Jewishness" a cultural rather than a religious designation, but if that was so, a gentile could not "become Jewish." In the Orthodox and Reform religious traditions, a non-Jew could convert to Judaism; in the secular realm, there was no such option. The concept of "secular conversion" to Judaism would not develop for another century.

For Elisheva's Zionist husband and his associates, many of whom were soon to move to Palestine, a new Jewish identity was emerging, one that jettisoned religious belief and substituted an ethnic and cultural definition of Jewish peoplehood. The Zionist hope was that the movement's struggles would be perceived by both Jews and non-Jews as part of the wider movement for national independence that followed the end of World War I. The fall of the Hapsburg, Wilhelmine, and Ottoman Empires liberated many different peoples from imperial rule. Now these national groups were demanding their independence. The "Spring of Nations" was the call of the hour. Zionism, its advocates argued, should be seen as part of that struggle for independence; therefore, the Zionist movement should be granted diplomatic and political recognition. But could a non-Jew participate in this new Jewish identity?

By marrying Bikhovsky, Elisheva was expressing her identification with Zionism and the revival of Hebrew literature, not with the Jewish religious tradition. She did not convert to Judaism at this time; nor did she choose to do so later in life, when it would have been to her great advantage. While Elisheva was married to Shimon Bikhovsky, his secular Jewish friends accepted her to some extent. Upon Bikhovsky's death, however, she would be on her own, as she had not pursued formal religious conversion, which in the end proved the only path to becoming a Jew.

In 1921 the influential Hebrew journal *Hatekufah* published some of Elisheva's Hebrew poems. As part of her growing prominence in early-twentieth-century Hebrew literature, Elisheva worked to translate, publicize and promote Hebrew writers to a Russian readership. She translated short stories and novels by emerging Hebrew writers like Brenner, Schoffman, and Gnessin, into Russian. But she did not neglect the Hebrew literary past. She also translated Yehuda Halevi's poems of Zion, written in the twelfth century, into Russian. And she began to craft her own literary essays in Hebrew. Some of these essays were about Hebrew writers; others were about Russian poets. Elisheva designed these essays to educate Hebrew readers both about emerging Hebrew poets and prose styles, and about new developments in Russian literature. Perhaps her most influential essay, *Meshorer ve-Adam*, which she wrote in 1924, examined the Russian symbolist poet Alexander Blok, whom she considered her greatest teacher. In the essay, she included Hebrew translations of Blok's Russian poems. Rather than attempt to convey the "wondrous structure" of Blok's poetry in the original, she chose to supply as literal a translation as possible. As she wrote, "In my eyes prose translation that is precise is far better than a second or third rate poetic translation."[5]

In 1925 Elisheva and Shimon Bikhovsky, with Mira, their one-year-old daughter, emigrated from Russia to Palestine. The Jewish population of Palestine had increased rapidly over the past few years, from 60,000 in 1918 at the end of World War I, to 120,000 when Elisheva and her small family arrived. This doubling of the Jewish population was the result of the *aliyot*, or mass emigrations of Jews from Europe. With this growing population came an increase in cultural activity. Music, especially classical music, flourished as Jewish musicians flocked to Palestine. A tradition of "Palestinian Jewish Art" developed and prospered at the Bezalel Academy of Arts and Design in Jerusalem and among artists in Tel-Aviv and Jaffa. Sir Ronald Storrs, Governor of Jerusalem under the British Mandate, encouraged this cultural flowering, which also included intellectual and literary pursuits. The Hebrew University was established in Jerusalem in 1925.

In Palestine Shimon Bikhovsky established his own publishing house, Tomer Press, which published Elisheva's work. This freed Elisheva from the ideological and stylistic constraints imposed on those Hebrew writers seeking publication in the establishment literary journals. But it also carried some risk. If Tomer Press were to fail, Elisheva would lose her access to the reading public and thus have little opportunity to get her work before the swiftly growing Hebrew readership. For several years Elisheva was a literary celebrity. Her poems and stories were published and read widely. Her first book, *Kos Ketanah (A Little Cup)*, was the first volume of Hebrew poetry by a woman published in Palestine. Soon Elisheva was hailed, along with Rachel Blaustein, Esther Raab, and Yocheved Bat Miriam, as one of the "four mothers" of modern Hebrew poetry.

After she published her first volume of Hebrew poetry, Elisheva turned to writing short stories in Hebrew. The characters in her stories are young Russian intellectuals and artists living in Moscow in the cultural ferment of the first years after the Russian Revolution. One of her signature stories, "A Small Matter," (*mikre tafel*) is narrated by a young Jewish woman whose Christian friends unwittingly reveal a deep-seated anti-Semitism. The theme of the young Jewish intellectual attempting to join Russian cultural life—an attempt that often seemed doomed to failure—is present in many of Elisheva's stories. At a party in a friend's house, the narrator of "A Small Matter" overhears a conversation about a "blood libel" trial then in the news. Hearkening back to a medieval trope, a Russian court has accused Jews of using the blood of Christian children in the Passover ritual. Though most of the narrator's friends find the accusations ridiculous, one young woman wonders aloud, "Perhaps it is true?" Through this ugly incident the story's protagonist gains some understanding of the social dynamics of anti-Jewish sentiment. But "A Small Matter" also operates on another level. Like many female characters in Elisheva's fiction, the protagonist finds herself alienated from the people who surround her, whether they are Christians or Jews. In response, she turns inward, "to her own inner spiritual dream world, which she inhabits with intensity."[6]

Once in Palestine, Shimon Bikhovsky devoted himself to Elisheva's career. He served as her agent, publisher, and publicist. He organized "Elisheva Soirees," where she read her poems to Jewish audiences. He capitalized on the "exotic" nature of her appeal to the Hebrew reader. The "chattering classes" of Jewish Palestine found the fact that a Russian Christian poet would decide to leave Russia and Russian culture and throw in her lot with the small Yishuv of Palestine nothing short of "miraculous." Jewish readers in the Yishuv and in the Jewish literary centers of Europe assumed that Hebrew language and literature were a Jewish project; an outsider joining the effort was both remarkable and unique.

At this point in the history of modern Hebrew literature, the masters of Hebrew poetry and prose were almost without exception former Yeshiva students who had left both the Yeshiva world and the strict orthodoxy it promoted and represented. As young men—and the Yeshiva world was a thoroughly male world—these students had mastered the classics of the Jewish textual tradition. This mastery shaped their efforts to establish a new, secular, Hebrew literature. The question arose, what could an outsider, a Christian and a woman, contribute to Hebrew literature? Neither Elisheva's religion nor her gender fit the classical model. But she did contribute, the critics of the time had to admit, to the birth of a new Hebrew literature. Her poems and stories were original, insightful, and promising. Some wondered, would Elisheva produce a novel?

A "NATIONALISTIC CONVERSION"

Elisheva never converted to Judaism, but many people remained convinced that she had, and her denials seemed to have had little effect on those who wanted, or needed, her to be Jewish in an "official" manner. Her situation revealed that the separation (though not the divorce) of Zionism from Orthodox Judaism, a separation that seemed self-evident to some secular Zionists of the early-twentieth century, never reached full fruition. In the 1920s, novelist and essayist Yosef Haim Brenner, a Jaffa resident, called for a break with the Jewish past. For Brenner, religion was a marker of that past. As he wrote, "Hebrew nationalism and the Hebrew language are the keys to a new Jewish future."[7] Brenner had been a close childhood friend of Elisheva's husband Shimon Bikhovsky, and the two men shared many ideas. The Zionist idea was actualized in the pre-state Yishuv of British Mandate Palestine, and within that community the "Jewishness" of the Zionist movement was strengthened, rather than weakened.

The idea that the new "Hebrew nation" could be separated from its Jewish religious roots, and from the Jews of the Diaspora, remained an undercurrent in Zionist and early Israeli thought, but not a powerful undercurrent. From the late-1940s to the mid-1960s, the "Canaanite movement," a literary trend that exerted some cultural influence in the first decades of Israeli statehood, articulated this idea. Canaanites called for a new "Semitic" sensibility, one that would break with the Jewish past, especially with the Jewish religious past, and embrace a Middle Eastern, rather than a western heritage. But this cultural position did not necessarily imply an affinity with the Arabs of Palestine.

Max Raisin, a prominent American Reform rabbi who met Elisheva on one of his visits to British Mandate Palestine, persisted in calling her a "righteous convert" to Judaism and publicizing her as "Ruth from the Banks of the Volga." He was evoking the biblical Ruth, the paradigmatic covert to Judaism.[8] But those familiar with Elisheva's life and literary work understood that though devoted to Zionism and the revival of Hebrew literature, she chose not to become a Jew through formal religious conversion. Jeremiah Frankel, a Zionist intellectual, dubbed her allegiance to the Zionist cause a "nationalistic conversion," in contrast to a religiously legal, *halakhic*, conversion, the normative manner in which a non-Jew would become a Jew.[9] Thus Elisheva's life and her choice not to convert to Judaism foreshadowed later Israeli debates about Jewish and Israeli identity. In the twenty-first century, some would attempt to assert a new type of identity—Israeli rather than Jewish, one Elisheva might have approved of.

In a 1934 letter, written nine years after she had arrived in Palestine, Elisheva reflected on the question of "religious identity" versus "national identity." She made it clear that religion had played no part in her attraction to Hebrew literature, or in her decision to settle in Palestine. She wrote, "Among all of the factors that brought me to live in the land of Israel and to participate to some extent in the life of the Jews in it, there was no religious element, neither external nor internal. Essentially, I never left a different religion, nor did I join in a formal manner the Jewish religion. As I said earlier this issue is highly personal, one that remains a matter of conscience."[10]

Decades later, Elisheva's daughter Mira Littel would characterize her mother's attraction to Palestine and Judaism as a consequence of her attraction to the Hebrew language: "My mother was drawn to Judaism because of the Hebrew language. It seemed very exotic and mystical to her that a language that was almost dead for two thousand years should come to life again through the efforts of one Eliezer ben Yehuda. For her, Judaism was like a secret society. Her brother was a linguist and thus it was natural that she went to study Hebrew at the 'Friends of the Hebrew Language Club.'"[11]

Elisheva was one of the few published women writers in Hebrew. Male voices dominated Hebrew literature, especially during its European phase (1880–1920). But as the writers of the Yishuv in Palestine took center stage in Hebrew culture, replacing those of Vilna, Odessa, and Warsaw, a handful of women writers—primarily poets—gained acceptance. Poetry was viewed as feminine; prose as masculine. In 1929, after four years in Palestine, Elisheva further impressed her readers with the publication of a three hundred page novel *Simtaot (Side Streets)*. Here, too, she was a literary pioneer. Like her book of Hebrew poetry, *Simtaot* was a first. It was the first Hebrew novel written by a woman. Elisheva had begun writing the novel in Moscow in 1925, before her departure for Palestine, and she completed it in Tel Aviv in 1929. In her essays, Elisheva argued that the composition of poetry was the greatest art, one that surpassed the writing of prose. As literary fate would have it, Elisheva is remembered today more as a novelist than as a poet. As

Israeli literary critic Dana Olmert has noted, "Looking back eighty years, it seems that in contrast to what she would have wanted, her literary excellence was demonstrated by her prose, not by her poetry. Outstanding in its excellence is the novel *Simtaot*."[12]

Simtaot is set among the literary and artistic bohemians of post-Revolution Moscow. Written in Hebrew, the book makes no reference to either Jewish settlement in Palestine or the revival of the Hebrew language there. The two main protagonists are Ludmilla, a Russian poet, and her lover and Hebrew teacher, Daniel. Like all of their friends, they are poor intellectuals and poets struggling to make ends meet.

On its initial publication *Simtaot* was not well received. Neither the growing Hebrew readership nor the influential literary critics of the day found it appealing. In the novel, powerful forces of attraction and repulsion between Jews and gentiles are at play. These forces are both erotic and cultural. Ludmilla is deeply attracted to her Hebrew teacher Daniel. As Dana Olmert has noted, "The power and vitality of the novel stem from the description of the erotic and power relationships between men and intellectual women who are sexually liberated and independent."[13] In addition to the portrayal of intelligent, liberated women, Elisheva offers a complex understanding of Jewish and Christian relationships and identities. As critic Yaffah Berlovitz noted in the 1990s, "Elisheva brought new themes, and a new style, to Hebrew prose. Among these themes were: a depiction of the 'new woman' of the post-World War I era; the self-portrait of woman-as-creator; and the dialogue between Christians and Jews as seen from a non-Jewish perspective."[14]

Sadly, these affirmations of Elisheva's literary talents came some sixty years after her death. In 1929 *Simtaot* was a novel—not unlike its author—ahead of its time; it would be "rediscovered" twice—once in 1977 and again in 2008. We might compare the reception of *Simtaot* to the reception of Henry Roth's *Call it Sleep*, which was first published in 1934 and then rediscovered in 1964. From Elisheva's correspondences with other Hebrew writers it is clear that she intended to write at least two more novels, and one imagines that they would have reflected her experiences as an immigrant to Palestine. But a drastic change in her circumstances would force her to abandon these plans. In reduced circumstances she would not be able to sustain the prolonged effort necessary to complete another novel.

By 1930 Elisheva seemed on the brink of accomplishing what she had set out to do some fifteen years earlier—master Hebrew poetry and prose and gain acceptance as a Hebrew writer in Palestine. Her poems were especially popular among women readers. Some critics have suggested that the fact that Elisheva's poetry was not bound by the weight of the Jewish textual past made her work accessible to a new readership of Hebrew prose and poetry, especially to women.[15] After the horrors of World War I, readers sought a poetry that was romantic and life-affirming. They found these elements in the poems of Elisheva, and in the poems of one of the other "mothers of Hebrew poetry," Rachel Blaustein. In the late 1920s some of Elisheva's poems were set to music. "In the Grove" (*Ba-hurshah*) became one of the most popular Hebrew songs of the era.

TRAGEDY, POVERTY, BITTERNESS AND DECLINE

Within a few years of her arrival in Palestine Elisheva's popularity began to wane. Perhaps Elisheva and her husband Shimon Bikhovsky had over-reached. They did not realize that the novelty of a "converted" writer, whether "converted" to Jewish nationalism or to the Jewish religion, could not sustain itself for more than a few years. Cultural celebrity is by its nature ephemeral. New writers moved into the limelight, though none of them were "converts" like Elisheva.

In 1932 Shimon Bikhovsky died in a car accident while he and Elisheva were on a literary tour of European Jewish cultural centers. Elisheva returned to Palestine to care for her eight-year-old daughter Mira. Elisheva was now forty-four years old and had no means of support. She had never converted formally to Judaism, and this put her daughter's status as a Jew in question. As the child of a gentile, Mira would be considered Jewish only if she pursued formal conversion to Judaism. The liberalism of the secular Jewish pioneers of the 1920s had hardened into a more conservative worldview. The deterioration of Arab-Jewish relations after 1929 reinforced conservative tendencies in the Yishuv. Shimon Bikhovsky's close friend Yosef Haim Brenner had been murdered in an Arab attack on a Jewish village, an increasingly common threat to the Yishuv. And as European anti-Semitism grew and the Nazi movement surged to power in Germany, the Jewish future seemed even more precarious. Many Jews reacted to the threat of anti-Semitism by "circling the wagons" both physically and metaphorically and protecting the borders of Jewish identity.

During their years in Palestine, Bikhovsky and Elisheva had not saved any money, nor had they acquired any property. After her husband's death, Elisheva was reduced to living in a shack near the beach in Tel Aviv's Montefiore neighborhood. Hayyim Nahman Bialik, who had achieved the status of "national poet" of the Yishuv in the 1920s, admired Elisheva's poetry and prose. He organized and contributed to a monthly stipend for the widowed writer and her daughter. Unfortunately, the stipend was barely enough to support Elisheva and Mira. When Rabbi Max Raisin, an American scholar who contributed to Elisheva's monthly stipend, met with her in Tel Aviv in 1935, she appeared exhausted and discouraged. As Raisin noted, "One could easily see that she was an unhappy woman, and the impression I got from our last conversation was that her unhappiness was due not merely to her material poverty, but also to the role she was forced to play as a member of the Jewish people."[16]

After her husband's death, Elisheva published very few poems. Her last major poem was in memory of her benefactor, the poet H. N. Bialik, who died in 1934. The opening stanzas of "In Memory of H. N. Bialik" contrast the eternity of the sea and the stars with the ephemeral nature of all human effort. People, the poem suggests, can only respond to the eternal with bitterness and jealousy. The poem ends with these lines: "I hold a book in my hands. Its pages yellow with age, it is marked with stains and with poems—the voice of a heart that has been stilled. Don't open the book—Jealousy is bitter. But the poems will live forever!"[17] From the publication of "In Memory of H. N. Bialik" until her death fifteen years later, Elisheva would publish only a few minor poems and some book reviews in the Hebrew press. She had produced the bulk of her Hebrew poetry and prose before her husband's death, before she was forty-five years old.

In a mid-1930s letter to the Hebrew writer Gershom Schoffman, Elisheva spoke of her isolation and loneliness. She was disillusioned with the new activist society she saw emerging in Jewish Palestine and felt that there would be no place in it for writers who were not politically "useful" or engaged. As she wrote to Schoffman, "You and I, and other writers not fit for 'real life' should really pick up and go to London or some other place and write Hebrew literature that no one 'needs.'"[18] Though she was, of course, saddened by her husband's early demise, her loneliness, she explained, had preceded his death. "Of course I feel very alone here . . . but if you want to know the truth, I felt this way before my husband died and have felt this way ever since we have moved to Palestine."[19]

Other Hebrew poets of the period expressed a similar sense of dislocation, displacement and alienation, but in Elisheva's case the alienation and disappointment ruled her life. More than poetic musings, these deep-seated emotions ruled her daily reality. It was during this period that she began to speak openly of her "two souls" in conflict. "There are two souls in me, one Russian and one Hebrew" she wrote.[20] While other Hebrew writers, many of whom emerged from Russian culture, might have spoken of having "two souls," they would not have described these souls as being in conflict. For Elisheva the conflict between her Russian origins and her adopted Hebrew culture, a culture which had disappointed and rejected her, was overwhelmingly painful. But her concern with doubleness and conflict was not new. Early in her career in her essay on the Russian symbolist poet Alexander Blok, she wrote of Blok's being torn between the idealism of his youth and the harsh realities of adulthood: "There is nothing sadder, or more frightening than to witness a soul torn in two. This is what we witness in Blok's later poems. How astute was the comment of one of Blok's commentaries 'that we, the readers, sit and delight in these poems—but the living soul of the poet is damned.'"[21]

The darker side of history soon intruded on Elisheva's life. When World War II broke out in Europe the Jews of Palestine were both alarmed and exhilarated. Many had come to Palestine to escape from the Nazis; now the Nazis were threatening not only Europe but also, by extension, the Middle East. The British had blocked the entry of Jewish refugees into Palestine, but many in the Yishuv aided "illegal" immigration whenever and wherever possible. Elisheva, living in a poor area of Tel Aviv, was naturally concerned about her future, and the future of her daughter Mira, who was at the time in her late teens. The outbreak of war brought prosperity to Tel Aviv. The British Army, already deployed in Palestine, greatly increased its number of troops. Jewish suppliers and merchants prospered providing for the needs of this expanding British military. Many Jews also joined the British forces, eager to fight as Palestinian Jews under the British flag. But Elisheva saw no benefit from this prosperity and enthusiasm. Her daughter, Mira, who had enlisted in the British Army, fell in love with and married a British soldier, before moving with him to England. Elisheva was now left completely alone, and her bitterness and disillusion only deepened.

Elisheva felt that publishers and booksellers had profited from her work while she was left in dire poverty. She had contributed to the emergence of a new Hebrew culture; its establishment figures now shunned her. In a 1944 letter to Mira, who was then serving in the British Army, Elisheva wrote, "One day I'll write about my twenty years in this country. The devil pushed me to devote myself to its ideals and to end up in it with all of my 'goyishe' naiveté. And I'll write about all the people who exploited me and how I ended up as someone's sacrificial lamb. Eventually I became one of the 'useless people' who have no place in the 'New' Yishuv that is coming into being. In short, I've become someone that those around me define with such self-confidence as a person who doesn't know how to help herself."[22]

LATER YEARS

By the mid-1940s, the literary life of the new nation and the emerging Israeli national consciousness shunned and ignored Elisheva. With only a meager stipend for support, she endured seventeen years of grinding poverty followed by illness and death. She was a woman, a non-Jew, a widowed mother, and an outsider to the Hebrew literary establishment, an establishment increasingly linked to the nationalist cause and the political-military struggles against the British and the Arabs. If readers of Hebrew literature thought of her at all, it was as "Ruth from the Banks of the Volga," the Russian Christian woman who had converted to Judaism and moved to the Holy Land.

Despite the failure of her campaign against this designation, Elisheva never gave up trying to counter the notion that she had converted to Judaism. In November 1947 she wrote to her American benefactor, Rabbi Max Raisin, who had coined the phrase "Ruth from the Banks of the Volga," to explain her despondent frame of mind. "I am not a Jewess, and just to make believe that I am one is something I cannot do."[23] The assumption of her readers that she was Jewish took a heavy toll on her.

In 1943 the *Encyclopedia of Literature*, a guide to the work of Hebrew writers, described Elisheva as "a convert to Judaism." Elisheva was incensed when she read the description. She found the editor, Baruch Krew, at his office, and demanded that the entry be corrected.[24] This incident, once it became known, alienated the few readers who were still interested in her work.

In 1945 Elisheva's collected poems were published, but the establishment critics did not pay much attention. As interest in her work was fading, the poems of another of the "mothers of Hebrew poetry" Rachel Blaustein, later known to generations of Israelis simply as "Rachel," were becoming immensely popular. But neither of these women would achieve the highest level of authorial prestige in the emerging Hebrew culture. That position was reserved for male authors alone. We do not know of Elisheva's reaction to the declaration of Israeli statehood in May 1948, though we can assume that she was as elated about it as were her fellow citizens. Her joy, however, was perhaps diluted by her failure to maintain her position as an important writer.

But Elisheva was not without friends. Poets and writers of her generation paid occasional visits to her Tel Aviv shack, but she did not encourage this socializing and the visits soon dropped off. She was not a bohemian; cafés and literary salons held no attraction for her. Her colleagues in the *Agudat Hasofrim*, the Hebrew writers' guild, made sure that her small stipend reached her, but they could not do much about her diminishing literary reputation. As Elisheva's daughter Mira remembered, "There were people who tried to help my mother, but she was a proud and hard woman, with strong principles. . . . She was very critical of others. It angered her that there was a lot of corruption in the country and that each person worried only about himself. It's no wonder that folks kept their distance from her."[25]

Israeli statehood, and the establishment of an official rabbinate, influenced Elisheva's fate. While "Jewishness" had been somewhat fluid and ill-defined under the British Mandate government, the Orthodox rabbis appointed by the new state now had the power to say who was and who was not a Jew. But it was not only the rabbis who wanted Jews and Judaism defined. The Nazis had been obsessed with defining Jews and "Aryans," and this obsession, with all of its murderous consequences, had a profound psychological effect on the members of the Yishuv and on Jews throughout the world. Definitions of "Jewishness" were now weighted with greater historical and political meanings. There was more at stake in the definition of a Jew than ever before. Elisheva, in her youth, had been attracted to the more universalistic aspects of Jewish life. But during and after World War II, she found these aspects diminished. As the question "Who is a Jew?" arose more frequently, universalism was no longer an option for most Jews, especially for the Jews of Palestine.

In Elisheva's case, the question "Who is a Jew?" played out in a bizarre way at her death. In 1949 Elisheva was planning to move to England and live with her daughter, Mira. Learning of this impending move, her friends in the writers' guild paid for Elisheva to go to Tiberias for a brief vacation at the town's famous hot springs. Despite her protestations and her tendency to alienate people, she still had some friends and admirers among these Hebrew writers. They hoped that resting in Tiberias would help her regain her strength before her long journey. But in Tiberias Elisheva took ill, and within a week her condition had deteriorated. When she went to the hospital complaining of weakness and chronic exhaustion, the doctors found her body riddled with cancer. She died soon afterwards in March 1949.

Her friends in the writers' guild sought to bury her in the cemetery of Kibbutz Kinneret, next to the poet Rachel Blaustein, who had been interred there in 1931. In keeping with Jewish custom, they wanted to bury her immediately—if not before the sun went down, then at least within twenty-four hours of her death. But the local rabbis protested. Elisheva was not Jewish according to the Orthodox definition of the term. Therefore, she could not be buried in a Jewish cemetery.

In 1955, six years after Elisheva's death, the question of "Who can be buried as a Jew?" would arise in a more public and painful manner with the Steinberg case. When a six-year-old Israeli boy whose mother was not Jewish died after a long-lingering illness, the rabbinate told his immigrant parents that they could bury their child in a fenced-off plot only at the edge of the local Jewish cemetery. This heart-breaking story with its rich and disturbing religious and cultural resonances would catch the attention of the local and international media and ultimately heighten *dati-hiloni* (religious-secular) tensions within Israel.[26] More than half a century later, how and where one is buried in the State of Israel remains a contentious issue. Religious authorities (Jewish, Muslim, or Christian) continue to administer and determine burial rites, much as they oversee other civil aspects of life like marriage and divorce. Some secular Israelis have advocated for civil burial, much as they have advocated for civil marriage, but they have yet to carry the day. Only in the last few years have non-denominational cemeteries begun to appear.

Only after the intervention of several major establishment literary figures, among them Asher Barash and Yaakov Fichman, did the Tiberias rabbis relent and allow Elisheva's burial service to proceed. *Davar*, the Yishuv's semi-official newspaper, did not mention this scandal in its obituary of "the poet Elisheva." Rather, it presented the funeral as a dignified and significant event: "The funeral procession of the poet Elisheva began at the Schweitzer Hospital in Tiberias. The casket, covered with flowers, was accompanied by members of the city council, members of the workers guild, and teachers from the local schools. At 5 p.m. the casket reached the Kinneret Cemetery, where a grave had been dug next to that of the poet Rachel. At the open grave, poet Anda Finkerfeld read Elisheva's poem 'Kinneret.' Abraham Broides read a eulogy and took leave of Elisheva in the name of the Hebrew Writers Guild. The children of both Degania Kibbutzim, accompanied by their teachers, placed a wreath on the poet's grave. Representing the agriculture settlements, L. Ben Ammitai eulogized Elisheva. One of the local workers recited the kaddish."[27] It is interesting to note the fusion of the secular (wreaths, flowers) and the religious (reciting the kaddish, the traditional memorial prayer). Eleven months later, as is the Ashkenazi Jewish custom, a tombstone was placed at Elisheva's grave. The inscription reads simply, "Elisheva Bikhovsky, Poet." Thus for many decades, when Elisheva was remembered at all, it was as a poet. Her prose, and especially her novel *Simtaot*, seemed consigned to literary oblivion.

The emergence of the Israeli feminist movement in the 1970s and 1980s would rectify this situation. Israeli feminist critics made a concerted effort to recover "lost" works of Hebrew literature written by women. This effort led to the rediscovery of the "mothers of Hebrew poetry," though the most popular, Rachel, had never left the public consciousness. Rachel's poems were set to music and became hit recordings. In addition to the rediscovery of Elisheva's poetry, Israeli feminists featured her novel *Simtaot*, the first modern Hebrew novel by a woman, as an early feminist manifesto. Literary critic Yaffah Berlovitz best demonstrated the feminist enthusiasm for Elisheva's work with her observation that the republication of *Simtaot* "reveals a creative diversity that enriched modern Hebrew poetry and prose with a feminine voice all its own—a voice that offered not only content and range but an inner rhythm with its own unique meter and cadence."[28]

Elisheva's divided soul sprang from a cultural conflict, not a religious conflict. Elisheva and her husband Shimon Bikhovsky had adopted a secular Hebrew culture, a culture they hoped would overcome Jewish-Christian religious difference. But their naïve expectations were not fulfilled. At the time of Elisheva's death, a year after the establishment of the State of Israel, religious difference still mattered greatly—even to those Israeli Jews who professed a secularist and universalist ideology. Over the subsequent decades of Israeli history, they would matter even more. The enthusiasm with which Elisheva and her literary works were met in the 1920s had by the late 1940s turned into ambivalence, hostility, or worst of all, indifference. In turn Elisheva's ambivalence toward her adopted home and culture—Israel and Hebrew literature—came to define her life, directly and tragically.

While Elisheva had no interest in religion, powerful religious impulses would come to motivate the protagonist of our next chapter, Oswald Rufeisen of Poland. He, too, immigrated to Palestine, and like Elisheva found that he "had two souls" within him. We shall see how he managed to reconcile these two souls, and to both inspire and irritate many people in the process.

NOTES

1. On writers and their 'wounds' see Wilson, *The Wound and the Bow*.
2. Bikhovsky, *Simtaot*, 297, n. 11.
3. Ibid., 298.
4. Ibid.
5. Bikhovsky, *Poet and man; Essay on the Poetry of Alexander Blok*, 1.
6. Berlovitz, "Elisheva Bichovsky."
7. Brenner, article/book, page.
8. On the "Ruth" theme see Miron, *Founding Mothers, Stepsisters*, 190–91.
9. Miron, *Founding Mothers, Stepsisters*, 189.
10. Bikhovsky, *Simtaot*, 287.
11. Negev, *Intimate Conversations*, 7.
12. Olmert, "Afterword" in *Simtaot* (2008 ed.), 350.
13. Ibid.
14. Berlovitz, "Elisheva Bichovsky."
15. Miron, *Founding Mothers, Stepsisters*, 193–194; Olmert, "Afterword," in *Simtaot* (2008 ed.), 353.
16. Raisin, *Great Jews I Have Known*, 239.
17. Bikhovsky, "In Memory of H. N. Bialik," 1.
18. Quoted in Kinel, "Lo Haya Li."
19. Miron, *Founding Mothers, Stepsisters*, 188.
20. Bikhovsky, article/book title, page.
21. Bikhovsky, *Poet and man; Essay on the Poetry of Alexander Blok*, 363.
22. Negev, *Intimate Conversations*, 11.
23. Raisin, *Great Jews I Have Known*, 239.
24. Toren, *Elisheva: The Collected Poems*, 3.
25. Negev, *Intimate Conversations*, 14.
26. On the Steinberg case see Weiner, *The Wild Gates of Ein Gedi*, 1–7.
27. "The poet Elisheva."
28. Berlovitz, "Elisheva Bichovsky."

Chapter Seven

Apostasy and Citizenship: The Case of Brother Daniel (Oswald Rufeisen, 1922–1998)

In the struggle over the definition of modern Jewish identity, Oswald Rufeisen (1922–1998), later known as Brother Daniel, is a pivotal figure. The case
that Rufeisen took to the Israeli High Court of Justice in 1962 brought the
elusive question of "Jewishness" to Israeli and world public attention in a
new and startling manner. The court's decision greatly influenced both Israeli law and Israeli public opinion. Historian Michael Stanislawski has called
the Rufeisen case "a fundamental episode in the history of the Jewish state"[1]
With the story of Oswald Rufeisen's remarkable life as the necessary backdrop, this chapter demonstrates the validity of Stanislawski's assertion.

The Rufeisen decision continues to influence Israeli and Jewish identity.
From the vantage point of 2015, more than a half-century after the Israeli
High Court ruled on the case, it is now apparent that the decision has helped
to shape the recent history of Israel and of the Jewish people. The court's
decision to deny Israeli citizenship under the Law of Return to the Carmelite
monk Brother Daniel had implications for three of the central questions
addressed in this book: Who is a Jew?; What is the relationship between
religious identity and citizenship?; and What is the state of Christian-Jewish
relations—more specifically Catholic-Jewish relations—in the post–World
War II world?

EARLY YEARS

Growing up in the 1920s in Zadziele, a small town in southwestern Poland, Oswald Rufeisen was one of the few Jewish children in his elementary school. The other children were Polish or German Catholics. The Rufeisens kept a kosher kitchen, and Oswald's father Elias went to synagogue on Saturday mornings. The Rufeisen family's commitment to Jewish religious practice consisted of marking the Shabbath and following the dietary laws, but not much more. This degree of observance was not uncommon for the place and time. It situated the Rufeisens in the continuum between strict Orthodox observance of Jewish law and assertive secular rejection of that law. Oswald's Hebrew name was Shmuel, but he was known both at home and at school as Oswald. His brother Aryeh, also known as Ernest, was two years younger. Unlike the more introverted Ernest, Oswald was outgoing and athletic. From an early age he took up horse-back riding, then a very popular sport among Polish youths. Among young Jews, however, riding horses was not so popular. As Oswald's contemporary, the writer Isaac Babel, has one of his fictional characters note, "When a Jew gets on a horse, he ceases being a Jew and becomes a Cossack."

When he was a little boy, Oswald's parents had run a not-too-successful tavern. Later they owned a local general store. By the time Oswald and Ernest became aware of their father's profession he had become a middleman between peasant woodcutters and the local lumber mill. As this proved an exceedingly difficult way to make a living, the elder Rufeisen decided to move to a larger town and try to establish a business there. Neither town had a large enough Jewish community to warrant a Jewish school, so any Jewish religious instruction the young Rufeisen brothers received came directly from their parents. Like Aaron Lustiger's parents, Polish Jews who had moved to Paris in the early 1920s, Oswald's parents educated their children in Jewish folkways, but not in the Jewish textual tradition. Neither Rufeisen nor Lustiger received a traditional Orthodox Jewish education. For each of these Polish Jewish converts, the introduction to a life structured around religious practice would come from the study and practice of Catholicism.

In Zadziele's one-room schoolhouse the day began with Catholic prayers. Joining his classmates in these prayers, Oswald saw no reason to be excused from what seemed to him a rote exercise devoid of significance. Nor did his parents raise any objections to this morning ritual. That Oswald would some-day recite and eventually teach these prayers to others would have seemed inconceivable both to him and to his parents. Reflecting on his childhood relationship to religion, Oswald later wrote, "I was not a pious Jew but I was deeply religious. . . . As a child I wanted to know the truth. Already by eight or so, I began to pray to God and asked to meet someone very wise who would be able to lead me to the truth."[2] Oswald was contrasting the piety of

Orthodox Jews he knew with what we might today call "spirituality"—a sense of the sacred outside of the clearly defined rules of religious ritual.

Always a bright student, Oswald was soon ready for high school. His parents arranged for him to attend a Polish government school in a neighboring town. In that school too, Jews were a minority, but not as small a minority as they had been in the Zadziele grammar school. Oswald did well in high school and ranked among the school's best students. He excelled in the study of languages, mastering German. Paradoxically, it was in this Polish school that he encountered Jewish education for the first time. The government school provided weekly religious instruction; a priest taught the Catholic students and a rabbi taught the Jewish students. Through this religious instruction Oswald was first exposed to Zionism. He and his brother became ardent supporters of a Jewish state in Palestine and joined *Akiva*, the local chapter of a Zionist youth organization. In its ranks they studied Hebrew and considered settling in Palestine, a possibility made all the more urgent by the rise of anti-Semitism in 1930s Poland.

So far, this account of a Polish Jewish childhood in the early twentieth century is not unusual. But Oswald Rufeisen's story would be anything but prosaic. His intellectual and social abilities were preparing him for a remarkable life. To his Jewish and Catholic high school friends, however, Oswald did not seem at the time like a person fated to lead such an extraordinary life. Jacob Rubenfeld, who was Rufeisen's leader in the *Akiva* youth group, remembered him as "a good boy and a good friend, well behaved . . . I never would have predicted that he would become something extraordinary, a hero or anything like that."[3] For his friends and associates, Oswald's very kindness, displayed in many acts of consideration, made him an unlikely candidate for heroism in a time of war.

THE GERMAN OCCUPATION

When the Nazis invaded Poland on September 1, 1939, many Jews, Communists, and other anti-Fascists fled east into the areas occupied by the Russian Army. The Rufeisen brothers and their parents quickly fled Zadziele. After two days on the road along with thousands of other refugees, the elder Rufeisens, exhausted and terrified, turned back to their hometown. They did not have the strength to escape from the Germans, but they insisted that Oswald and Ernest continue without them. A few months later the German invaders would deport the elder Rufeisens to Auschwitz, where they would be murdered. Oswald and Ernest eventually reached the Lithuanian city of Vilna. In Vilna, Oswald and Ernest lived in the *Akiva* movement's "Urban Kibbutz," a communal apartment in the Jewish section of the city. The brothers were active and enthusiastic members of the kibbutz and often aided more desperate refugees. They spent a year and a half in Vilna, from December 1939 to June 1941.

In Vilna, Oswald apprenticed himself to a local Jewish shoemaker. In this way he learned the trade that would soon save his life. Through connections in the Zionist Youth Movement, Ernest, his younger brother, received a much-coveted young person's visa for Palestine. With this visa Ernest could escape the Germans; he arrived in Palestine at the beginning of 1941. At age nineteen Oswald was too old for an emigration certificate. He remained in Vilna and was in the city when the Germans attacked on June 22, 1941. The Germans had broken the Hitler-Stalin Pact and advanced on Russia with an army of more than two million soldiers. As part of "Operation Barbarossa," the German invasion of the Soviet Union, the Germans now directly targeted Jews in the Russian territories for extermination. In the wake of the invasion, the Russian army left Vilna, along with many civilians who feared capture by the Germans, and fled to the East.

The local police who were collaborating with the German occupiers soon apprehended Oswald and his companions as they were fleeing Vilna. The police arrested this small group and took them to prison, where a German S. S. officer interviewed each of the prisoners. When asked his profession, nineteen-year-old Oswald was unsure of what to say. Afraid to show uncertainty or hesitation he blurted out "shoemaker." As he had been apprenticing in that trade during the past few months in Vilna, the assertion had some truth to it.[4] Most of the Jewish prisoners did not possess skills useful to the Gestapo and so were summarily executed. But the Gestapo declared Oswald and a dozen or so of his shoemaker colleagues "Nutzlicher Juden," or "Necessary Jews." The implication was that all other Jews were "unnecessary" and doomed to extermination.

Whether he was deemed necessary or unnecessary, Oswald Rufeisen did not look like the Nazi caricature of "the Jew." He was athletic and carried himself like an outdoorsman, the result of his years of horseback riding. He was also fluent in German. The great irony here was that Oswald had perfected his German in the religious classes on Judaism offered in his Polish high school. These skills would not only help Oswald deceive the Nazis and survive the war, but also enable him to save many other people from the Nazis.

Oswald spent several months, from July to September of 1941, as a slave-laborer in a Gestapo prison near Vilna, before the Nazis decided to transfer him and other "necessary Jews" to a different prison. During this transfer, Oswald and a friend managed to escape. As he spoke fluent German and did not fit the Nazi stereotype of a Jew, Rufeisen was able to "pass" as a Pole. He destroyed his "Nutzlicher Juden" document and his Star of David armband. At this point Rufeisen made a daring, and one might stay, astounding move. Having heard from escapees and refugees that German officers in the occupying forces were in dire need of Polish translators, Oswald offered his services as a translator to an officer of the local military police in the Russian town of Mir. Interrogated about his ethnic origins, he identified himself as a Volksdeutsche, a Pole of German origin. He knew that he was walking into a veritable lion's den. Two weeks before Oswald arrived in Mir, German soldiers had murdered some fifteen hundred of the town's two thousand five hundred Jews. The remaining Jews had been herded into a ghetto in the ruins of the town's castle.

From November 1941 through August 1942, as the Nazi extermination machine operated at full power, Rufeisen "hid in the open" in an official position. He served as a translator and interpreter for the local police chief and was soon asked to serve as the secretary of the regional police.[5] As Rufeisen was working as a translator for German officers they issued him an S. S. uniform and identity card, which gave him access to all restricted areas, including the ghetto where the surviving Jews of Mir lived under terrible conditions. With his "Aryan" appearance and linguistic abilities in Polish and German, Rufeisen remained undetected for nine months, during which time he was able to work against his German commanders and their local collaborators. The local Polish police enforced the occupiers' anti-Jewish regulations with little German supervision. In Rufeisen's most heroic action during this period he warned the Jews of the Mir ghetto that the Germans had ordered their "liquidation."

Rufeisen's anti-Nazi activities were not limited to saving fellow-Jews. He did all he could to warn all opponents of the German occupation, including the Communists in Mir, of impending actions against them. In December 1941 Oswald helped save forty Russian army prisoners who were incarcerated in the town. He informed his superiors that as these prisoners were weak and demoralized the guards could relax their watch and reduce the number on duty. This ruse enabled all forty prisoners to escape.[6]

But Rufeisen could not save all of the people imprisoned by the Nazis in the Mir area. He was present when the police murdered individual Jews. He told an Israeli TV interviewer in 1984 that on three occasions he had had to translate execution orders from German to Polish and then stand by and witness the executions. But, in the impossible situation in which he found himself, complicity in these smaller crimes made his superiors trust him and this trust enabled him to prevent a larger crime, the elimination of all of the remaining Jews in Mir. Rufeisen provided the resistance fighters in the Mir ghetto with guns and ammunition from German supplies, which they used to organize a breakout. More than three hundred Jews escaped.[7] Unfortunately, hundreds of others did not dare break out and so remained in the ghetto, where they were soon murdered.

The police suspected that the escapees from the Mir ghetto had received inside assistance. A jealous associate in the police department betrayed Rufeisen, and the local authorities arrested him. When his commanding officer asked Rufeisen if he had warned the Jewish Partisans of the intended German *aktion*, Rufeisen admitted as much and confessed to being a Jew. As Rufeisen later recalled, "When he accused me, I couldn't answer. But then I did. I was satisfied that I had saved the Jews of Mir. I admitted that I was a Jew."[8] Oswald's commanding officer had taken a liking to his young translator and decided not to betray him to the Germans. Despite Rufeisen's transgression, the officer allowed him to escape. In August 1942, Rufeisen fled to a Catholic convent not far from the police station, where he received sanctuary.[9]

CONVERSION: BECOMING A POPULAR LOCAL PRIEST

Rufeisen spent a little over a year in the Catholic convent, which was associated with the Carmelite Order. When German officers searched the nunnery, Rufeisen would hide. In November 1943, he left the convent to join the local partisans. Outwardly, Rufeisen seemed unchanged, but inwardly he had been transformed. While in hiding. he came to believe in Jesus as the Messiah and decided to become a Christian. Baptized only three weeks after he arrived, Rufeisen left the convent a practicing Catholic.

What had prepared Rufeisen for this transformation? In later interviews, he alluded to his need to see the miraculous in the "world at war" around him. During his refuge in the convent, he came across a Polish Catholic periodical with an illustrated article on the pilgrimage to Lourdes. Studying the photos in the article and reading the accounts of pilgrims who had been healed there, Oswald came to believe that miraculous cures were real. At the same time he was reading and rereading the Gospels. Jesus's healing miracles and the miracles at Lourdes converged in his mind. Oswald was looking for signs of the miraculous, and in the darkness of the surrounding war he found them.

In letters sent to his brother Ernest after the war Oswald attempted to convey the strength of his new religious convictions and the power of the war-time experiences that led him to become a Christian. Reading the accounts of healing at Lourdes in conjunction with studying the New Testament was at the center of his conversion account. He told his brother, "The New Testament is a holy scripture, written almost exclusively by Jews, the disciples of Jesus Christ, and almost in its entirety, without changes, preserved till our time. It was not easy to believe it, but now I am ready to give my life for this truth."[10]

Almost forty years after his conversion, in an interview with the author Nechama Tec, Rufeisen related his first reading of the New Testament to his sense of attachment to the Land of Israel. For Rufeisen, as for many other Christians of his day, the Land of Israel was Jesus's land. The Zionism of his youth was now transformed from a political program to an idea based on Christian religious belief. Oswald believed in the idea of a Jewish return to Zion, but it was now a return to Zion in which Jesus had fulfilled Jewish messianic yearnings. Previously Rufeisen's Jewish Zionism had been a secular ideology; now his Zionism was anchored in Christian belief.

Conversion accounts often focus on a previously unknown scripture, which once read, moves the reader to discover and adopt a new set of beliefs. The seeking reader discovers a text that was previously inaccessible or forbidden in his own religious culture. Among the examples in this book are Donato Manduzio, whom we met in chapter 4, who turned to Judaism upon reading an Italian translation of the Old Testament, and Rabbi Israel Zolli of Rome, whom we met in chapter 5, who turned to Christianity upon reading the New Testament.

Remembering his first months in the convent at Mir, Rufeisen said, "I felt very much like a Jew, I identified with the plight of my people. I also felt like a Zionist. I longed for Palestine, for my own country. In this frame of mind I became exposed to the New Testament, a book that describes events that were taking place in my fatherland, the land I was longing for. This, in itself, must have created a psychological bridge between me and the New Testament."[11] There is a paradox here: it was the New Testament that encouraged Rufeisen's Zionist yearnings. Generally, the Hebrew Bible/Old Testament inspired in modern Jewish readers a sense of attachment to the land in which the biblical narratives took place. This also tended to be true for Christian readers. For Rufeisen, as for Lustiger and our two other Jewish converts to Christianity, reading the Old Testament and the New Testament as a single unit led to the realization that there was a bridge between the two scriptures. The New Testament awakened sympathy for Zionism by instilling a yearning for the landscape of Israel, where Jesus had lived and taught.

Reading the New Testament had a stunning effect on Oswald Rufeisen. He wrote to his brother, "In the convent, all alone, among strangers, I created an artificial world for myself. I pretended that the two thousand years never happened. In this make-believe world of mine I am confronted by Jesus from Nazareth.... If you will not understand this, you will not understand my struggle for the right to my Jewish nationality. Soon I begin to move more and more towards the position taken by Jesus. I find myself agreeing with Jesus's approach and view of Judaism. His sermons appeal to me strongly. In this process I somehow disregard all that happened later in the relationship between the Jews and the Christians."[12]

Explaining to an interviewer why the figure of Jesus appealed to his religious sensibilities, Rufeisen said, "I always wanted to know a truly beautiful person, someone I could rely on and who would tell me what to do. When I read the New Testament I cried all day and felt that I had leaped back two thousand years. I came to believe in miracles, and I asked for a miracle. I wept, and prayed, and then asked to be baptized. So I became a *meshummad*, an apostate, and was granted a new life. I decided to dedicate my life to Jesus."[13]

Rufeisen remained in the convent from August 1942 to November 1943. From November 1943 to August 1944 he fought with the Bielski Partisans, who were situated in the vast Nalibocki forest of western Belorussia/White Russia.[14] In August 1944, the partisan groups enthusiastically welcomed the Russian troops who liberated White Russia.[15] After the war, Oswald joined the Carmelite Monastery in Cracow. The Polish Provincial of the Order suggested that Rufeisen take the name Daniel because "he had been like Daniel in the lion's den and survived." From 1945 to 1949 Rufeisen lived as a monk in Cracow, taking his final (lifelong) vows in 1949. He was twenty-seven years old at the time.

Following their separation in Vilna in 1941, Ernest Rufeisen, who had immigrated to Palestine, had no idea if his brother Oswald was alive or dead. In 1945 Oswald wrote to Ernest of his wartime experiences and of his conversion to Christianity while in the convent.[16] A year after he joined the Carmelite Monastery in Cracow, Rufeisen embarked on the course of study to prepare himself for the Catholic priesthood. In 1952, at the age of thirty, he was ordained as a priest.[17] This was the same period in which Aaron Lustiger, another converted Jew whom we met in chapter 3, was studying for the priesthood in France. Lustiger was ordained a year later, in 1953. Oswald/Brother Daniel asked that his ordination ceremony be held in his home town of Zadziele, despite the fact that his parents, who had been the only Jewish couple in the town, had been deported from there to Auschwitz and murdered. At the time of his ordination there were no Jews living in Zadziele. Oswald would now return to his parents' home town as the only Jew—and as the town's newly-ordained Catholic priest.

Oswald's superior, the head of the Cracow Monastery, feared that the local Catholic population would object to the ordination of a Jew as a priest. But Rufeisen persisted in his insistence that the ceremony be held in his home town. To the surprise of the Church hierarchy, the local residents celebrated the ordination with great enthusiasm. From the time of his ordination until 1959 Rufeisen served as a popular local priest. His local fame led to invitations to preach throughout the Catholic churches of Poland.

ISRAEL, THE STELLA MARIS MONASTERY, AND A HEBREW CHURCH

Though a respected and beloved priest in Poland, Brother Daniel never gave up his dream of living in the Land of Israel. He had become a Catholic priest, but he remained a Zionist. On a number of occasions during his years as a priest in Poland he had requested that the Carmelite authorities allow him to move to the order's monastery in Haifa. But they always deferred or declined his requests. In an early-1950s application to the Polish government for permission to travel overseas Rufeisen wrote that he was "requesting permission to travel to Israel for permanent residence and also for a passport. I base this application on the ground of my belonging to the Jewish people, which I have continued to do although I embraced the Catholic faith in 1942 and joined a monastic order in 1945. . . . I chose an order which has a chapter in Israel, having regard to the fact that I would receive leave from my superiors to travel to the land for which I have yearned since my childhood when I was a member of the Zionist Youth Organization. . . . I fully believe that by emigrating I shall be able to serve Poland which I love with all my heart, by helping her sons scattered all over the globe and in particular those who are in the land to which I am going."[18] In 1958, after years of Oswald's importuning, the Carmelite authorities and the Polish Government agreed to his request, but he still had to convince the Israeli authorities to admit him.[19] In addition to the difficulties of obtaining permission from the Polish authorities and the Catholic Church to settle in Israel, Rufeisen was anxious about his reception by the Israeli authorities and public. He knew that the Jewish state would not readily welcome a Jewish Catholic Priest.

Rufeisen, who followed Israeli current events from his parish in Poland, was concerned about immigrating to Israel at a time when the question of Jewish identity was so much in the public eye. In 1958, the question of "Who is a Jew?" was the cause of a parliamentary crisis in Israel, and it was generating a great deal of public discussion, debate, and argument. The 1952 Law of Return granted citizenship to anyone who was a "member of the Jewish people." Promulgated against the background of the *Shoah*, the law specified requirements for membership in the Jewish collective that were not based on religion. Rather, the definition of Jewishness was a reaction to the criteria that the Nazis had used to persecute and murder Jews. If a person "returning" to Israel had at least one Jewish grandparent, he or she was entitled to citizenship under the Law of Return.

In 1959, Rufeisen arrived at the Israeli port of Haifa in his Carmelite monk's cassock and asked to be granted citizenship under the Law of Return. Could a Catholic monk be considered a Jew? There had been and would continue to be incidents in which a particular immigrant's status as a Jew was in doubt, but no other legal case would frame the question of Jewish identity so starkly. Israeli government officials refused Rufeisen's request for citizenship. They agreed to give him a one year residence permit. Thus, for a time Rufeisen was officially stateless, a "man without a country." He had spent the past sixteen years as a Polish citizen and devout Catholic, and the past six years as a monk in the Carmelite order. He was now poised to encounter— and to influence—the State of Israel and the world at large.

Rufeisen, "determined to challenge the meaning of the Law of Return, approached the Ministry of the Interior."[20] The ministry agreed to admit him to the country and offered him naturalization, a process that would lead to full citizenship within a few years. But Rufeisen had something other than "naturalization" in mind. He insisted that the State of Israel, under the terms of the Law of Return, accept him as a Jew despite his conversion to Catholicism and his vocation as a priest. As historian Michael Stanislawski has noted, "Brother Daniel was committed to receiving public and legal sanction for his deeply held belief that he was indeed a Jew—a Jew by nationality and a Catholic by religion; this was, he claimed, totally in line with the basic Zionist redefinition of Jewishness as a nationality like all other nationalities, entirely independent of religious commitment."[21] What Rufeisen did not understand was that Zionism's "redefinition" of Jewishness was not complete or total. It was in fact not independent of religious commitment at all. The state's political leadership was secular, but traditional ideas about Jewish identity still held sway. Decades later, Rufeisen recalled a poignant conversation with Israeli government officials: "The interior minister, Moshe Haim Shapira, invited me to talk. I had an hour-long conversation with him, his juridical counsel and the ministry's director general. He offered me citizenship, but told me, 'Don't go to the High Court, because not everybody will understand. They'll see it as discrimination against a baptized Jew.'" As journalist David B. Green noted in 1998, the problem for Moshe Haim Shapira "was not personal resentment of Daniel, but rather the question [still with us] of who is a Jew, and what was to be the identity of the Jewish state."[22]

When Rufeisen arrived in Haifa, his brother Ernest/Aryeh, who had immigrated to Palestine at the beginning of the war, welcomed him. Before leaving Poland, Rufeisen had made contact with monks of the Carmelite order who resided in Haifa. He intended to establish residence in the Stella Maris Monastery. But the Carmelite Monastery in Haifa would not be an escape from the world; rather, Rufeisen would use the monastery as his base of operations in a campaign to serve as a Catholic priest and yet be accepted as a Jew in the Jewish state.

The Carmelite monastery in Haifa is located on a peak in the Carmel mountain range, overlooking the Mediterranean. Many centuries before the first monastery was established there, this peak was a sacred site. In the Biblical Book of Kings we read of Elijah's defending the worship of the God of Israel over that of the Canaanite god Baal. In a dramatic contest held on Mount Carmel, Elijah confronted four hundred prophets of Baal and four hundred prophets of the goddess Asherah. Elijah as the prophet of the God of Israel triumphed over them, establishing the God of Israel as the true god. This narrative is situated in the ninth century B.C.E. during the reign of the Israelite rulers Ahab and Jezebel. Later, the Greeks too worshipped at the site. The historian Tacitus mentions an oracle on Carmel that the general Vespasian consulted before his campaign against Judea in 70 C.E.

Crusader Knights established the Carmelite order in the twelfth century, settling near the traditional cave of Elijah on Mount Carmel. After the fall of the Crusader Kingdom in Palestine the order moved to France and England. It did not return to Mount Carmel until the mid-seventeenth century. It was this monastery that Brother Daniel was to join upon his arrival in Israel.

A legend that circulated in seventeenth- and eighteenth-century England, "asserted that Elijah established a community of hermits on Mount Carmel, and that this community existed without break until the Christian era and was nothing else than a Jewish Carmelite order, to which belonged the Sons of the Prophets and the Essenes. Members of it were present at St. Peter's first sermon on Pentecost and were converted, and built a chapel on Mt. Carmel in honor of the Blessed Virgin Mary, who, as well as the apostles, enrolled herself in the order."[23] In the nineteenth century, Church historians debunked these tales, but the emphasis on "Jewish Carmelites" is remarkable when we consider some of the figures who joined the order, including not only St. John of the Cross and St. Teresa of Avila, both sixteenth century descendants of Spanish Jewish families, but also twentieth century Jewish converts Edith Stein (St. Teresa Benedicta), Elias Friedman, Oswald Rufeisen, and Aaron Lustiger.

Rufeisen did not intend to live a life of monastic seclusion in the Stella Maris Monastery. He wished to engage with the larger Israeli society and to minister to those "Hebrew Catholics" in the Haifa area who were in need of a Polish-speaking priest. In the late-1950s and early-1960s there were thousands of Eastern European Catholic residents in Israel, many of them Polish women married to Jewish men. There were also Romanians, Czechs, Bulgarians and other in the same situation.[24] Before Rufeisen's arrival in Haifa there had been one Polish-speaking Catholic priest who served in the area. This priest often expressed anti-Semitic prejudices, and his parishioners yearned for someone more sympathetic to their situation as Catholics married to Jewish spouses.

Rufeisen soon realized that modern Hebrew was the common language among his parishioners, and he established a special ministry for these believers. In a 1980s interview Rufeisen recalled, "Eventually, as I worked with these people, I found Hebrew as a common language for all of them. From this grew the idea of a Hebrew Church. This was a gradual evolutionary development."[25] In 2015, this Hebrew Catholic vicariate in Israel has grown to include thousands of members, many of whom are Israeli-born. It is led by Father David Neuhaus S.J., a Jewish convert to Catholicism.[26]

When Brother Daniel arrived at the Stella Maris Monastery in 1959, there were fifteen monks in residence. Brother Daniel, however, was not the only converted Jew among them. Father Elias Friedman, a Jewish physician from

South Africa, had converted to Catholicism while serving in the South African Army during World War II. Like Brother Daniel, Friedman had joined the Carmelite order. He arrived at Stella Maris in 1954 and had been living there for five years when Brother Daniel arrived from Poland.

As monks in the Haifa monastery, both Friedman and Rufeisen could fulfill their Zionist aspirations and their monastic vows. Each man saw himself as ministering to both Jews and Christians, but in different ways. Friedman sought to organize a distinctively Jewish community within the Catholic Church that would remain "Jewish" in perpetuity. Rufeisen too had a Jewish-Christian synthesis in mind, though of a different sort. As he explained to journalist David Green, "I am not missionizing. But I think that for those people who came to Israel who are not Jewish, if they wish to remain Christian, we must help them. We who are inside must help them find a form that can be eventually accepted."[27]

The purpose of Friedman's Hebrew-Catholic association was to create a "community framework" for Jewish converts to the Catholic Church. Friedman argued that a Jew resists conversion because of the Church's current "regime of assimilation, which systematically ignores the specific elements of his identity." Jews therefore "perceive the regime of assimilation as an expression of gentile contempt for Jewish identity and a real menace to their historical survival." Father Friedman proposed a community within which "the convert would be free to develop his new identity in harmonious continuity with his past, to assure the Hebrew education of his children and God willing, to establish a mutually beneficial relation with the Jewish People."[28] The Israeli authorities had little tolerance for Friedman's approach, as they considered it missionary activity on the part of the Catholic Church. The Israeli government was interested in bringing apostates back to Judaism, not in facilitating the apostasy of Israeli Jews to Catholicism. Friedman, though a more systematic thinker than Rufeisen, did not influence Israeli Jewish society in the way that Rufeisen, as an activist, did. In March of 2010 when I visited the Stella Maris Monastery in Haifa, I asked one of the resident monks, Father John Landy, how these two very different personalities, Brother Daniel and Father Elias Friedman, had gotten along. He replied, "Two Jews in a Monastery? They argued all the time!"

THE LAW OF RETURN AND THE FIGHT FOR ISRAELI CITIZENSHIP

The Israeli officials who first looked into Rufeisen's application for citizenship were well aware of the difficulties Rufeisen would face if he pressed his case to be accepted as a Jew and granted citizenship under the Law of Return. They advised him to work with the Ministry of Interior to find a less public way to achieve Israeli citizenship. Looking back at the case from the vantage point of the early twenty-first century, when questioning the parameters of Israeli Jewish identity is much more common, we can appreciate Ernest/ Aryeh Rufeisen's comment that it was too early in Israeli history to challenge accepted notions of Israeli identity. "Aryeh Rufeisen warned his brother that the country was not ready for such a move and that he was born at least fifty years too early."[29] Speaking to an interviewer in the 1980s Brother Daniel concurred with his brother's judgment.

The year before Brother Daniel arrived in Israel, the Israeli government had clarified the Law of Return in a way that limited its application and made Rufeisen's case more difficult to advance. On July 20, 1958 the Israeli government, referring to the debate about the definition of Jewish nationality, stated, "Anyone declaring in good faith that he is a Jew, *and who does not profess any other religion*, shall be registered as a Jew."[30] The statement arose from a case in which Israeli parents, a Jewish father and a non-Jewish mother, wished to have their child registered as a Jew. The Ministry of the Interior rejected the request, because the mother was not Jewish and had not converted to Judaism. But Haim Cohn, chief legal counsel to Prime Minister Ben Gurion at the time and one of the authors of the Law of Return, decided that because both parents agreed on the child's religious identity (and under Israeli Law a wife's opinion is as relevant as that of a husband's) the child should be registered as a Jew by the state.[31]

Cohn's decision ignited a parliamentary crisis. The Orthodox parties, offended by the challenge to rabbinic law, according to which a child could be considered Jewish only if the mother was Jewish, threatened to leave the government coalition. The parties defused the situation with an odd sort of compromise: Israeli identity cards would have separate spaces for "religion" and "nationality."[32] This "solution" soon became the basis of additional dissension and confusion. If the Law of Return was amended so that anyone who had "professed another religion" would be excluded, then Rufeisen, as a monk and a priest, would surely be excluded. He knew this, and for this reason decided to challenge the law.

Haim Cohn would be a key figure in the Brother Daniel case. As mentioned earlier, Cohn, as Ben Gurion's legal counsel, had been one of the authors of the 1950 Law of Return. Raised in an Orthodox Jewish home in Germany, Cohn underwent a conversion experience almost as radical as that of Oswald Rufeisen. Cohn had come to British Mandate Palestine as an Orthodox Jew planning to study in the Hebron Yeshiva, the most rigorous of Talmudic academies, but soon after his arrival he transformed himself into an assertively secular Jew. During his long and productive career in the legal profession, Cohn helped create and shape a new Israeli Jewish secularism. By the time Brother Daniel's case came to court in 1962, Haim Cohn had become not just a major figure in Israeli legal affairs, but an Israeli Supreme

Court justice. He has been described as "arguably the most controversial, complex, and creative jurist in Israeli history."[33]

Brother Daniel's conversion to Catholicism, which took place in 1942, brought him before the Israeli Supreme Court in 1962. Haim Cohn's "conversion" to secularism and his advancement in the legal profession brought him to serve on that Supreme Court. In 1930s Palestine, Cohn and many other Jewish intellectuals had become convinced of the historical necessity to create "the new Jew." The new Jew had to jettison the burden of rabbinic law and create a revolutionary new "Hebrew" culture, one that would replace traditional Jewish religious culture. For Cohn, as a student and practitioner of Western law, this meant formulating a new "Hebrew Law," in contrast to "Jewish law" with its rabbinic underpinnings. In his dissenting opinion on the Brother Daniel case, Cohn, like Rufeisen, was at least fifty years ahead of his time.

Rufeisen's request to be accepted as a Jew under the Law of Return came before the Israeli High Court in March of 1962, two months after the conclusion of the Eichmann trial. Eichmann had been sentenced to death by hanging, but he was entitled to an appeal, which was also before the court at this time. Though there were no official or legal connections between the two cases, there were circumstantial, psychological, and emotional connections. As Michael Stanislawski has noted, "It was inevitable, then, that the Rufeisen case would be played out against the backdrop of the Eichmann case with its unprecedented detailing before the Israeli public of the history of anti-Semitism and the particulars of the mass murders of the Jews."[34] Formally, Rufeisen's suit was against the Minister of the Interior, "asking for an order to compel him to grant the certificate and to issue the identity card" which would identify Rufeisen as a Jew.[35] Informally, on an emotional level, Rufeisen's case overlapped the Eichmann trial. Rufeisen, who had saved hundreds of Jews from the Nazis, was well-known for his heroic deeds. When he settled in Israel, the Jewish survivors of the German *aktion* in Mir, who had been saved by Rufeisen's deception of his superior officers, celebrated his arrival and welcomed him warmly.

It was difficult for Rufeisen to find legal counsel. Lawyers that he approached saw little chance that the judges would decide in his favor. Reading the accounts of Rufeisen's efforts one gets the sense that his was very much a one-man campaign, one he embarked upon without financial or organizational support of any kind. He needed the permission of his superiors at the Stella Maris Monastery to take the case to court, permission they eventually granted. His friends, among them Father Joseph Stiassny of Jerusalem's Ratisbonne Monastery, helped raise money to pay the two lawyers—the advocates Yaron and Kushnir, both affiliated with the Leftist Mapam party— who agreed to represent him.[36] For the lawyers and their political allies, the case was part of a larger struggle against the religious authorities at the

Ministry of Interior, who controlled aspects of Israeli life such as the registration of marriages, divorces, and funerals.

Rufeisen sought to set a precedent for other "Jewish Christians" who immigrated to Israel. They too should be eligible for citizenship under the Law of Return. Rufeisen knew that because of his prominence, his citizenship request could be fulfilled through a naturalization process, but other petitioners might not have the same advantages. In the mid-1990s, reflecting on the failure of his appeal to the Supreme Court, Rufeisen said, "My head was too hot at the time." But he did not express regret that he had taken his case to the highest court in the land. The controversy around the case had brought the issues of Israeli identity and Jewish-Christian difference into the court of public opinion, where they have remained for more than half a century.

THE ISRAELI SUPREME COURT

The five judges who presided at the hearing understood their job to be two-fold: first, "to define who is a Jew under the Law of Return," and then to decide whether Oswald Rufeisen/Brother Daniel fit that definition. The court spelled this out in its summary statement: "The question which the court now has to decide is: What does the word Jew in the Law of Return mean? Does it also include a Jew who has changed his religion, converted to Christianity and was baptized but feels himself and sees himself a Jew in spite of his conversion?"[37] Ultimately, the court rejected Brother Daniel's appeal by a four-to-one decision, concluding that a baptized Jew was no longer a Jew under the Law of Return and thus not eligible for citizenship.

Thus, the Ministry of the Interior would not be compelled to grant Rufeisen an identity card identifying him as a Jew. Judge Berenson in the majority opinion stated, "A Jew who changed his religion cannot be counted as a Jew in the sense and the spirit that the Knesset (Parliament) meant in the Law of Return and as it is accepted among our people today. I don't think that we the judges have the permission to be the pioneers in front of this whole nation and decide that which would be happening in the years to come. The law follows in the footsteps of life. Life does not follow in the footsteps of the law."[38]

Judge Berenson's last sentence may be an accurate description of civil law, but it is not an accurate description of rabbinic law. In rabbinic understanding, life follows in the footsteps of the law, though the law may at times be adjusted to the circumstances of life. But Berenson and the three judges who joined the majority opinion based their definition of a Jew not on rabbinic law, in which the child of a Jewish mother is deemed Jewish, but on the "sense and spirit that the Knesset meant in the Law of Return and as it is accepted among our people today."[39] In that sense, according to the judges' understanding of Israeli public opinion, a Jew who converted to Catholicism would not be considered a Jew.

Under a strict interpretation of rabbinic law, Brother Daniel's case might very well have been decided differently. His mother was Jewish; therefore, according to rabbinic law, there was no question; he was a Jew. "However, the justices unanimously rejected the relevance of religious law in considering the question before them. The term 'Jew' in the Law of Return, declared Justice Silberg, does not refer to the Jew of religious law, but to the Jew of secular law."[40] Rabbi Aaron Lichtenstein, a prominent Orthodox scholar, noted in 1963 that the question "Who is a Jew?" admitted of no single answer. There were various categories and circumstances of Jewish identity. Rufeisen, in the eyes of Orthodox Jews, was a *meshummad*, an apostate, but he was still a Jew. Born and raised in a Jewish family, his conversion to Catholicism would disqualify him from participating in some Jewish religious activities, such as leading prayers. But he could, depending upon the circumstances, be considered a Jew for other purposes, such as burial.[41]

The dissenting voice in the court's four-to-one decision against Brother Daniel's appeal was that of Haim Cohn. Judge Berenson in his majority opinion states that the court should not act as "pioneers in front of the nation" and challenge Israeli public opinion regarding who counts as a Jew. Judge Cohn disagreed. He understood the complexities of Rufeisen's situation and could see the implications for Israel's future. Cohn's assertive secularism made him the odd man out on the court. He had been selected to serve on the Rufeisen case because of his expertise both on the question "Who is a Jew?" and on the Law of Return (1950), which he had helped write.[42] In response to Judge Silberg's observations on the importance of maintaining and respecting "Jewish continuity"—and therefore rejecting as untenable a "Jewish-Catholic" identity—Cohn in his dissent posits a new *Israeli* definition of identity. He writes, "I don't subscribe to this type of 'historical continuity.' . . . Quite to the contrary, the nature of historical processes is that times and concepts change, as do ideas and cultural values. The result is a continual improvement of ways of life and of the law." Cohn describes the establishment of the State of Israel as "the most revolutionary event in the history of a people living dispersed among the nations." The larger framework of Cohn's thinking was this: While dispersed, Jews were either threatened or persecuted. They had to define and maintain their identity with complete integrity. But now that Jews constituted a majority population in their own state, a state which claimed equal status among the family of nations, they must adopt new social attitudes, attitudes very different than those they held in the Diaspora. Within the new state the foreigner and "the stranger" within the Jewish majority must be treated with the utmost respect. Should Israel treat those wishing to live in the state as Jews were treated by the Christian states of

Europe? If Rufeisen wanted to be admitted to Israel as a Jew, claimed Haim Cohn, it was the state's obligation to accept him. For, no democratic state has the right "to limit the freedom of an individual to declare his national and religious identity as his conscience sees fit."[43]

In contrast to his colleagues, Justice Cohn considered Brother Daniel a Jew because he had been born a Jew and because he declared himself a Jew. We could think of Cohn as honoring a subjective definition of "Jewishness," while the majority of the court sought to establish an objective definition. The four judges of the majority reasoned that for Israelis of that time, Rufeisen, having apostatized, was no longer a Jew.

Each of the majority judges used somewhat different reasoning to substantiate this claim. According to Judge Silberg, "To permit a Christian to be a Jew . . . would renounce all those spiritual values for which we have been martyred throughout the different periods of our long exile until today."[44] In contrast to Silberg's religious Zionist view, Justice Landau stressed "the importance for this case of the manner of construction of Jewish identity by the founders of Zionism."[45]

Judge Berenson's summation of the judgment echoed Judge Silberg's thinking about the historical relationship between Judaism and Christianity:

> A fresh wind is blowing even in the world of religious creeds. Understanding and cooperation on a scale never known before until recent times are gradually replacing hatred and strife. . . . But this kind of thing is only at the beginning and does not yet play any part in the consciousness of people at large. It will take a long time still, so it seems, before convictions change and that sense of grievance so deeply felt by the Jews for all the wrong that Christianity had done to their people, whose history is soaked with the blood of martyrs who died in order to sanctify the Holy Name, will disappear. Until that day dawns it is not possible to recognize the petitioner as a Jew for the purpose of the Law of Return.[46]

CONCLUSION

Having lost his case in the Israeli high court, Brother Daniel was nevertheless able to become an Israeli citizen through naturalization, which he completed in 1964. After several years in Haifa, he was granted citizenship on the basis of residence in the country. He now had all of the responsibilities and privileges of citizenship, including opportunities of employment to supplement his meager stipend as a monk. The monastery provided a place for him to live, but no more than that. He soon realized that his many charitable and pastoral efforts required outside funding, and that he needed a steady source of income. Beginning in 1965, Brother Daniel supported himself by serving as a licensed Israeli tour guide. From the mid-1960s to the mid-1980s he guided groups of Christian tourists to holy sites throughout Israel. At those sites he would conduct a mass and read appropriate passages from Scripture. Brother Daniel was so well-respected by those who took his tours that word of his popularity eventually reached the Government Tourist Agency. The agency, which still retains control over Israel's lucrative tourist industry, hired Brother Daniel to teach government-approved tour guides about the history and geography of Christianity in the Holy Land.

By the mid-1980s Brother Daniel was able to give up his job as a tour guide. He had attracted a group of supporters, particularly in Germany, who sent him money on a regular basis to support his work. With that money he established an old age home which he had founded in the coastal town of Nahariya. He also continued to minister to the members of his Hebrew-speaking Catholic community, which had grown considerably during his tenure. By the end of his life there were some eight thousand members.

Unlike the other converts examined in this book Brother Daniel was not a systematic thinker or writer. He did not publish any books or engage in extensive correspondence, but we still can see his theology evolving and developing over the decades. By the mid-1990s he had articulated his ideas about Hebrew Catholics in a more precise manner. The growing number of immigrants to Israel who were "not Jewish" according to the Israeli Rabbinate became the focus of his concern. Though he was fully engaged in the effort to form a Hebrew Catholic community in Israel, Brother Daniel was reluctant to help native-born Israeli Jews convert to Christianity. He knew that outright missionary activity directed at Jews would exacerbate the hostility already expressed toward him by the Israeli Rabbinate. Similarly, he distanced himself from Jews for Jesus, an organization founded in the United States in the early-1970s and active in Israel from the late-1980s onward. Brother Daniel considered their teachings to be "present-day ideas about Jesus as represented by the different Protestant sects,"[47] not the "Universal Christianity" of Catholicism that he was seeking to promote. In the following chapter we will examine the history of Jews for Jesus and its founder Martin "Moishe" Rosen, and the impact they have had on Jewish identity.

NOTES

1. Stanislawski, "A Jewish Monk," 548.
2. Tec, *In the Lion's Den*, 9.
3. Ibid., 13.
4. Ibid., 37.
5. Ibid., 85.
6. Trunk, *Jewish Responses to Nazi Persecution*, 291.
7. Tec, *In the Lion's Den*, 134–148.
8. Gera, "Brother Daniel: The Last Jew."
9. United States Holocaust Memorial Museum. "Resistance plans and escape from the Mir ghetto"; Gera, "Brother Daniel: The Last Jew."
10. Rufeisen in 1945, quoted in Tec, *In the Lion's Den*, 208.

11. Tec, *In the Lion's Den*, 166.

12. Ibid., 167.

13. Gera, "Brother Daniel: The Last Jew."

14. Tec, *In the Lion's Den*, 185.

15. Ibid., 202.

16. Ibid., 208.

17. Ibid., 214.

18. Jackson, "Brother Daniel: The Construction of Jewish Identity in the Israeli Supreme Court," 116–117.

19. Tec, *In the Lion's Den*, 217–219.

20. Ibid., 226–227.

21. Stanislawski, "A Jewish Monk," 553.

22. Green, "The 'Troublemaker,'" 98.

23. Chisholm, "Carmelites," 358.

24. Tec, *In the Lion's Den*, 235.

25. Ibid., 235.

26. Galili, "An unorthodox aliyah."

27. Green, "The 'Troublemaker,'" 102.

28. E. Friedman, "Original Manifesto of the Association of Hebrew Catholics." For more on Father Friedman see Kinzer, *Post-Missionary Messianic Judaism.*

29. Tec, *In the Lion's Den*, 227.

30. Jackson, "Brother Daniel: The Construction of Jewish Identity in the Israeli Supreme Court," 117.

31. H. Cohn, *Being Jewish*, 143, 164–165.

32. Ibid., 143.

33. Stanislawski, "A Jewish Monk," 653.

34. Ibid., 565.

35. Galanter, "A Dissent on Brother Daniel," 11.

36. Tec, *In the Lion's Den*, 228.

37. Court record, quoted in Tec, *In the Lion's Den*, 229.

38. Trial manuscript, quoted in Tec, *In the Lion's Den*, 230.

39. Ibid.

40. Galanter, "A Dissent on Brother Daniel," 11.

41. See Lichtenstein, "On Conversion" and Donniel Hartman, *The Boundaries of Judaism.*

42. H. Cohn, *Being Jewish*, 141–148.

43. Ibid., 185.

44. Quoted in Galanter, "A Dissent on Brother Daniel," 15.

45. Jackson, "Brother Daniel: The Construction of Jewish Identity in the Israeli Supreme Court," 123.

46. The Ministry of Justice, "Judgment," 70.

47. Tec, *In the Lions' Den*, 245.

Chapter Eight

Moishe Rosen, Founder of Jews for Jesus (1932–2010)

Historian of religion Yaakov Ariel has described missionary to the Jews Leopold Cohn as having "laid the foundation for what would later become the largest mission to the Jews in America."[1] For decades, Cohn and his son Joseph Hoffman Cohn led the American Board of Missions to the Jews (ABMJ), which was founded in the early twentieth century. The elder Cohn (1862–1937) was a European Jewish convert to Christianity who claimed to have served as an Orthodox rabbi in Slovakia. After his conversion to Christianity, Cohn served as a Baptist missionary to New York's Jewish community. Seventy-five years after its founding an offshoot of the ABMJ, Jews for Jesus, would achieve national prominence under the leadership of Martin "Moishe" Rosen, and it would succeed in converting many Jews.

When Leopold Cohn's son Joseph (1886–1953) took over the ABMJ in 1923, he turned the missionary group into a national organization with a large and effective workforce. "By the early 1940s, the mission fulfilled its aspirations and operated throughout the United States in virtually all large Jewish communities."[2] The organization grew, but it was not very successful in bringing Jews to Christianity. In many instances, these Christian attempts to convert Jews led to greater cohesiveness within American Judaism. To both the Christians who supported the ABMJ and the Jews to whom the missionary message was addressed, the Cohns emphasized that only Jewishly-educated Jews could persuade other Jews of "the Christian truth." For this reason, the Cohns argued, Jewish missionaries needed a basic education in the Jewish traditions, for it was only on the basis of that education that Christian theological arguments directed to Jews would be convincing. The effectiveness of this strategy would wane somewhat over the course of the

149

century, as younger Jews became less familiar with the Jewish textual tradition and more secular in outlook.

From within the ranks of the ABMJ, a new organization, Jews for Jesus,
would emerge in the early 1970s. In 1972 the group's founder Martin
"Moishe" Rosen was forty years old, and he had been a missionary for more
than fifteen years. Unlike many members of his generation Rosen had neither
the inclination nor the resources to "tune in, turn on and drop out"; he did not
embrace the emergent youth culture. But Rosen understood, as no other
missionary of his time did, that the alternative style of the counterculture
could be put to effective use in Christian missions to young Jews.

Rosen's new approach was a far cry from that of the ABMJ, a formal and
theologically conservative missionary organization. To promote his missionary aims, Rosen changed his look and presentation. He let his hair grow long.
He wore jeans and a motorcycle jacket. He peppered his speeches and broadsides with countercultural idioms. He read Saul Alinsky's *Rules for Radicals*
and used it to hone his organizing skills and tactics. Here again, Rosen had an
insight that no other conservative thinker had expressed, much less tried to
implement. While the majority of conservatives had dismissed Alinsky's
book as a leftist tract, Rosen saw it as a valuable tool for conservative
activists.[3]

Rosen's single most effective move, however, was to change his first
name from Martin to Moishe. Doing so allowed him to present himself as
more "authentically Jewish" both to the Christians who were his financial
and organizational supporters, and to the Jews attracted to Christianity who
were his missionary target. In the age of the television series *Roots*, which
celebrated the search for ethnic origins, "Moishe" rather than Martin played
well. When many Jews were anglicizing their names, Rosen would Hebraize
his. Martin was now Moishe, and as such he would endeavor to make evangelical Christianity appeal to Jews disaffected with American culture in general and American Judaism in particular.

According to Rosen family lore, Martin Rosen's paternal grandfather
called him "Moishe," the Yiddish form of the Hebrew name "Moshe," or
Moses.[4] When he started Jews for Jesus in the early 1970s, Rosen chose to
adopt this Yiddish form of his Hebrew name. Doing so signaled to both
fellow missionaries and potential converts that he was "authentically" Jewish, though he had formally converted to Christianity. He told potential Jewish converts that they too could retain their Jewish identity. Emulating Rosen, other members of the core leadership of Jews for Jesus changed their
first names to highlight their "Jewishness." Some whose parents had angli-
cized their Jewish last names chose to return to those Jewish names as well.

In an interview with Juliene Lipson, a University of California, Berkeley
researcher who was writing a doctoral dissertation on the early years of Jews
for Jesus, Rosen complained of his early "gentilization." He explained that

by the late 1960s he "had become an uptight religious organization man."[5] The "uptight religious organization" that Rosen was referring to was the ABMJ, which had employed Martin Rosen since 1954. A year earlier, in 1953, Rosen and his wife Ceil had been baptized at the First Baptist Church of Lakewood, Colorado not far from their hometown of Denver.[6] Soon after his baptism Rosen sought employment as a missionary to Jews, which he found with the ABMJ.

Joseph Cohn had died in 1953, a year before Rosen became affiliated with the missionary group.[7] Cohn and his large staff were political and theological conservatives. They opposed liberal Protestant ideas that were emerging in the 1950s, particularly the idea articulated most famously by theologian Rein hold Niebuhr that Christians should not proselytize to Jews. According to Niebuhr, Jews had their own religious traditions; they were not in need of Christian "help." But Cohn, who followed a pre-millennialist theology, could not accept Niebuhr's argument. For the pre-millennialists, Israel's conversion at the End of Time was an essential component of their theology. The conversion of the Jews to Christianity was a necessary prelude to the return of Jesus. Rosen would forefront these ideas throughout his career, especially after his organization opened a branch in Israel.

YOM KIPPUR AND CONVERSION

In Rosen's account of his awakening to Christianity, Yom Kippur, or the Day of Atonement, played a pivotal role.[8] As we have seen with other converts in this book, it is not unusual to find conversion narratives intimately intertwined with this Jewish holiday. Rabbi Zolli of Rome wrote of "seeing Jesus" in the synagogue on Yom Kippur, and of Jesus telling him that in the next High Holiday season he would no longer be attending synagogue. Soon after this vision Rabbi Zolli resigned his post and joined the Roman Catholic Church. Aaron Lustiger, who was baptized as a young man and eventually became a Cardinal in the Roman Catholic Church, continued throughout his life to attend Yom Kippur services in the Chief Rabbi's synagogue in Paris. On that solemn Day of Atonement, he would recite the *Yizkor*, the memorial prayer, in honor of his parents. According to family tradition, the Lustigers were descended from Levites. For Cardinal Lustiger, participation in Yom Kippur prayer was linked to the Levites' service in the Temple on the Day of Atonement; it was a practice for which he was destined.

Growing up, Moishe Rosen did not find the atmosphere at home particularly religious. As he noted, "My father's belief, that 'religion is a racket', made more and more sense to me as I got older."[9] Despite this seemingly anti-religious attitude, the family still celebrated the Jewish high holidays. As Rosen wrote, "Though my father was disenchanted with Jewish religious leadership, he expected the family to observe certain traditions. He always got off work on *Yom tov*, or holidays such as Yom Kippur and Rosh Hashanah, and we went to my grandfather's house and to synagogue."[10]

At age six he read in the Yom Kippur prayer book about *Kaparot*. *Kaparot* is a pre-Yom Kippur ritual in which Orthodox Jews enact a symbolic sacrifice by holding a chicken above one's head and reciting this prayer: "This is my *kaparah*—my substitute and atonement. May this chicken die and I live a long and good life." From his discovery of this ritual at such a young age, Rosen developed a life-long fascination with the concept of atonement and the Jewish rituals surrounding it. In his 1974 book *Jews for Jesus*, Rosen recounts the trajectory of this fascination. He tells of a chance meeting with a young man at a Denver bus stop on Yom Kippur of 1949. Rosen writes, "I had just attended a service at a synagogue—out of respect for traditions, not God."[11] The young man, on hearing that Rosen had been to prayers, asks why. Rosen replies, "For Yom Kippur services. It's the one day in the year when the Jews go to synagogue to ask for forgiveness of sins." His new acquaintance then explained the Christian concept of forgiveness, which could be mediated only through Jesus. He gave Rosen a pocket New Testament, and Rosen promised that he would read it. As Rosen remembered, "After we parted at my stop, I had a lot to think about. I had fasted all day but I wasn't aware of being hungry. I had never heard anyone explain the Christian faith so well, and I wondered if I might have to revamp my definitions of 'Gentile' and 'Christian.'"[12]

Rosen goes on to note that on that same afternoon his girlfriend Ceil Starr forced him to break the Yom Kippur fast by insisting that he have an ice-cream cone. "Ceil was a professed atheist who reacted violently against the restrictive customs that her family had imposed on her. I generally tried to observe the main fast days, such as Yom Kippur, the Day of Atonement, but she had nothing but contempt for such practices. I remember we were together . . . on Yom Kippur . . . she made a special point of buying me an ice-cream cone."[13]

In 1950 Martin married Ceil, whose given name was Rita Elfbaum. The bride and groom were both eighteen years old, and they married under the *Chupah*, or bridal canopy, in a traditional Jewish wedding ceremony.[14] Unlike Martin, Ceil had been raised in an Orthodox home. Years later she would tell her daughter Ruth that her "experience of Orthodox Judaism reminded her of her mother: arbitrary, heavy-handed, all-consuming, and never satisfied, no matter how hard one tried to comply."[15] Ceil was drawn to Christianity several years before Martin, and she would play a decisive role in bringing him to Christian belief and practice. In 1953, in the third year of their marriage, Ceil and Martin Rosen formally converted to Christianity, largely at Ceil's urging. They were baptized in Trinity Baptist Church near Denver.

SEVENTEEN YEARS AT THE ABMJ

Martin joined the staff of the ABMJ in 1954, one year after his marriage to Ceil. Recognizing his leadership potential, the ABMJ agreed to support Rosen and his family for three years while he attended Northeastern Bible Institute in New Jersey. This evangelical institution was started as a Baptist Bible School in 1950, but by the time Rosen enrolled it had been renamed a Bible Institute.[16] The seminary's conservative approach to the study of the Bible and Christian theology would influence Martin throughout his life.[17] Professors at the institute emphasized the doctrine of biblical inerrancy, the claim that everything in the Bible was literally and historically true. This training influenced Rosen deeply. As he wrote, "On my graduation from Bible College, I was firmly committed to a ministry with ABMJ."[18]

Martin had wanted to enroll at the Moody Bible Study Institute of Chicago, the premiere school for the education of missionaries, but the ABMJ wanted him to be near New York City, hence the choice of New Jersey's Northwestern Bible Institute. The ABMJ expected Rosen to begin his missionary career in New York City's large and varied Jewish community while he was attending seminary. Rosen was eager to learn as much about missionary techniques as he could. In the mid-1950s when the Catholic Church in Manhattan offered a yearlong set of classes that focused on the practical aspects of mission work, Rosen enrolled for the entire sequence of courses. Ceil also attended this missionary training by the Catholic Church. She would become a full partner in her husband's mission to the Jews and a co-founder and leader of Jews for Jesus. With the conclusion of his seminary training in 1957, Rosen was ordained as a Conservative Baptist minister.[19] The ABMJ assigned him to their mission in Los Angeles. On the front of the house that the Rosen's rented there was a small sign that read, "Reverend Martin Meyer Rosen." He was not yet "Moishe" Rosen. The journey to "Moishe" would take fifteen years.

Rosen dubbed the Los Angeles mission the Beth Sar Shalom Hebrew Christian Fellowship (*Sar Shalom*, or "Prince of Peace"). ABMJ director Daniel Fuchs assiduously mentored Rosen in his new leadership position; Fuchs, also a Jewish convert to the Baptist church, was the author of *How to Reach the Jew for Christ*, which had been published in 1943.[20] He became the ABMJ director of missionary activity in 1955, a year after Rosen joined the organization. By the late 1950s he had emerged as the organization's *de facto* leader.[21] Under Fuchs' influence the ABMJ opened an Israeli office in the 1950s.[22] In 1958 Fuchs came to Los Angeles to spend ten days with the Rosens. Rosen wrote, "The ten days he spent with me revolutionized my life."[23] Thirty years later, Jews for Jesus would open its own office in Israel and through it achieve considerable success in "bringing Israeli Jews to Jesus." In the three intervening decades from the mid-1950s to the mid-1980s, the centrality of the State of Israel in conservative Christian doctrine grew even stronger. American-Christian missionaries, including Jews for Jesus, made Israel the focus of many of their efforts.

At some point during his tenure in Los Angeles Rosen stopped referring to himself as a "minister." By the time he arrived in New York City to head the ABMJ, he no longer identified himself as a clergyman. And when he founded Jews for Jesus in San Francisco in 1973, he had become simply "Moishe Rosen." The audience he sought to influence—Jews active in the counterculture—was not about to listen to a minister, or for that matter, to a rabbi. But they might listen to a fellow Jew with whom they could identify, both ethnically and culturally.

In Los Angeles in the 1960s Martin and Ceil worshiped at the First Baptist Church of Hollywood. Ceil taught Bible classes for children. Five years into Rosen's tenure in Los Angeles the ABMJ "went Hollywood," increasing its visibility and popularity in the entertainment industry. The organization purchased a mansion once owned by film star Mary Pickford and opened a center for missionary activities. The Rosen family purchased a home in nearby North Hollywood. By the early 1960s Rosen had become a prominent preacher and teacher in Southern California.[24]

In 1965 Daniel Fuchs asked Rosen to organize a training program for candidates in Jewish missionary work.[25] To initiate the program, missionaries in Los Angeles joined in a Christian "day of prayer and fasting" on Yom Kippur. The purpose of this day-long event was "to pray for the work of the gospel among Jewish people." Rosen's childhood Yom Kippur experiences no doubt played a role in his decision to highlight that particular Jewish holiday. In subsequent years, other Jewish holidays—Passover and Hanukah in particular—would be chosen for these prayer meetings. With the establishment of Jews for Jesus these days of prayer would shift from peripheral celebrations to central events. As Rosen pointed out, "Israel's feasts of Jehovah portray stages of God's dealings with humanity, which culminate in the completion of the plan of salvation."[26]

In April of 1973 Jews for Jesus conducted a public Passover Seder, for which Rosen wrote a *Haggadah* with Christological references.[27] The organizers served "Passover lamb," a practice contrary to the rabbinic rule that lamb was *not* to be eaten at the seder. The seder ritual evokes but does not re-enact the Passover ritual of Temple times in which each family ate of the lamb offered for sacrifice. According to the rabbis, a bone is placed on the seder plate as a reminder of the Temple ritual, but actual lamb meat is not to be consumed. Rosen, however, was not interested in rabbinic rules; he was creating a Christian Seder. In the Christian understanding of the Passover, the temple sacrifice served as a prefiguration of the passion of Jesus, which according to the New Testament took place at the time of Passover. Jesus, then, is the lamb. So for the Jews for Jesus seder, lamb would be served.

By the second half of the twentieth century Passover had become centered in the Jewish home, rather than in the synagogue. American Jews were more likely to observe this holiday than any other. And it was the holiday most Christians associated with Judaism. Rosen and Jews for Jesus recognized this American Jewish enthusiasm for Passover, and built on it. The seder and its association with the Last Supper thus became an ideal time for a meal-centered celebration of Christian fellowship and missionary outreach to Jews. Yom Kippur, a day of fasting set in the synagogue, could not compete with Passover in the American marketplace of religious celebrations. In the early twenty-first century there are numerous "Church Seders" conducted annually. I am not aware of any church Yom Kippur services.

From his post at the helm of the ABMJ in New York City, Rosen took a trip to northern California in 1967 which changed his approach to missionary work. He returned from the West Coast convinced that "outreach to hippies ought to be a primary focus of Jewish evangelism in New York."[28] According to Rosen, he had become "a self-satisfied religious bureaucrat who was more concerned with running an efficient organization than with showing compassion to other human beings."[29] After his trip to California, he was motived to organize a movement more in touch with the spirit of the times. In his 1974 book *Jews for Jesus*, Rosen speaks of the changes he underwent in the late 1960s as his "greening." As he writes, "I was getting involved in Jewish matters again, but this time my perspective was that of the young Jews from the so-called counterculture. . . . They were spiritually hungry and so full of energy and zeal."[30] As a young American Jew who lived in both San Francisco and New York in 1967 I can attest to the atmosphere of spiritual hunger, energy, and zeal. I vividly remember encountering Jews for Jesus members on the streets of both cities. They were competing with Hare Krishna devotees, Moonies, and others for the attentions of the young and the disaffected. But unlike these groups, Jews for Jesus had a built-in audience among young Jewish Americans.

JEWS FOR JESUS

In 1970, Rosen moved to San Francisco to start a new ministry. He would part ways with the ABMJ three years later. Jewish critics first used the name "Jews for Jesus" as a way of mocking Rosen's new mission. But as with other pejorative terms first coined by opponents of new religious movements (e.g., Shakers), this targeted group adopted the name with pride. According to Rosen's daughter Ruth, "When people used the phrase to try to dismiss the group, saying, 'you can't be Jews for Jesus,' Moishe realized that the slogan was invaluable and had it copyrighted. No other phrase and no other name brought the issue to the forefront so succinctly."[31]

A 1972 article in *Time Magazine* described Jews for Jesus as "part of the growing, nationwide Jewish wing of the Jesus movement." The magazine characterized the organization's participants as "young spiritual refugees from secularized Jewish homes, liberal synagogues, the drug culture or radical politics."[32] In search of a strong Jewish voice to speak in opposition to Jews for Jesus, the *Time* reporter quoted Rabbi Shlomo Cunin, the Habad-Lubavitch Rabbi at U.C.L.A. Rabbi Cunin bemoaned the "loss of Jewish youth" to Jews for Jesus. According to the *Time* article, "Rabbi Cunin estimates that young Jews are converting to Christianity at the rate of six to seven thousand a year." Thirty-five years later this same Rabbi Cunin would become the most fervent of Jewish messianists. On the 1994 death of the Lubavitcher Rabbi, M. M. Schneerson, Cunin was among those Hasidic leaders who declared openly that the *Rebbe* was the messiah, and that he would soon rise from the grave and redeem the Jewish people and the world. To historians of religion, the emergence of a new Jewish messianism in the late-twentieth century was a fascinating phenomenon. Many scholars pointed out that the rhetoric and scriptural references of the *Habad* messianists were remarkably similar to those of the early Christians, and to those of Jews for Jesus.

The 1972 *Time* article helped put Jews for Jesus on the very crowded counterculture map. But it was Rosen's success with the nation's disaffected youth that put him on a collision course with the politically and socially conservative leadership of the ABMJ.[33] It was not that Rosen had changed his theology; he remained as conservative as his ABMJ colleagues and their Baptist supporters. But he had changed his style, and this was a change that his evangelical Protestant supervisors could not tolerate. As Yaakov Ariel noted, "Jews for Jesus was an agent of evangelical Protestantism acting to Christianize Jews and bring them into the evangelical community."[34] But with Rosen's radical tactics, many evangelicals felt that they could no longer support him.

Rosen skillfully invoked Jewish law to counter claims that he and his fellow Jews for Jesus members, having been baptized, "were no longer Jews." As he wrote, "According to *Halakhah*, or Jewish law, a person is a Jew if his mother was Jewish or if he converts to Judaism. My mother was Jewish and the same goes for other Jews for Jesus, so we're Jewish under the law. We may be heretics in the eyes of some Jewish leaders, but we're still Jewish."[35] In discussions of the question of Jewish identity, Rosen cited the 1962 Israeli Supreme Court case of Brother Daniel. According to Rosen, the Israeli court had not considered seriously Brother Daniel's request to be recognized as both a Roman Catholic and a Jew. This was a serious error. Rather than deal with the claim directly, the court had "dodged the identity issue." Jews for Jesus would not skirt the issue.

In the three decades between founding Jews for Jesus in 1973 and his resignation from the organization in 1996 Rosen did not alter his theological orientation. He changed the *style* of his missionary work, but not the content. At the age of forty he was able to adapt his missionary message to the mood and needs of the time. His older associates in the ABMJ proved much less flexible. Young Jews soon found them anachronistic and out of touch. As a consequence Rosen was highly successful in attracting Jews to Christianity. He influenced thousands of Jews to convert, though not as many as he would later claim.

A sympathetic journalist described Rosen's situation in the early 1970s in this way: "He was a successful director of a Jewish mission, shielded by a receptionist, a secretary, and two assistants. He was part of a world of respectable, ambitious achievers. The hippies ambling the streets in ragged jeans and tee-shirts were losers. But his conscience was pricked: 'I have become more concerned with administrative processes than with people. How can I get to know the hippies?'"[36]

In his 1974 book *Jews for Jesus*, written with William Proctor, Rosen explained his choice of style and method. "As crazy as we may look there is a certain method to our sartorial madness. In street clothes, denims, or informal dress we're able to identify with the culture and age group of the people we most want to encounter."[37] Rosen called his method of evangelizing "Holy Boldness," because it involved direct confrontation with the public. "We successfully choose the street or campus as our place of confrontation, not the pulpit or the pew. And vocal confrontation for us is not merely shouting slogans and chants, but being able to verbalize our feelings with conviction and tell them to others."[38] One of Rosen's maxims was that "'Friendship evangelicalism' is no evangelism at all."[39]

In another astute move that appealed to children of the counterculture, Rosen formed a Jews for Jesus rock and roll band, Liberated Wailing Wall. The band toured the United States and Europe throughout the 1970s. It recorded four popular albums—"Hineni!"; "I Am Not Ashamed"; "We Were Like Dreamers"; and "Who Hath Believed Our Report?"—and attracted a large fan base.

From the early 1970s onward a hallmark of Rosen's style was an emphasis on ethnic Jewish markers. His newly adopted name Moishe, his focus on the Passover Seder as a Jewish-Christian experience, and his constant references to Jewish food and family customs set Jews for Jesus apart from other missions to the Jews. Rosen combined the emphasis on Jewish ethnicity with a call to converted Jews to worship in conservative evangelical congregations, and to adopt and adhere to a strict Protestant theology. The conservative theology that Rosen had studied and absorbed during his early years at Northeastern Bible Institute remained the basis of his teaching until the end of his life; it did not change.

Rosen's deep-seated conservatism put him in early opposition to an emerging religious movement, "messianic Judaism."[40] Initially, Rosen did not support those Jews in the Jesus movement who insisted that after conversion to Christianity Jewish believers in Jesus should constitute their own distinct community and retain some Jewish religious practices. Mark Kinzer, a theoretician of Messianic Judaism, has defined the movement as "the attempt of Jewish Yeshua-believers to sustain their Jewish identity and religious expression as intrinsic to and required by their faith in Yeshua."[41] In contrast to Rosen's call for converted Jews to join local churches after their baptism, messianic congregations called on their members to practice a syncretic "Jewish Christianity," or "Christian Judaism," and worship in messianic synagogues under the direction of messianic rabbis. Eventually, Rosen and Jews for Jesus would make an uneasy peace with these emerging messianic Jewish congregations. Rosen would compromise on this issue, but at the end of his life he seemed to regret this decision.

In the late 1970s the success of Jews for Jesus alarmed the leadership of the major American Jewish organizations. Not only was Jews for Jesus highly visible, getting a great deal of media attention and receiving funding from main-line churches, but the organization's appeal could be measured in actual numbers of Jews baptized. The Anti-Defamation League denounced Jews for Jesus as "deceptive." The Jewish Community Relations Council of New York City established a "task force on missionary activity" whose stated purpose was "to alert and educate the Jewish community and to develop appropriate responses."[42] This task force commissioned two eminent Jewish scholars to write a short book that would counter the arguments put forth in the many broadsides distributed by Jews for Jesus. In 1978 David Berger and Michael Wyschogrod, both Orthodox rabbis, published *Jews and "Jewish Christianity."*[43] The book, a brief 71 pages, had two stated objectives: "First, to persuade Jews who have been attracted by 'Jewish Christianity' to take another look at the issues. Second, to familiarize other readers with a Jewish approach to what has become a controversial and hotly debated topic."[44] What sets *Jews and "Jewish Christianity"* apart from other Jewish anti-missionary publications of the time is its respectful attitude toward the young reader. The book neither mocks nor condemns Jews who are interested in Christianity. "There will be no attempt here to 'explain away' your interest in Christianity by reducing it to a psychological or educational problem."[45] Young American Jews drawn to Jews for Jesus would have likely encountered such a dismissive attitude from their parents, rabbis and school teachers. In contrast, Berger and Wyschogrod note, "We have tried, sincerely and respectfully, to explain the Jewish point of view concerning Jews who have embraced or are thinking of embracing Christianity. In the final analysis it is you who must make the decision."[46]

The text of the book does not mention Jews for Jesus by name, but the back cover does. According to the back cover copy, the book has been "written both for Jews who have been attracted to Christianity, especially to Jews for Jesus and similar groups which claim to be Christian and Jewish simultaneously."[47] Throughout the book the authors emphasize that they are not writing an anti-Christian polemic. Christians, they explain, can be counted among "the righteous of all nations, who have a place in the 'world to come.'" But Jews, "who are born into the covenant of Abraham . . . must remain loyal to the faith of their people."

Rosen's ability to attract future leaders to the organization was remarkable. Despite a leadership style that was "top down" and a personality that was domineering, he created a cadre of young leaders who would shepherd Jews for Jesus into the twenty-first century. This group included David Brickner, Rosen's chosen successor, as well as Rosen's daughter Ruth. From 1980 until his retirement in 1996, Rosen explained his responsibilities as "chiefly working as a strategist, trying to discern the best places to spend my energy and the energy of Jews for Jesus. I had pretty much taught the staff all that I could teach them in doing the work, and a lot of my new work was putting out fires, making things work according to their principles and practices."[48] From 1996 onwards, the younger leadership ran the organization. David Brickner, Rosen's protégée and the son of two of the group's founders, became chairman of the organization at that time.

Those Jews who converted to Christianity under the auspices of Jews for Jesus were for the most part young people from non-Orthodox Jewish families. Their childhood experiences of Judaism tended to fall within the parameters of the Reform or Conservative denominations, or within cultural and secular forms of Jewish expression.[49] In contrast, American Jewish converts to Christianity during the first half of the twentieth century had come for the most part from Orthodox families. Thus it had been essential for missionaries like those of the ABMJ, who wished to influence Jews raised in Orthodox homes, to be as familiar with Jewish texts as their "targets" were. For later missionaries like Rosen of Jews for Jesus, however, knowledge of the Jewish textual tradition was less important. Their missionaries did not need to read Hebrew, or know the Bible, or the Talmud. Their "targets" did not know these texts either. Rosen trained his missionaries to appeal to cultural forms of "Jewishness" that included ethnic solidarity, folkways, and a sense of mutual responsibility, rather than to the religious aspects of Jewish identity.

LATER YEARS

By the 1980s Jews for Jesus had grown into a large international organization with an annual budget in the tens of millions of dollars.[50] As Rosen's financial supporters, impressed with his success as organizer and propagandist, steadily increased their support, his allies in conservative theological circles sought to honor him. Though he had shed the title of "minister" decades earlier, Rosen was not averse to receiving academic honors. In 1986, Western Conservative Baptist Seminary, based in Portland, Oregon, granted him an honorary Doctor of Divinity degree.

The major American Jewish organizations continued to object to Rosen's efforts, and they organized campaigns attempting to discredit Jews for Jesus. In 2001 the Anti-Defamation League (ADL) released a report titled *With Subterfuge and Deception: 'Jews for Jesus' Targets Jews.* The report asserted, "Once again, Jews for Jesus is trying to distort Jewish identity as part of their deceptive and offensive campaign to impose Christian beliefs on Jews." Abraham H. Foxman, ADL National Director, took particular issue with a Jews for Jesus campaign that featured Holocaust survivors professing their belief in Jesus. He wrote, "By emphasizing the Holocaust, Jews for Jesus is using the darkest chapter in the history of Judaism—the persecution and annihilation of European Jews—to attempt to mislead survivors and their children about their history and faith. It is impossible for a person who is Jewish to worship Jesus Christ. That is the fundamental distinction that sets these faith systems apart."[51] Foxman also had objected to the activities of another converted Jew, Cardinal Lustiger. When an interfaith group had sought to honor Lustiger for advancing Jewish-Catholic relations, Foxman had objected: "I don't think he should be honored because he converted out, which makes him a poor example."[52] For Foxman, Lustiger, like Rosen, was not only blurring the lines between Judaism and Christianity, but also invoking the memory of the Holocaust to do so.

In 2014, the ADL was again at loggerheads with Jews for Jesus over its production of the short internet film *That Jew Died for You.* The black and white YouTube film shows Jesus carrying his cross as he approaches the gates of Auschwitz. At the gates, the Nazi guards sentence him to death in the gas chamber. On a Web site supporting the video, the producers of the film explained, "Jesus has often been wrongly associated with the perpetrators of the Holocaust. In reality he is to be identified with those who were the victims. As a Jew, if he were in Europe at this time, Jesus may well have suffered the same fate of the six million who perished in the concentration camps." According to Foxman and the ADL, the film was "an outrageous cheapening of the tragedy of the six million Jews and millions of others who perished in the Holocaust."[53]

Opposition to Jews for Jesus came from liberal Protestants as well. In the second half of the twentieth century, Reinhold Niebuhr's assertion that Christians need not proselytize to Jews had become widely accepted. Rosen challenged this consensus. In a statement titled "Why Witness to the Jewish People" Rosen once again argued against disapproval of missions to the

Jews. "Some who want to be politically correct say, 'The Jews have their own religion, an ancient and noble religion that predates Christianity.' . . . But God demonstrated—not only through scripture, but through the Incarnation at Bethlehem—that if anyone needs Jesus, the Jewish people do. . . . Religion is not enough without the reality of the redeemer."[54]

In 1991 Rosen wrote a book on prophecy and the millennium that hearkened back to his Baptist theological training. In *Overture to Armageddon*, which was published by Campus Crusade for Christ in the wake of the First Gulf War, Rosen writes in the conversational and confrontational style that he had developed over his decades as a polemicist. Like many other "prophecy" books of the period, Rosen presents the 1991 Gulf War in biblical terms: "When things began happening in the land that in ancient times was called Babylon, and when it became more than ancient history, and the prophecies seemed so relevant, I thought this would be a good time to write and tell you about the modern times' Y'shua and what he wants from you."[55] Unlike Hal Lindsey in his 1972 book *The Late Great Planet Earth* and his many emulators, Rosen is cautious about predicting the future and correlating biblical prophecy with current events. His pronouncements are more circumspect. As he says, "We have no idea exactly how prophetic events will play themselves out. . . . Our hope for the future should be centered not on a series of predicted events, but on a predicted person—Jesus, Y'shua, the Messiah."[56]

From his 1996 retirement as chairman of Jews for Jesus to his death in 2010, Rosen remained active in the organization he founded. Beset in later years by medical problems, including diabetes and its attendant circulatory complications, he developed prostate cancer in 2007. When Rosen died in May of 2010, his family found great meaning in the fact that he died on *Shavuot*, the Jewish Pentecost. His daughter Ruth recalled that in his youth Rosen "had made his first public profession of faith in Jesus on Pentecost Sunday."[57] She was referring of course to the Christian Pentecost, which commemorates the day that the Holy Spirit descended on the early community of Christians. *Shavuot*, or the Jewish Pentecost, commemorates Moses's receiving the Torah on Mt. Sinai. But for Jews for Jesus devotees, there was no appropriation or contradiction here. The two Pentecosts, separated as they were by some two thousand years, were bound together.

On Rosen's death, the Jews for Jesus Web site published his final message to the faithful: "I hope I can count on you to show love and respect for the Jewish people, but Jewishness never saved anybody. Judaism never saved anybody no matter how sincere. Romans 10:9 and 10 make it clear that we must believe in our hearts and confess with our mouths the Lord Jesus in order to be saved. There are no shortcuts. There is no easy way. Within Judaism today, there is no salvation because Christ has no place within Judaism."[58] Thus Rosen, on his deathbed, returned to an earlier uncompromising position and sought to distance Jews for Jesus from messianic Jewish theology which called on Jewish believers in Jesus to maintain a degree of separation from fellow Christians. Rosen saw no reason to sustain a separate Jewish identity within Christianity.

Rosen also objected to the growing emphasis among messianic Jews on the religious significance of the State of Israel. Like the ultra-Orthodox rabbis we encountered in the story of Ruth Ben David, Rosen expressed reservations about an End-Time understanding of the State of Israel. Like those rabbis, Rosen hearkened back to the classical Jewish idea that the redemption of Israel, both the people and the land, would occur as a result of divine agency, not through human effort. He wrote, "I hear a lot of Jewish believers talking about moving to Israel, making aliyah, going home. Basically, this presents a theological problem to me. The Diaspora, or Scattering, took place according to God's prophesied judgment. See Deuteronomy 28. I believe that when our time comes, God Himself will gather the Jews together in Israel, and the Diaspora will be over. I'm willing to believe that the establishment of Israel in 1948 could be the beginning of the return. But the return is more like what is described in Zechariah 12:10."[59]

Rosen's understanding of the messianic age was, of course, still Christological, as his citation of Zechariah demonstrates. While Rosen agreed with the Orthodox rabbis that divine agency would bring about the redemption of Israel, he understood the Hebrew Bible as predicting the life, death, resurrection, and return of Jesus. In contrast to this reading of biblical narrative, the Jewish tradition asserts that prophecy ceased after the last three prophets of the Hebrew Bible—Haggai, Malachi, and Zechariah. The rabbis understood prophecies, including that of the late sixth century B.C.E. prophet Zechariah, as referring to the building of the Second Temple, an event close to their own time, and to the eventual destruction of that temple. But when Rosen cites Zechariah, he understands the prophet to be speaking of the distant eschatological future, when Jesus will return, and the Jews will mourn for "the one whom they have pierced," accept Jesus as the messiah, and be restored.

Thus in his final statements, Rosen remained a prophecy-oriented, conservative Christian, not a messianic Jew or a supporter of *aliyah*, immigration to Israel. In the edited volume dedicated to him, *Jews and the Gospel at the End of History: A Tribute to Moishe Rosen*, editor Jim Congdon makes clear that Rosen and his ideological colleagues oppose those Protestants who call for an end of Christian missions to the Jews. "Christians who read their Bible know that when the end of history arrives, the Jew will be there. At that time they will look on him whom they pierced, repent and be restored (Zechariah 12:10). And until that day, those who truly love 'the apple of God's eye' will want to introduce them to God's messiah."[60]

So was Moishe Rosen a master of "subterfuge and deception," as the ADL's Abraham Foxman put it? Or was he, as a journalist for an evangelical journal put it, "The most colorful Jewish evangelist of the twentieth century—perhaps since the apostle Paul?"[61] Opinions remain sharply divided on the question, but no one would deny that Moishe Rosen's missionary activities resulted in converts. Rosen claimed that the number of converts was in the tens of thousands, but reliable figures are difficult to come by. In 2014 it is estimated that the number of believers who identify themselves as "messianic Jews" is close to a quarter of a million. Some of these are Jews by birth who have confessed their belief in Jesus; some are Christians. In the United States, more than three hundred houses of worship consider themselves messianic Jewish congregations. In Israel it is estimated that there are more than one hundred messianic congregations. Some 10,000 Israeli Jews identify with Jews for Jesus or other messianic groups.[62]

NOTES

1. Ariel, *Evangelizing the Chosen People*, 30.
2. Ibid., 107.
3. M. Rosen and Proctor, *Jews for Jesus*, 91–93; R. Rosen, *Called to Controversy*, 218–19, 301.
4. Lipson, "Jews for Jesus," 166.
5. Ibid., 20.
6. R. Rosen, *Called to Controversy*, 73.
7. Ibid., 119.
8. Ibid., 50–54.
9. Ibid., 21.
10. M. Rosen and Proctor, *Jews for Jesus*, 17.
11. Ibid., 17.
12. Ibid., 21–23.
13. Ibid., 21.
14. R. Rosen, *Called to Controversy*, 56.
15. Ibid., 59.
16. Ibid., 85.
17. For M. Rosen's affiliation with Western Seminary in Portland, Oregon, and with the International Council on Biblical Inerrancy, see R. Rosen, *Called to Controversy*, 236–237.
18. M. Rosen and Proctor, *Jews for Jesus*, 39.
19. R. Rosen, *Called to Controversy*, 130.
20. Ariel, *Evangelizing the Chosen People*, 85.
21. Ibid., 113.
22. Ibid.
23. R. Rosen, *Called to Controversy*, 140.
24. Ibid., 153–153.
25. For details, see M. Rosen and Proctor, *Jews for Jesus*, 54.
26. See C. Rosen and M. Rosen, *Christ in the Passover*.
27. M. Rosen and Proctor, *Jews for Jesus*, 107–110.
28. R. Rosen, *Called to Controversy*, 175.
29. M. Rosen and Proctor, *Jews for Jesus*, 57.
30. Ibid., 62.
31. R. Rosen, *Called to Controversy*, 197.
32. See *Time Magazine*, "Religion: Jews for Jesus."
33. See R. Rosen, *Called to Controversy*, 197–203.
34. Ariel, *Evangelizing the Chosen People*, 211.
35. M. Rosen and Proctor, *Jews for Jesus*, 95.

36. Quoted in Congdon, *Jews and the Gospel at the End of History*, 64. Also see Damato, "The Man Behind the Jews for Jesus."

37. M. Rosen and Proctor, *Jews for Jesus*, 89.

38. Ibid.

39. Tucker, "Remembering Moshe Rosen."

40. See Ariel, *Evangelizing the Chosen People*, 296; and R. Rosen, *Called to Controversy*, 261.

41. Kinzer, *Post-Missionary Messianic Judaism*, 11.

42. Berger and Wyschogrod, *Jews and "Jewish Christianity,"* 7.

43. See Berger and Wyschogrod, *Jews and "Jewish Christianity."*

44. Ibid., 9.

45. Ibid., 14.

46. Ibid., 67.

47. Ibid., back cover.

48. R. Rosen, *Called to Controversy*, 257.

49. Ariel, *Evangelizing the Chosen People*, 211, 320.

50. Ariel, "Counterculture and Mission," 247; R. Rosen, *Called to Controversy*, 257.

51. See Anti-Defamation League, "ADL Says Jews for Jesus Ads are Deceptive and Offensive."

52. See Malcolm, "Jewish Group Criticizes Honor for Converted Prelate."

53. See *The Times of Israel*, "ADL flogs Jews for Jesus over Holocaust clip."

54. R. Rosen, *Called to Controversy*, 302.

55. M. Rosen and B. Massie, *Overture to Armageddon*, 9.

56. Ibid., 75.

57. R. Rosen, *Called to Controversy*, 294.

58. See M. Rosen, "He being dead still speaks. (Hebrews 11:4)."

59. See M. Rosen, "35 Things about Me, Moishe Rosen," and M. Rosen and B. Massie, *Overture to Armageddon*, 153–158.

60. Congdon, *Jews and the Gospel at the End of History*, 11.

61. Tucker, "Remembering Moshe Rosen."

62. See Posner, "Kosher Jesus: Messianic Jews in the Holy Land."

Epilogue

When I embarked on the research for *Jewish–Christian Difference and Modern Jewish Identity*, I told myself that the great debates about Jewish identity were a thing of the past, albeit the recent past. The year 2008, the sixtieth anniversary of the founding of the State of Israel, was, I felt, a point from which one could survey the history and consequences of the "Jewish identity wars" of the twentieth century and reflect on them with some distance and scholarly objectivity.

But it was in 2008 that another crisis in the battles over the definition of Judaism erupted in Israel. As is often the case, that crisis affected Jewish communities around the world, especially the American Jewish community. The question of whether conversions performed by Conservative or Reform Rabbis would be valid in Israel has long been part of the debate about Jewish identity. Now, rifts within Orthodox Judaism about the validity of conversions were evident. Ultra-Orthodox Rabbis on the high court of the Israeli Rabbinate declared that thousands of conversions that were overseen by Rabbi Haim Druckman, a Religious Zionist rabbi, were invalid. This declaration precipitated another set of court cases, challenges, and negotiations about the increasingly complex issue of who is authorized to oversee conversion to Judaism.

This book's accounts of religious conversion were my key for probing the borders of Judaism and for chronicling the ways in which those borders were being challenged, redefined, and, by some, re-imagined. But, as the 2008 cases indicated, the debates and redefinitions continued unabated. During the six years in which I was researching and writing this book (from 2008 to 2014) new debates and public controversies concerning Jewish identity arose. Each of these were, by definition, related to the historical and cultural past. But the most intriguing and stimulating of these controversies had a new and surprising spin. The issues may have been centuries old, but the manifestations were strikingly modern.

The stories of conversion in *Jewish–Christian Difference and Modern Jewish Identity* are tales of intense personal struggle and engagement with religious questions. But, as we have seen, each story of a personal spiritual quest had a public face. The Brother Daniel case of 1962 is a prime example; the rejection of his appeal to be recognized as a Jew influences Israeli public policy to this day. Jews around the world now look to Israel when considering "Who is a Jew?"—though they don't necessarily adhere to the decisions of the Israeli courts. But there is no doubt that the increasing centrality of Israel to Jews around the world makes what transpires there an unavoidable factor in deliberations and decisions about Jewish identity.

As we follow the "Jewish identity wars" into the twenty-first century it seems that Israel and the public face of Jewish identity dominate the conversation; personal religious questions tend to receive less attention. One startling American news story about Jewish identity was the 1997 *Washington Post* story that Secretary of State Madeleine Albright was in fact the daughter of Jewish parents who had converted to Roman Catholicism. Albright's given name at birth was Marie Korbel. Secretary Albright told the press that her parents had hidden her Jewish past from her, and that she was completely surprised by the discovery. Her parents, politically active Czech Jews who met and married in the mid-1930s, saw the looming dangers of German military aggression and anti-Semitism. They obscured their Jewish identity and joined the Catholic Church. The Korbels escaped from Czechoslovakia in 1938 and made their way to England. After the War, they returned to Czechoslovakia and Joseph Korbel served as Czech ambassador to Yugoslavia. With the 1948 Communist takeover of Czechoslovakia the Korbels immigrated to the United States. The young Marie was eleven years old at the time. Her parents never told her that her grandparents were Jews and that three of them were murdered by the Nazis during the war.

Scholars of Holocaust history have documented thousands of cases of European Jews who hid their identities to escape the Nazis and their collaborators. What is striking about the Albright story is that Madeleine Albright, who converted to the Episcopal Church when she married, was not aware of how successful her parents' conversion to Catholicism was. Mrs. Albright, a student of history with a PhD from Columbia University, was oblivious to the religious dimension of her own rich history.

In the past six years international news stories have highlighted unresolved issues of Jewish identity and attest to this question's continuing significance. The first of these stories, which made headlines in the United Kingdom, is a saga of exhumation and reburial involving Britain, Austria, and Israel. Theodore Herzl, the founder of political Zionism, who died in 1904, was buried in Vienna. In his will he requested that "when the Jewish state was founded" (such was his certainty), he and his children should be reburied in Jerusalem. In 1949 Herzl's body was exhumed and reburied in a cemetery on the mountain in Jerusalem named in his honor. His children's bodies, buried in Europe after their deaths in 1930, were not exhumed. Hans was buried in 1930 in England, where he had lived since his father's death in 1904. In that same year Herzl's daughter Pauline had died of a drug overdose and was buried in France. For decades, the Israeli Rabbinate had opposed both reburials. But in 2006 the Chief Rabbinate declared that the actions of both Herzl children were the result of the mental illness with which they had long been afflicted. Therefore they could be buried in a Jewish cemetery.[1]

In 2009, two years after that decision, the British Chief Rabbi, and the British government, had to confront the issue of identity in a public policy question. In November 2009, Britain's Supreme Court ruled that the Jews' Free School of London could not apply Orthodox Jewish standards in formulating its admissions policies. At issue was the application of a twelve-year-old boy whose mother was a convert to Judaism from Roman Catholicism. The conversion was supervised by a Liberal rabbi and was therefore unacceptable to the Orthodox rabbis who set the school's admission standards. For these Orthodox rabbis Jewish identity was defined in a very specific manner. The child of a Jewish mother is Jewish, as is any person who converts to Judaism under the guidance of Orthodox rabbis. Anyone whose mother is not Jewish or whose conversion was supervised by a rabbi of a more liberal denomination, would not be Jewish in their definition. Britain's Chief Rabbi, Jonathan Sacks, is Orthodox and he decided that as the boy's mother had not converted according to Orthodox norms, her son was not "a member of the Jewish people." Therefore, Rabbi Sacks reasoned, the school was correct in refusing him admission.

The British court, however, saw this standard as an ethnic, rather than a religious test, and criticized the school's admission criterion as a "test of ethnicity which contravenes the Race Relations Act." The seven Judges of the Supreme Court of the United Kingdom viewed the exclusion of the boy as an act of racial discrimination, prohibited by law. The school had to admit the child. As a result of this ruling, relations between Britain's Jewish communities have worsened. Liberal Jewish leaders expressed resentment that the Orthodox sector has shunned and excluded them. Orthodox Jews spoke of an irreparable break with their liberal co-religionists. And the case has had repercussions in other British religious communities as well. As religious schools in Britain are state-funded, many groups, including Muslims and Hindus, are reconsidering their own school admissions policies. Who can they include or exclude? How will the legal system deal with these policies? Thus the British court's decision about a Jewish school is having an impact on government policies, inter-faith relations, and intra-communal relations within the United Kingdom.[2]

Another Jewish identity story, which made headlines in Israel and Russia in 2010, involves Russia, Israel and the United States. Within the State of Israel the thorny question "Who is a Jew?" (and thus the question "Who is not a Jew?") has been a permanent feature of public and private life. The issue has surfaced dramatically in the past few years. After the fall of the Soviet Union, one million people emigrated from Russia to Israel. About one-third of these immigrants are not Jewish according to Orthodox standards, which, under Israeli law, are authoritative. Their claim to Jewish identity was based on their marriages to Jewish spouses or their descent from one Jewish grandparent. Some people in this non-Jewish group are committed members of the Russian Orthodox Church. For them and for others, their wish to be accepted as Israeli Jews has encountered many obstacles.

Thus in the 1990s many Russian immigrants to Israel were caught in the indeterminate status of a "Jew with rights" who is not a Jew according to the Rabbinate. That is to say that they were "Jewish enough" to be granted the Right of Return under Israeli law, but they were not "fully Jewish" in the eyes of the official rabbis of the state. Among these cases was that of Lev Paschov. Paschov immigrated to Israel with his parents and subsequently served in the Israeli army. In 1993 he was killed in a firefight in Southern Lebanon. He was given a military funeral and buried in one of Israel's sprawling military cemeteries. That might have been the end of a tragic story, but the tale did not end with Paschov's death. After his burial, the army rabbinate discovered that while Paschov's father was Jewish, his mother was not. Therefore, they decided he could not be buried in 'consecrated ground.' His body was exhumed and he was reburied in a cemetery for non-Jewish soldiers. This case sharpened the already contentious issue of Israeli identity and Jewish identity, and embittered the antagonists in this issue.

That was the story of an individual tragedy, but there is, of course, a larger communal problem concerning Russian Jews in Israel. As circumcision was not practiced in the Soviet Union, all Russian males who came to Israel in the 1990s and wished to convert to Judaism needed to be circumcised. *Operation Abraham*, run by an Israeli medical team, has circumcised over 80,000 of these immigrants to Israel. And there are many more in the pipeline.

In July 2010 this internal Israeli issue made headlines in the international press. Israeli Parliament members of the Yisrael Beiteinu ("Israel is our home") party, which represents many emigrants from the Russian Federation, allied itself with the State Rabbinate, the body that would approve the conversions of large numbers of men undergoing circumcision. They introduced a bill that would place authority over all conversions to Judaism in the hands of the official Rabbinate and thereby bring all Conservative and Reform conversions into question (including conversions conducted outside of Israel). The ensuing protest from the leaders of the large American Jewish organizations was loud and clear, and in the end very effective. Within a few weeks of the protests Prime Minister Netanyahu said he would oppose the Yisrael Beiteinu bill, as it would "tear apart the Jewish people."

These twenty-first century stories show us that the question "Who is a Jew?" and the related question, "Who is an Israeli?" are very much alive. It is an insider question for Jewish communities and an outsider question that has an effect on the European and American societies in which Jews reside. Answers to these questions also have an effect on the Arab citizens of Israel, who make up 20 percent of the population. As the idea and reality of Israeli identity become more strongly tied to Jewishness, a tendency that has been strengthened during the Netanyahu years, the 'Israeliness' of the country's Palestinian citizens is more and more marginalized.

In the American Jewish community, identification with Israel is now a hallmark of Jewish identity, and there is some truth to the assertion that "Zionism is now the religion of American Jews." The success of the "Birthright" program, in which more than 300,000 American Jewish college students have gone on free two-week trips to Israel, has further strengthened this identification. Here too the question "Who is a Jew?" rises to the fore. To be eligible for Birthright, one does not have to be Jewish according to Orthodox rabbis: any Jewish ancestry or identification is sufficient. Thus American college students are given the message that the State of Israel is their "birthright." The implication is clear: Israel is not the birthright of the Arabs of the country, or of the Palestinians in the territories and in exile.

But it is not only the American Jewish community who are engaged with Jewish and Israeli identity; Americans of all religious groups seem engaged with these issues. In 2011 the issue of Jewish identity entered the American public conversation with the shooting of Representative Gabrielle Giffords of Arizona. In the decade prior to the shooting, Representative Giffords, who was born to a Christian mother and Jewish father, had embraced what she identified as her "Jewish heritage." This embrace was the result of an Israeli-government-sponsored tour of Israel to which members of the US Congress were invited. On her return to Arizona, Giffords began to identify herself as a Jew. She joined a Tucson, Arizona Jewish congregation; the rabbi of this congregation is described as the former congresswoman's spiritual advisor. When Giffords was shot, many people in liberal synagogues throughout the United States prayed for her recovery, including, as one member described them, "many synagogues in which . . . Giffords would not be considered sufficiently Jewish to receive an *aliyah* to the Torah."[3]

Representative Giffords's sense of Jewish identity, catalyzed by her visit to Israel, had been a *personal* issue before she was shot in Tuscon. After she was shot her identity became a Jewish communal issue. Concern for her moved many in the Jewish community to identify with her—and thus the question of her religious identity was linked to a larger communal issue: "Who is a Jew, and who is not?"

Within Israel a new challenge to the state's definition of a Jew was offered by one of the country's best-known public intellectuals. In May 2011 the prominent Israeli novelist Yoram Kaniuk asked the Ministry of the Interior to "change his status on the population register from 'Jewish' to 'no religion.'" He was not the first Israeli Jew to propose this idea. But no one had made any headway on this issue. As a public figure and a chronicler, in his novels and memoirs, of Israel's dramatic history, Kaniuk had the resources and notoriety to publicize, and perhaps win, such a case. As in the case that moved Ben Gurion to send letters to fifty-one Jewish intellectuals in 1958, it was the ethnic-religious status of a child that brought his case to court and to the public's attention. Kaniuk was also well-known in academic circles in the United States. He had been a visiting professor at several universities and a writer-in-residence at Dartmouth College. At Dartmouth in the 1980s, Kaniuk and I co-taught an Israeli literature course, and we had many opportunities to discuss the vagaries and contradictions of the Jewish identity question. Thus, I was not surprised when he took his case to the Israeli Supreme Court.

Kaniuk's grandson, born in 2010, was at his parents' request, registered as "without religion." Kaniuk's American-born wife is Christian, and she and their Israeli-born daughter are registered with the government as "Christian." The baby's parents wanted their child registered without religious designation and their request was granted. Grandfather Yoram Kaniuk was inspired by this unexpected concession to ask the government to describe his identity in the same way as it had described his grandson's. But as Yoram Kaniuk had been listed as a "Jew" for all of his life, the population registry refused his request. Kaniuk appealed the decision in the Tel Aviv district court. He told the judge that while he did not want to convert to another religion, he had never identified as a religious Jew. To the surprise of many Israel-watchers, both within the country and abroad, the judge, Gideon Ginat of the Tel Aviv District Court, granted Kaniuk's request. He could now identify as an Israeli, not a Jew. The basis of his decision was that Israel's 1948 Declaration of Independence upheld "freedom of religion." Kaniuk's lawyer told the *Jerusalem Post* that the right to define oneself is a "fundamental right that should be taken for granted, without any restrictions."[4]

In the aftermath of the Kaniuk decision, many secular Israeli Jews applauded Kaniuk's victory and said they planned to make similar appeals. And in 2013, twenty-one Israeli Jewish citizens led by the eminent linguist Uzzi Ornan petitioned the Supreme Court to grant them the same status Yoram Kaniuk was granted, the national designation of "Israeli" rather than the religious designation of "Jew." But the court neglected their appeal. Designating citizens as "Israeli," the justices asserted, would have "weighty implications." They agreed with a lower court ruling on the issue that stated that the question of "Israeliness" "has public, ideological, social, historic, and political character—but not a legal character. This issue is a national-political-social question and it is not the court's place to decide it."[5] Too, some Israeli Arab intellectuals expressed hope that the Kaniuk decision might secularize the notion of Israeli identity, which had become infused with religious meaning. But as the Israeli social critic Gershon Gorenberg noted, the victory was a limited one. Kaniuk and others might now define themselves as Israelis of no religion, "but only according to the inadequate categories of nationality and religion. Real freedom of conscience would require the state to stop registering religious and ethnic identity."[6] And that, one might add, is very unlikely, especially in the light of late 2014 developments within the Israeli government and parliament. In December of that year the government coalition led by Prime Minister Benyamin Netanyahu's Likud Party broke down and new elections were called for. A key issue of contention between the political factions was Netanyahu's support of a series of "nationality bills." These bills would emphasize the "Jewish character" of Israel and bring its claim to protect the equal rights of all of its citizens into question. These bills would "remove Arabic as an official language alongside Hebrew and increase the influence of Jewish law."[7]

Giving more power to the state-sponsored rabbinic authorities would make conversion to Judaism all the more restricted and difficult, and would emphasize Jewish rather than Israeli identity. Thus, we can see that in the middle of the second decade of the twenty-first century the vexed questions "Who is a Jew?" and "Who is an Israeli?" are as vital and contentious as ever.

NOTES

1. See Associated Press, "Herzl's children buried alongside their father in Jerusalem."
2. See Weiler, "Discrimination and Identity in London."
3. See Fendrick, "Beyond 'Yes or No' Jewishness."
4. See Paraszczuk, "Writer Yoram Kaniuk to be registered as 'no religion.'"
5. See "Supreme Court Rejects Citizens' Request."
6. On the Kaniuk Case of 2011 see Barker, "Israeli Court Separates Church from State"; Gorenberg, "A Jew of No Religion"; Kerby, "Israeli author Yoram Kaniuk wins court battle"; Paraszczuk, "Writer Yoram Kaniuk to be registered as 'no religion'"; and Zarchin, "Israeli Court grants author's request."
7. See "Israel Struggles With Identity Crisis."

Bibliography

Allitt, Patrick. *Catholic Converts: British and American Intellectuals Turn to Rome*. Ithaca, New York: Cornell University Press, 1997.

Alter, Alexandra. "Rewriting the Rules of Summer Fiction." *The Wall Street Journal*, May 24, 2012. http://online.wsj.com/article/SB10001424052702304840904577424142251963680.html.

Alter, Robert. "The Shalit Case." *Commentary*, July 1, 1970. http://www.commentarymagazine.com/article/the-shalit-case/.

Anti-Defamation League. "The Conversion Crisis: The Current Debate on Religion, State and Conversion in Israel." Anti-Defamation League Online, 2001. http://www.adl.org/israel/conversion/intro.asp.

Anti-Defamation League. "ADL Says Jews for Jesus Ads are Deceptive and Offensive." News release, April 27, 2001. http://www.adl.org/presrele/rel_chstsep_90/3817_90.asp.

Ariel, Yaakov S. "Counterculture and Mission: Jews for Jesus and the Vietnam Era Missionary Campaigns." *Religion and American Culture*, Vol. 9, No. 2 (Summer 1999): 233–257.

———. *Evangelizing the Chosen People: Missions to the Jews in America, 1880-2000*. Chapel Hill: University of North Carolina Press, 2000.

Associated Press. "Israeli Court Rules Jews for Jesus Cannot Automatically be Citizens." *The New York Times*. December 27, 1989. http://www.nytimes.com/1989/12/27/world/israeli-court-rules-jews-for-jesus-cannot-automatically-be-citizens.html.

Associated Press. "Herzl's Children Buried Alongside their Father in Jerusalem." *Haaretz*, September 20, 2006. http://www.haaretz.com/news/herzl-s-children-buried-alongside-their-father-in-jerusalem-1.197723.

Banki, Judith H. "Historical Memories in Conflict." In *Memory Offended: the Auschwitz Convent Conflict*, edited by Carol Rittner and John K. Roth. New York: Praeger, 1991.

Barker, Anne. "Israeli Court Separates Church from State." *The World Today Online*, October 11, 2011. http://www.abc.net.au/worldtoday/content/2011/s3336673.htm.

Barnett, J. L. "Tales of a City: A Time to Mourn, and a Time to Dance." *The Jerusalem Report*, June 13, 2005.

Barzilai, Gad. "Who is a Jew? Categories, Boundaries, Communities and Citizenship Law in Israel." In *Boundaries of Jewish Identities*, edited by Susan Glenn and Naomi Sokoloff, 27–42. Seattle: University of Washington Press, 2010.

Baseheart, Mary Catherine. *Person in the World: Introduction to the Philosophy of Edith Stein*. Dordrecht: Kluwer Academic Publishers, 2010.

Batzdorff, Susanne M. *Aunt Edith: The Jewish Heritage of a Catholic Saint*. Springfield, Illinois: Templegate Publishers, 2003.

Becker, Fritz. "The New Jews of San Nicandro: Some Latter-Day Recruits to the Covenant." *Commentary*, April 1948. https://www.commentarymagazine.com/article/the-new-jews-of-san-nicandrosome-latter-day-recruits-to-the-covenant/.

Beilin, Yossi. *His Brother's Keeper: Israel and Diaspora Jewry in the Twenty First Century.* New York: Schocken Books, 2000.

Ben-David, Joseph. "San Nicandro: A Sociological Comment." *The Jewish Journal of Sociology* (1959): 250–57.

Ben David, Ruth. Typescript in Harvard's Houghton Library.

Ben-Rafael, Eliezer. *Jewish Identities: Fifty Intellectuals Answer Ben Gurion.* Boston: Brill, 2002.

Ben-Sasson, Haim Hillel. "Apostasy." In *Encyclopedia Judaica*, Vol. 3, 202–211. Jerusalem: Keter, 1972.

Ben Sasson, "Anuism," *The Jewish Virtual Library*, 2008. http://www.jewishvirtuallibrary.org/jsource/judaica/ejud_0002_0002_0_01173.html.

Ben-Simon, Daniel. "He'd say kaddish for his mother." *Haaretz*, August 7, 2007. http://www.haaretz.com/print-edition/news/he-d-say-kaddish-for-his-mother-1.227018.

Berenbaum, Michael. "The Struggle for Civility." In *Memory Offended: the Auschwitz Convent Conflict*, edited by Carol Rittner and John K. Roth. New York: Praeger, 1991.

Berger, David, and Michael Wyschogrod. *Jews and 'Jewish Christianity'.* New York: KTAV, 1978.

Berger, David. *The Rebbe, the Messiah, and the Scandal of Orthodox Indifference.* Portland, Oregon: Littman Library of Jewish Civilization, 2001.

Berlovitz, Yaffah. "Elisheva Bichovsky." In *Jewish Women: A Comprehensive Historical Encyclopedia.* March 1, 2009. Jewish Women's Archive. http://jwa.org/encyclopedia/article/elisheva-bichovsky.

Bernstein, Fred. "Onetime Catholic Priest Abraham Carmel Celebrates his 25th year as an Orthodox Jew." *People Magazine*, March 26, 1979. http://www.people.com/people/archive/article/0,,20073218,00.html.

Bikhovsky, Elisheva. *Poet and man; Essay on the Poetry of Alexander Blok.* Tel-Aviv: Tomer, 1929.

———. *Simtaot: A Novel.* Tel-Aviv: Tomer, 1929.

———. *Simtaot: A Novel.* Bene Berak: ha-Ḳibuts ha-me'uḥad, 2008.

———. "In Memory of H.N. Bialik."

Birnbaum, Eliyahu. "Manduzio—Father of many people" (English). *Shavei Israel*, November 7, 2007. http://www.shavei.org/communities/san_nicandro/articles-san_nicandro/manduzio-father-of-many-people/?lang=en.

Birnbaum, Eliyahu. "Manduzio—Father of many people" (Hebrew). *Shavei Israel*, November 7, 2007. http://www.shavei.org/communities/san_nicandro/articles-san_nicandro/manduzio-father-of-many-people/?lang=he.

Blau, Ruth. *The History of Yossele Schumacher.* Booklyn, N.Y.: Yitsḥak Brakh, 1993.

Blau, Ruth. *Shomrei Ha'Ir—Guardians of the City.*

Blau, Uri. "Women of Many Faces." *Haaretz*, November 3, 2008.

Cabaud, Judith. *Eugenio Zolli ou Le Prophéte d'un Monde Nouveau.* Paris: O.E.I.L., 2000.

Cargas, Harry James, ed. *The Unnecessary Problem of Edith Stein.* Studies in the Shoah, 4. Lanham, Maryland: University Press of America, 1997.

Carlebach, Elisheva. *Divided Souls: Converts from Judaism in Germany, 1500–1750.* New Haven: Yale University Press, 2001.

Carmel, Abraham I. *So Strange My Path.* New York: Bloch Publishing, 1964.

———. "My Chosen People." Typescript in author's personal collection.

Carozzi, Pier Angelo. *Israel-Eugenio Zolli: Un Semitista tra religioni e storia.* Padua: Il Poligrafo, 2009.

Cashman, Greer Fay. "No Stranger to Controversy." *The Jerusalem Post*, March 8, 2000. http://web.archive.org/web/20010119125400/http://www02.jpost.com/Editions/2000/03/05/Features/Features.3576.html.

Cassin, Elena. *San Nicandro: The Story of a Religious Phenomenon.* London: Cohen and West, 1957.

Central Conference of American Rabbis. "Apostate in the Synagogue." CCAR Responsa, 2011. http://ccarnet.org/responsa/tfn-no-5753-13-81-85/.

Chisholm, Hugh, ed. "Carmelites." In *The Encyclopaedia Britannica: A Dictionary of Arts, Sciences, Literature and General Information*, 11th ed, Vol. 5, 358–359. New York: The Encyclopaedia Britannica Company, 1910.

Cicognani, Amleto G. to Israel Zolli. October 1953. University of Notre Dame Archives.

Cohen, Asher, and Bernard Susser. "Jews and Others: Non-Jewish Jews in Israel." *Israel Affairs*, 15:1, 2009. 52–65.

Cohen, Shaye. *The Beginnings of Jewishness: Boundaries, Varieties, Uncertainties.* Berkley: The University of California Press, 1999.

Cohn, Elliot. "The Use of Holocaust Testimony by Jews for Jesus: A Narrative Inquiry." *Melilah* 4 (2009): 1–24.

Cohn, Haim. *Being Jewish* (In Hebrew). Israel: Kinneret, Zmora-Bitan, Dvir, Or Yehuda, 2006.

Cole, Tim. *Selling the Holocaust: From Auschwitz to Schindler; How History is Bought, Packaged, and Sold.* New York: Routledge Press, 2000.

Congdon, Jim, ed. *Jews and the Gospel at the End of History.* Grand Rapids: Kregel Academic Publishing, 2009.

Corroler, Catherine. "Jean-Marie Lustiger, mort d'un cardinal d'action." *Libération*, August 6, 2007. http://www.liberation.fr/societe/0101108527-jean-marie-lustiger-mort-d-un-cardinald-action.

Damato, Catherine. "The Man Behind the Jews for Jesus." *Power for Living*, September 2, 1979.

Davis, John. *The Jews of San Nicandro.* New Haven: Yale University Press, 2010.

Davison, Neil. "Still an Idea Behind it: Trieste, Jewishness, and Zionism in Ulysses." *James Joyce Quarterly* 38: 3–4 (Spring/Summer 2001), 373–394.

Davar. "The Poet Elisheva."

"Declaration of Israel's Independence 1948." Yale Law School: The Avalon Project, 2008. http://avalon.law.yale.edu/20th_century/israel.asp.

Diamond, James A. *Converts, Heretics, and Lepers: Maimonides and The Outsider.* South Bend, Indiana: University of Notre Dame Press, 2007.

Eisenberg, Dennis, Uri Dan, and Eli Landau, *The Mossad: Israel's Secret Intelligence Service: Inside Stories.* New York: Paddington Press, 1978.

Elgot, Jessica. "Jews for Jesus Founder Moishe Rosen dies." *The Jewish Chronicle*, May 21, 2010. http://www.thejc.com/news/world-news/31908/jews-jesus-founder-moishe-rosendies.

Elkoshi, Gedalyah. "Elisheva," In *Encyclopedia Judaica*, Vol. 6, 671–672. Jerusalem: Keter Publishing House, 1972.

Ellenson, David, and Daniel Gordis. *Pledges of Jewish Allegiance: Conversion, Law, and Policymaking in Nineteenth- and Twentieth-Century Orthodox Responsa.* Stanford: Stanford University Press, 2012.

Endelman, Todd M. *Jewish Apostasy in the Modern World.* Teaneck, New Jersey: Holmes & Meier Publishers, 1987.

Ettinger, Yair. "Notes on a Scandal." *Haaretz*, July 23, 2010. http://www.haaretz.com/weekend/week-s-end/notes-on-a-scandal-1.303654.

Fein, Leonard. "Open a Secular Door to Judaism." *The Jewish Daily Forward*, December 2, 2005. http://forward.com/articles/2372/open-a-secular-door-to-judaism.

Fendrick, Susan P. "Beyond 'Yes or No' Jewishness." *The Forward*, February 16, 2011. http://forward.com/articles/135474/beyond-yes-or-no-jewishness/.

Fermi, Laura. *Mussolini.* Chicago: The University of Chicago Press, 1974.

Fishman, Sylvia B. *Double or Nothing?: Jewish Families and Mixed Marriage.* Waltham, Massachusetts: Brandeis University Press, 2004.

Foa, Anna. "The Rabbi Who Studied Jesus." *L'Osservatore Romano*, February 20, 2010. http://chiesa.espresso.repubblica.it/articolo/1342271?eng=y.

Fox, Margalit. "Moishe Rosen Dies at 78; Founder of Jews for Jesus." *The New York Times*, May 22, 2010. http://www.nytimes.com/2010/05/22/us/22rosen.html.

Friedman, Elias. "Original Manifesto of the Association of Hebrew Catholics." Association of Hebrew Catholics, 1979. http://www.hebrewcatholic.net/original-manifesto-of-the-ahc/.

Friedman, Menachem. "The First Confrontation Between the Zionist Movement and Jerusalem Orthodoxy after the British Occupation of 1918." *Zionism: Studies in the History of the Zionist Movement 1*. Tel Aviv: Tel-Aviv University, 1975.

Friedman, Philip. "The Fate of the Jewish Book During the Nazi Era." *American Jewish Year Book*, Vol. 15 (1957–58): 81–94.

Gaboriau, Florent. *The Conversion of Edith Stein*. Translated by Ralph McInerny. South Bend, Indiana: St. Augustine's Press, 2002.

Galanter, Marc. "A Dissent on Brother Daniel." *Commentary*, 36 (July 1963):10–17. https://www.commentarymagazine.com/article/a-dissent-on-brother-daniel/.

Galili, Lily. "An unorthodox aliyah." *Haaretz*, April 22, 2010. http://www.haaretz.com/weekend/week-s-end/an-unorthodox-aliyah-1.284722.

Gallo, Patrick J. "To Halt the Dreadful Crimes." In *Pius XII, the Holocaust and the Revisionists: Essays*, edited by Patrick J. Gallo, 110–135. Jefferson, North Carolina: McFarland & Company, 2005.

Garber, Zev, and Bruce Zuckerman. "Why do we call the Holocaust 'The Holocaust?' An Inquiry into the Psychology of Labels," *Modern Judaism*, 9 (May 1989): 197–211.

Gaster, Moses, ed. "R. Jehiel of Paris, the Learned Bishop and the Two Demons." In *Ma'aseh Book: Book of Jewish tales and legends*, 505–10. Philadelphia: Jewish Publication Society of America, 1981.

Gera, Amir, dir. "Brother Daniel: The Last Jew." Israeli documentary film, 2001.

Gildea, Robert. *Marianne in Chains: Daily Life in the Heart of France During the German Occupation*. New York: Metropolitan Books, 2002.

Ginsberg, Rachel. "Guardian of the City: The Secret Life of Ruth Blau." *Mishpacha*, January 27, 2009: 56–62.

Glückel of Hameln. *The Memoirs of Glückel of Hameln*. Tanslated by Marvin Lowenthal. New York: Schocken Books, 1987.

Goldman, Shalom L. *Zeal for Zion: Christians, Jews, and the Idea of the Promised Land*. Chapel Hill: The University of North Carolina Press, 2009.

———. The Yeshiva of Flatbush in Brooklyn, New York. January 2008.

Gorenberg, Gershom. "A Jew of No Religion." *The American Prospect*, October 19, 2011. http://prospect.org/article/jew-no-religion.

Green, David B. "The 'Troublemaker.'" *The Jerusalem Report*, May 14, 1998, 96–103.

Haberman, Clyde. "Jerusalem Journal: the Cardinal Visits and the Chief Rabbi is Pained." *The New York Times*, April 28, 1995. http://www.nytimes.com/1995/04/28/world/jerusalem-journal-the-cardinal-visits-and-the-chief-rabbi-is-pained.html.

Halbertal, Moshe, and Donniel Hartman, eds. *Judaism and the Challenges of Modern Life*. Volume 2 of Kogod Library of Judaic Studies. New York: Continuum, 2007.

Hamans, Paul. *Edith Stein and Companions*. Translated by Sister M. Regina van den Berg, F.S.G.M. San Francisco: Ignatius Press, 2010.

Harel, Maayan. "Review of *Simtaot*." *Haaretz*, September 3, 2008.

Hartman, David. *Israelis and the Jewish Tradition: An Ancient People Debating Its Future*. New Haven: Yale University Press, 2000.

Hartman, Donniel. *The Boundaries of Judaism*. Volume 1 of Kogod Library of Judaic Studies. Reprint. New York: Continuum, 2007.

The Hebrew Catholic, No. 85, Winter-Spring 2008. http://www.hebrewcatholic.net/85-winter-spring-2008/.

Herbstrith, Waltraud. *Edith Stein: A Biography. The Untold Story of the Philosopher and Mystic Who Lost Her Life in the Death Camps of Auschwitz*. Translated by Father Bernard Bonowitz, OCSO. San Francisco: Ignatius Press, 1992.

Hobsbawm, Eric J. *Primitive Rebels: Studies in Archaic Forms of Social Movement in the 19th and 20th Centuries*. Manchester, Great Britain: The University of Manchester Press, 1959.

Hovel, Revital. "Supreme Court rejects citizens' request to change nationality from 'Jewish' to 'Israeli.'" *Haaretz*, October 3, 2013. http://www.haaretz.com/news/national/.premium-1.550241.

Inside the Vatican. "My Father Never Stopped Being a Jew." February 1999. http://www. catholicculture.org/culture/library/view.cfm?recnum=1067.

Israeli Prime Minister's Office, Overseas Division. *A Study in Fanaticism: The Neturai Karta Extremist Group.* Jerusalem, 1964.

Jackson, Bernard S. "Brother Daniel: The Construction of Jewish Identity in the Israeli Supreme Court." *International Journal for the Semiotics of Law*, VI (1993): 115–146.

The Jerusalem Post, "Apostate French cardinal dies at 80." August 6, 2007. http://www.jpost. com/Jewish-World/Jewish-News/Apostate-French-cardinal-dies-at-80.

Katz, Robert. *Black Sabbath: A Journey Through a Crime Against Humanity.* New York: Macmillan, 1969.

Kerby, Rob. "Israeli author Yoram Kaniuk wins court battle to be ethnic Jewish, but not religious." BeliefNet. http://www.beliefnet.com/columnists/news/2011/10/israeli-author-yoram-kaniuk-wins-court-battle-to-be-ethnic-jewish-but-not-religious.php.

Kertzer, David I. *The Kidnapping of Edgardo Mortara.* New York: Vintage, 1998.

Kimmerling, Baruch. *The Invention and Decline of Israeliness: State, Society, and the Military.* Berkeley: The University of California Press, 2001.

Kinel, S. "Lo Haya Li." *Haaretz*, 12 June 2008.

Kinzer, Mark. *Post-Missionary Messianic Judaism: Redefining Christian Engagement with the Jewish People.* Grand Rapids: Brazos Press, 2005.

Klein, Emma. *The Battle for Auschwitz: Catholic-Jewish Relations Under Strain.* Portland, Oregon: Vallentine Mitchell, 2001.

Koren, Doron. "Hebrew Love, circa 1929." Ynet, June 14, 2011. www.ynet.co.il.

Krauss, Yitzhak. "Judaism and Zionism." *Ha Ziyonut*, 22 (2000): 38–60.

Lando, Michal. "Israeli Reunites with NY Woman Who Helped in His Abduction." *The Jerusalem Post*, June 7, 2007. http://www.jpost.com/International/Article.aspx?id=64144.

Lapide, Pinchas E. *Three Popes and the Jews.* New York: Hawthorn Books, 1967.

———. *The Prophet of San Nicandro.* New York: Beechhurst Press, 1953.

Lapide, Phinn. "San Nicandro's New Jews in Israel: Progress Report." *Commentary*, September 1951. http://www.commentarymagazine.com/article/san-nicandros-new-jews-in-israelprogress-report.

Latorre, Alberto. "Eugenio Zolli: apostata o profeta?" *Studia Patavina: Revisita di Scienze Religiose* 49.3 (2002): 29–64.

———. "Israel Zoller." In *Israel-Eugenio Zolli: Un Semitista tra religioni e storia*, edited by Pier Angelo Crozzi. Padua: Il Poligrafo, 2009.

———. "Tra Wissenschaft des Judentums, Modernismo e Psicoanalisi" in *Israel-Eugenio Zolli: Un Semitista tra religioni e storia*, edited by Pier Angelo Crozzi. Padua: Il Poligrafo, 2009.

Lau, Rabbi Israel Mir. *Out of the Depths: The Story of a Child of Buchenwald Who Returned Home at Last.* New York: Sterling Publishing, 2011.

Le Figaro. "Les obsèques du cardinal Lustiger célébrées vendredi." August 5, 2007.

Lev-Ari, Shiri. "She chose the Jewish People." *Haaretz*, July 17, 2002. http://www.haaretz. com/culture/arts-leisure/she-chose-the-jewish-people-1.39528.

Levine, Samuel. *You Take Jesus, I'll Take God: How to refute Christian Missionaries.* Los Angeles: Hamoroh Press, 1980.

Lichtenstein, Aharon. "On Conversion." In *The Conversion Crisis: Essays from the Pages of Tradition*, edited by Aharon Lichtenstein, Emanuel Feldman, and Joel B. Wolowelsky. New York: KTAV, 1990.

Lipson, Julienne G. "Jews for Jesus: An Anthropological Study," Ph.D. diss., University of California Berkley, 1978.

Luconi, Stefano. "Recent Trends in the Study of Italian Anti-Semitism Under the Fascist Regime." *Patterns of Prejudice*, Vol. 38 No. 1 (2004): 1–17.

Lustiger, Jean-Marie. *Dare to Believe: Addresses, Sermons, Interviews, 1981–1984.* New York: Crossroad, 1986.

———. "How Can We Believe in God Today?"

———. *The Promise.* Grand Rapids, Michigan: Wm. B. Eerdmans Publishing, 2007.

Lustiger, Jean-Marie, Jean-Louis Missika, and Dominique Wolton. *Choosing God, Chosen by God: Conversations with Jean-Marie Lustiger*. San Francisco: Ignatius Press, 1991.

Magarik, Raphael. "The Very First of the Jews for Jesus: Moishe Rosen's Controversial Story, Told by his Daughter." *The Forward*, April 13, 2012. http://forward.com/articles/154180/the-very-first-jew-for-jesus/?p=all.

Magnus, Shulamit S. "Good Bad Jews: Converts, Conversion and Boundary Redrawing in Modern Russian Jewery, Notes toward a New Category." In *Boundaries of Jewish Identity*, edited by Susan Anita Glenn and Naomi B. Sokoloff, 132–60. Seattle: University of Washington Press, 2010.

Malcolm, Teresa. "Jewish Group Criticizes Honor for Converted Prelate." *National Catholic Reporter*, November 6, 1998, 11.

Malham, Joseph M. *By Fire into Light: Four Catholic Martyrs of the Nazi Camps*. Leuven: Peeters Publishing, 2002.

Matalon, Ronit. "What do women want?" *Yediot Ahronot*, June 3, 2010.

Mathis, Father, to Father Raphael Simon. September 1953. University of Notre Dame Archives.

Matthews, T. S. "Religion: Greatest Tragedy." *Time Magazine*, Vol. 46, February 26, 1945, 68.

Medwick, Cathleen. *Teresa of Avila: The Progress of a Soul*. New York: A. A. Knopf, 1999.

Mendes-Flohr, Paul, and Jehuda Reinharz. *The Jew in the Modern World: A Documentary History*. 3rd ed. New York: Oxford University Press, 2010.

Michaelis, Meir. *Mussolini and the Jews: German-Italian Relations and the Jewish Question 1922–1945*. New York: Oxford University Press, 1979.

The Ministry of Justice. *Judgment: High Court Application of Oswald Rufeisen v. The Minister of the Interior, State of Israel, The Supreme Court*. Jerusalem: The Ministry of Justice, 1963.

Miron, Dan. *Founding Mothers, Stepsisters: The Emergence of the First Hebrew Poetesses and Other Essays*. Tel Aviv: Hakibbutz Hameuchad, 1991.

Moorehead, Caroline. *A Train in Winter*. New York: HarperCollins Publishers, 2011.

Moseley, Ray. *Mussolini's Shadow: The Double Life of Count Galeazzo Ciano*. New Haven: Yale University Press, 2000.

Negev, Eilat. *Intimate Conversations*. Tel Aviv: Yediot Aharonot, 1995.

Newman, Louis I. *A "Chief Rabbi" of Rome Becomes a Catholic: A study in Fright and Spite*. Ashuelot, New Hampshire: The Renaissance Press, 1945.

Novick, Peter. *The Holocaust in American Life*. Orlando: Mariner Books, 2000.

Olmert, Dana. "Afterword." In *Simtaot: A Novel*. Tel Aviv: Hakibbutz Hameuchad, 2008.

Paraszczuk, Joanna. "Writer Yoram Kaniuk to be registered as 'no religion.'" *The Jerusalem Post*, October 2, 2011. http://www.jpost.com/NationalNews/Article.aspx?id=240278.

Pizzi, Katia. *A City in Search of an Author: The Literary Identity of Trieste*. New York: Sheffield Academic Press, 2002.

Pope Benedict XVI. "Auschwitz: Benoît XVI évoque d'emblée «les victimes de la terreur nazie»." *Zenit*, May 25, 2006. http://www.zenit.org/article-12902?l=french.

Pope John Paul II. *John Paul II: On Jews and Judaism*. Washington, D.C.: USCCB Publishing, 1987.

———. "Auschwitz: « Il n'est permis à personne de passer avec indifférence »." *Zenit*, 27 January 2005. http://www.zenit.org/article-9568?l=french.

Sarah Posner, "Kosher Jesus: Messianic Jews in the Holy Land," *The Atlantic*, November 29, 2012.

"Priest who Converted to Judaism to Speak." *The Day* (New London, Conn.), May 18, 1978, 22.

Rabinowicz, Tzvi. *Hasidim and the State of Israel*. Madison: New Jersey: Fairleigh Dickinson University Press, 1982.

Rabkin, Yakov. *A Threat From Within: A Century of Jewish Opposition to Zionism*. New York: Zed Books, 2006.

Raisin, Max. *Great Jews I Have Known: A Gallery of Portraits*. New York: Philosophical Library, 1950.

Ravenna, Alfredo. "The Converts of San Nicandro." *The Jewish Journal of Sociology* (1959): 244–249.

Reichman, Herschel. "The Cardinals Visit: Thoughts of a Rosh Yeshiva." *The Commentator* (Yeshiva University), February 17, 2004.

"Religion: The Converts of San Nicandro." *Time Magazine*, September 15, 1947.

Riggs, Bryan Mark. *Hitler's Jewish Soldiers: The Untold Story of Nazi Racial Laws and Men of Jewish Descent in the German Military.* Lawrence, Kansas: University Press of Kansas, 2002.

Rosen, Moishe. *Y'shua: The Jewish Way to Say Jesus.* Chicago: Moody Press, 1982.

———. "35 Things about Me, Moishe Rosen," July 29, 2009. http://moisherosen.org/2009/07/29/35-things-about-me-moishe-rosen/.

———. "He being dead still speaks (Hebrews 11:4)." http://blog.jforj.com/moisherosen/writings-by-moishe/he-being-dead-still-speaks-hebrews-114/.

Rosen, Moishe, and Bob Massie. *Overture to Armageddon: Beyond the Gulf War.* San Bernardino: Here's Life Publishers, 1991.

Rosen, Moishe, and Ceil Rosen. *Christ in the Passover.* Chicago: Moody Publications, 2006.

Rosen, Moishe, and William Proctor. *Jews for Jesus.* Old Tappan, New Jersey: Revell Co., 1974.

Rosen, Ruth. *Called to Controversy: The Unlikely Story of Moishe Rosen and the Founding of Jews for Jesus.* Nashville: Thomas Nelson, 2012.

Rosenstock-Huessy, Eugen, and Franz Rosenzweig. *Judaism Despite Christianity: The Letters on Christianity and Judaism Between Eugen Rosenstock-Huessy and Franz Rosenzweig.* Birmingham: University of Alabama Press, 1969.

Rossner, Rena. "The Rabbi, The Pope, and The Cardinal." *The Jerusalem Post*, November 4, 2005. http://rabbidavidrosen.net/press/The%20rabbi%20the%20pope%20and%20the%20cardinal.doc.

Rubenstein, Richard L. *After Auschwitz.* 2nd ed. Baltimore: Johns Hopkins University Press, 1992.

Rudoren, Jodi. "Israel Struggles With Its Identity." *The New York Times*, December 8, 2014. http://www.nytimes.com/2014/12/09/world/middleeast/israels-nationality-bill-stirs-debate-over-religious-and-democratic-identity.html.

Sarfatti, Michele. *The Jews in Mussolini's Italy: From Equality to Persecution.* Madison: University of Wisconsin Press, 2006.

Satlow, Michael. *Jewish Marriage in Antiquity.* Princeton, New Jersey: Princeton University Press, 2001.

Schoeman, Roy. *Honey from the Rock: Sixteen Jews Find the Sweetness of Christ.* San Francisco: Ignatius Press, 2007.

Scrivener, Jane. *Inside Rome with the Germans.* Auckland, New Zealand: Holloway Press, 2007.

Segal, Alan. *Paul the Convert: The Apostolate and Apostasy of Saul the Pharisee.* New Haven: Yale University Press, 1990.

Selzer, Michael. *Zionism Reconsidered: The Rejection of Jewish Normalcy.* New York: Macmillan, 1970.

Semi, Emanuela Trevisan. *Jacques Faitlovitch and the Jews of Ethiopia.* Portland, Oregon: Vallentine Mitchell, 2007.

Shva, Shlomo. "Elizaveta Ivanova Zirkova." *Davar*, May 9, 1969, 29.

Smith, Shoham. "Review of 'Queen of the Hebrews and Other Stories.'" *Haaretz*, November 6, 2002.

"Songs by Elisheva." http://www.zemer.co.il.

Stanislawski, Michael. "A Jewish Monk? A Legal and Ideological Analysis of the Origins of the 'Who Is a Jew' Controversy in Israel." In *Text and Context: Essays in Modern Jewish History and Historiography in Honor of Ismar Schorsch*, edited by Ismar Schorsch, Eli Lederhendler, and Jack Wertheimer, 548–77. New York: Jewish Theological Seminary of America, 2005.

Stein, Edith. *Life in a Jewish Family: Her Unfinished Autobiographical Account.* Edited by Lucy Gelber & Romaeus Leuven, OCD. Translated by Josephine Koeppel, OCD. Washington, D.C.: ICS Publications, 1999.

————. *The Hidden Life: Essays, Meditations, Spiritual Texts (The Collected Works of Edith Stein, Vol. 4)*. Edited by Lucy Gelber and Michael Linssen. Translated by Waltraut Stein. Washington, D.C.: ICS Publications, 1992.

Stille, Alexander. *Benevolence and Betrayal: Five Italian Jewish Families Under Fascism*. New York: Picador, 1991.

Tagliabue, John. "Jean-Marie Lustiger, French Cardinal, Dies at 80." *New York Times*, August 6, 2007. http://www.nytimes.com/2007/08/06/world/europe/06lustiger.html?pagewanted=all.

————. "Polish Prelate Assails Protests by Jews at Auschwitz." *New York Times*, August 11, 1989. http://www.nytimes.com/1989/08/11/world/polish-prelate-assails-protests-by-jews-at-auschwitz-convent.html.

Talmon, J. L. "Who is a Jew." *Encounter* (May 1965): 28–36.

Tec, Nechama. *In the Lion's Den: The Life of Oswald Rufeisen*. New York: Oxford University Press, 1990.

The Times of Israel. "ADL flogs Jews for Jesus over Holocaust clip." April 24, 2014. http://www.timesofisrael.com/adl-flogs-jews-for-jesus-over-holocaust-clip/#ixzz3P1X8ZIEn.

Time Magazine. "Religion: Jews for Jesus." Vol. 99, No. 24. June 12, 1972.

Toren, Haim, ed. *Elisheva: The Collected Poems*. Tel Aviv, 1970.

Trunk, Isaiah. *Jewish Responses to Nazi Persecution*. New York: Stein and Day, 1979.

Tucker, Ruth. "Remembering Moishe Rosen: Jews for Jesus founder left his mark on evangelism." *Christianity Today*, May 21, 2010. http://www.christianitytoday.com/ct/2010/mayweb-only/30-52.0.html.

United States Holocaust Memorial Museum. "Resistance plans and escape from the Mir ghetto." *The United States Holocaust Memorial Museum Encyclopedia of Camps and Ghettos, 1933–1945*, June 20, 2014. http://www.ushmm.org/wlc/en/article.php?ModuleId=10007238.

Wakin, Daniel J., and Laurie Goodstein. "In Upper Manhattan, Talmudic Scholars Look Up and Find Cardinals Among the Rabbis." *New York Times*, January 20, 2004. http://www.nytimes.com/2004/01/20/nyregion/in-upper-manhattan-talmudic-scholars-look-up-and-find-cardinals-among-the-rabbis.html.

Walker, Ken. "The Godfather of Jewish Evangelism." *Charisma Magazine*, 28 February 2010. http://www.charismamag.com/index.php/features/26301-the-godfather-of-jewish-evangelism.

Weiler, J. H. H. "Discrimination and Identity in London: The Jewish Free School Case." *Jewish Review of Books*, Number 1, Spring 2010. http://www.jewishreviewofbooks.com/publications/detail/discrimination-and-identity-in-london-the-jewish-free-school-case.

Weiner, Herbert. *The Wild Goats of Ein Gedi*. New York: Doubleday, 1961.

Weisbord, Robert G., and Wallace P. Sillanpoa. *The Chief Rabbi, the Pope, and the Holocaust: An Era in Vatican-Jewish Relations*. New Brunswick, New Jersey: Transaction Publishers, 2008.

Wengeroff, Pauline. *Rememberings: The World of a Russian-Jewish Woman in the Nineteenth Century*. Edited by Bernard D. Cooperman. Translated by Henny Wenkart. Bethesda: University Press of Maryland, 2000.

Wilensky, David A.M. "What would you call me?: Patrilineal Jew Laments Need for 'Conversion.'" *The Jewish Daily Forward*, April 20, 2012. http://forward.com/articles/154650/what-would-you-call-me/.

Wilson, Edmund. *The Wound and the Bow: Seven Studies in Literature*. New York: Oxford University Press, 1947.

Wolf, Hubert. *Pope and Devil: The Vatican Archives and the Third Reich*. Translated by Kenneth Kronenberg. Cambridge: The Belking Press of Harvard University Press, 2010.

World Jewish Congress. "Statement of the World Jewish Congress on the Death of French Cardinal Jean-Marie Lustiger." *PRNewswire-USNewswire*, August 6, 2007. http://www.prnewswire.com/news-releases/statement-of-the-world-jewish-congress-on-the-death-of-french-cardinal-jean-marie-lustiger-57899882.html.

Yahil, Leni. *The Holocaust: The Fate of European Jewry, 1932–1945*. New York: Oxford University Press, 1987.

Yahuda, A. S. "The Conversion of a 'Chief-Rabbi': What the Jewish Community Knows about Dr. Zoller." *The Jewish Forum* (New York), September 1945, 170–80.

"Yeshivat Chovevei Torah: Is It Orthodox?" *Yated Ne'eman*, July 12, 2009.

Zarchin, Tomer. "Israeli Court grants author's request to register 'without religion.'" *Haaretz*, October 2, 2011. http://www.haaretz.com/print-edition/news/israel-court-grants-author-s-request-to-register-without-religion-1.387571.

Zeveloff, Naomi. "Patrilineal Descent Jews Still Find Resistance: Denominations Stick To Traditional Definition Of Who Is Jewish." *The Huffington Post*, April 4, 2012. http://www.huffingtonpost.com/2012/04/04/patrilineal-descent-jews-still-find-resistance-_n_1403385.html.

Ziprin, Nathan. "On the Record: They Can Have Him." *Detroit Michigan Jewish News*, August 1953.

Zlotowski, Michel. "The Jewish Archbishop Speaks About the 'Shoah.'" *The Jerusalem Post*, April 28, 1989. http://www.institutlustiger.fr/documents/OC/JML_1989_04_28_Jerusalem_Post_Itw_The_Jewish_archbishop_speaks_about_the_Shoah.pdf.

Zolli, Eugenio. "The Status of the State of Israel." *The Catholic World*, Vol. 169, No. 1013 (August 1949): 326–329.

———. *The Nazarene: Studies in New Testament Exegesis*. Reprint. Birmingham, Alabama: New Hope Publishers, 1999.

———. *Before the Dawn: Autobiographical Reflections by Eugenio Zolli, Former Chief Rabbi of Rome*. Reprint. San Francisco: Ignatius Press, 2008.

Zubrzycki, Genevieve. *The Crosses of Auschwitz: Nationalism and Religion in Post-Communist Poland*. Chicago: The University of Chicago Press, 2006.

Index

About the Author

Shalom Goldman is professor of Religion and Middle Eastern studies at Duke University. He is the editor of the pioneering volume *Hebrew and the Bible in America* and author of four scholarly books and many articles in academic and popular journals. His works in the performing arts includes his collaboration with composer Philip Glass on the opera *Akhnaten*.